Apologetics in the New Age

A Christian Critique of Pantheism

David K. Clark
and Norman L. Geisler

BAKER BOOK HOUSE
Grand Rapids, Michigan 49516

Copyright 1990 by
Baker Book House Company
Printed in the United States of America

Library of Congress Cataloging-in-Publication Data

Clark, David K.
    Apologetics in the New Age : a Christian critique of pantheism / David K.
Clark and Norman L. Geisler.
      p.   cm.
    Includes bibliographical references.
    ISBN 0-8010-2544-3
    1. Pantheism—Controversial literature. 2. New Age movement—Controversial
literature. 3. Apologetics—20th century.
    I. Geisler, Norman L. II. Title.
    BT1185.C57   1990
211'.2—dc20   90-32058
                                                                    CIP

Contents

Introduction
Philosophy in the New Age

Christians today stand again on Mars Hill.

In the first century, Saint Paul debated two groups of Greek philosophers at a place in Athens called Mars Hill. Paul's antagonists were the Epicureans and the Stoics. Like Paul, Christians in the West today are locked in debate with both Epicureans and Stoics.

When the American Atheists met in Denver recently, Madalyn Murray O'Hair declared that there is no God. Shirley MacLaine soon came to town to pronounce that she and all her listeners are gods. Shortly thereafter, in a Denver crusade, Billy Graham preached that Jesus alone is God.[1] These well-known champions of three world views have rekindled that ancient Mars Hill debate.

O'Hair is the contemporary embodiment of the Epicureans. Speaking broadly, modern Epicureans are Secular Humanists. Those who adopt the atheistic perspective of these modern Epicureans have been the primary critics of the Christian faith for several centuries. For this reason, the talents of Christian defenders generally have been turned Westward in response to atheists and agnostics.

In recent decades, the dialog between world views has once again become a trialog. The modern counterpart of Stoicism in our culture is mystical pantheism. MacLaine, the Oscar-winning actress, is the new pantheistic kid on the Western metaphysical block. Pantheists, despite great variety, agree that God is the world and the world is

---

1. *Rivendell Times*, Sept. 1, 1987; quoted in Russell Chandler, *Understanding the New Age* (Waco: Word, 1988), p. 26. For an excellent introduction to these three world views, see the debate among John Kennedy, Aldous Huxley, and C. S. Lewis as imagined by Peter Kreeft in *Between Heaven and Hell* (Downers Grove: InterVarsity Press, 1985).

God. From this perspective, individual humans are part of God's being.

The Pantheism of the New Age

Pantheism etymologically means "All is God." The word was first used by John Toland, an Irish deist, in 1705. The world view is built on the key idea that all of reality is one. (This is called 'monism.') Anything real is interrelated with everything else that is real. There may be forms or levels of reality, but in the final analysis, all reality is unified ontologically, that is, in its being. No qualitative distinctions can differentiate kinds of real things. There is no infinite contrast between an eternal Creator and a temporal creature. The ultimate reality, God, alone is real. Insofar as we are real, you and I are part of God.

This world view finds practical application in Hindu life and culture. For example, some ancient Hindu paintings depict humans with a picture of God in the middle of the chest. God resides within, not in a relationship of love or communion, but in actual, metaphysical union—a literal oneness of being. When Hindus greet one another, they place their hands together like a steeple and bow. "I worship the god that is in you," they are saying. God is I; I am God.

To clarify this, Eastern gurus and masters use a helpful illustration. To live on earth is to be like a drop of spray tossed up by the sea. There may be a period of seeming isolation from the ocean, but the drop's individual existence will be over shortly, and the drop will fall back into the sea, the Source of its being. Like the drop, we will return to God's being to be reunited with the All. The skin of surface tension that seems to isolate us from God will break, and our being will merge with the infinity of the Ocean.

Expressions of this shift in thought toward Oriental concepts, what Harvey Cox calls "the turn east,"[2] are easily identified in our culture. For example, polls show that nearly one of three young people in America believes in reincarnation. Popular movies like the *Star Wars* series (which grossed over one billion dollars) powerfully present pantheism. Actor Billy Dee Williams quotes Irvin Kershner, director of *The Empire Strikes Back*, as saying, "I wanna introduce some Zen here because I don't want the kids to walk away just feeling that everything is shoot-'em-up, but that there's also a little something to think about in terms of yourself and your surroundings."[3] Millions of Americans are taking lessons in meditation, yoga, or the martial arts, all of which spring out of pantheistic thought. Fortune 500 corpora-

2. Harvey Cox, *Turning East: The Promise and Peril of the New Orientalism* (New York: Simon and Schuster, 1977).

3. Interview with Billy Dee Williams, *Rolling Stone,* July 24, 1980, p. 37.

tions are hiring consulting firms specializing in the development of human potential through an awareness of the deity within each person.

For several decades, Oriental gurus, in a seemingly endless stream, have attracted crowds of Western followers. These gurus have cashed in on their connections with entertainment demigods to thrust themselves into public consciousness. They appear on television talk shows, receive the accolades of doting celebrities, buy full-page ads in major papers. Their disciples accost us in airports. We no longer react with surprise.

A modern version of Stoic pantheistic philosophy is the New Age movement. The New Age movement has been called "the fastest growing alternative belief system in the country."[4] The movement is a loosely knit network of personalities, groups, and institutions tied together by the belief that a New Age of international peace, ecological sensitivity, and social enlightenment can be inaugurated. New Age advocates look for the dawning of a new world. They are optimistic, evolutionary, and utopian. They share a vision of a literal heaven on earth where personal and social problems are overcome and a new era of peace and prosperity emerges.[5]

New Age proponents generally claim that their utopian hope will be realized when enough people achieve 'Higher Consciousness.' Anyone can reach this personal enlightenment by using any of a variety of means including the martial arts, meditation, yoga, drugs, hypnosis, or even biofeedback. Marilyn Ferguson, author of the New Age book, *The Aquarian Conspiracy,* says that humans have access to a source of "transcendent knowing, a domain not limited to time and space."[6]

This level of consciousness is possible because of the pantheistic underpinning of reality: every person participates in the divine. Swami Muktananda, the guru who got former California governor Jerry Brown, among others, into yoga, put it this way: "Kneel to your own self. Honor and worship your own being. God dwells in you as you."[7] *Time* reports that Shirley MacLaine defended this key tenet of New Age thinking at a $300-per-person meeting in New York (part of a fifteen-city tour that earned $1.5 million). As MacLaine was leading meditation, a voice from the audience called, "With all due respect, I

4. *The Christian Herald* (February 1988), p. 51.

5. J. Gordon Melton, *Encyclopedic Handbook of Cults in America* (New York: Garland, 1986), p. 113.

6. Marilyn Ferguson, *The Aquarian Conspiracy: Personal and Social Transformation in the 1980s* (Los Angeles: J. P. Tarcher, 1981), p. 176.

7. Swami Muktananda, quoted in Tom Minnery, "Unplugging the New Age," *Focus on the Family* (August 1987), p. 2.

don't think you are a god." Not missing a beat, MacLaine replied, "If you don't see me as God, it's because you don't see yourself as God."[8]

It would be one thing if this pantheistic mentality were confined to small communes populated by true believers. But such is not the case. The uninitiated will find the infiltration of this mode of thinking into various aspects of American culture quite surprising. New Agers actively promote their beliefs in the arts, in education, and even in the corporate world.

Consider several examples. The blasphemous film *The Last Temptation of Christ* presents Jesus wrestling not only with lustful temptations, but also with his messianic identity. Nikos Kazantzakis, author of the novel on which the film was based, explains the reason he has Christ struggling with self-identity: Jesus represents the "yearning . . . of man to attain God, or more exactly, to return to God and identify himself with him."[9] Two professors of business at Stanford University are teaching a course called "Creativity in Business" in which they promote New Age meditation techniques. They have taken their course into the business arena with the publication of a book by the same title. As they introduce yoga, they give their rationale by quoting favorably from Swami Muktananda: "Everything is contained in the Self. The creative power of this entire universe lies inside every one of us. The divine principle that creates and sustains this world pulsates with us as our own Self."[10]

Some Eastern imports are less metaphysically blatant than this swami. But some movements that play down overt religious connotations nevertheless have pantheistic overtones. Transcendental Meditation (TM), while promoting its medicinal benefits as a form of relaxation, incorporates clearly pantheistic ideas into its approach. Though the techniques can be learned in a purely mechanical way, answers to "How?" and "Why?" inevitably take the novice into the realm of Eastern philosophy. When we ask these questions, we find that the techniques give us inner harmony and lower stress levels because we have God within.

The fundamental identity between the human self and the divine Self makes the New Age utopian dream possible. Ultimately, if enough people meditate, the inner harmony will grow to global proportions. Douglas Groothuis, a leading evangelical critic of the New Age, put it this way: "The underlying theme of the New Age is that as self-realized gods, we inherit the supernatural. New Age disci-

8. Otto Friedrich, "New Age Harmonies," *Time* (December 7, 1987), p. 64.

9. Nikos Kazantzakis, *The Last Temptation of Christ*, trans. P. A. Bien (New York: Simon and Schuster, 1960), pp. 1–2.

10. Michael Ray and Rochelle Myers, *Creativity in Business* (Garden City: Doubleday, 1986), p. 28.

plines teach that as lords of our own universe, we create our own reality by the power of our thoughts. . . . The prerogatives of the Godhead are ours for the taking."[11] What an intoxicating vision!

Historical Foundations

Where do the historical roots of this movement lie? In the words of one commentator, the New Age Movement has been "fed by many tributaries, but cannot be reduced to any single one. The strands of the ancient wisdom . . . are now all aswirl, one virtually indistinguishable from the next, and all drawing on one another."[12]

Several sources can be identified from the recent past. The Transcendentalists—Walt Whitman, Henry David Thoreau, and Ralph Waldo Emerson—introduced Eastern thought into American culture in the middle of the nineteenth century. While at Walden, for example, Thoreau read the *Bhagavad Gita*, an influential Hindu writing. Another source is the mental healing or inner healing movement, whose founders included Friedrich Anton Mesmer's (1733–1815) Spiritualism (note *mesmerize*), Mary Baker Eddy's (1821–1910) Christian Science, and Madame Helena Petrovna Blavatsky's (1831–1891) Theosophy. In our century, the introduction of Zen to the West by D. T. Suzuki and Alan Watts and the arrival of gurus like Swami Muktananda and Maharishi Mahesh Yogi (founder of TM) are important. These influences coalesced with the beatnik, hippie, and psychedelic movements (c. 1950s to 1970s).

Some may be surprised that the New Age movement has roots in the last century. But mixed with these influences are more ancient parallels in occult, gnostic, pagan, and even native American religions. The occult, though different from the New Age movement per se, shares with it practices like divination and consulting mediums. (This is known in the New Age movement as "channeling.") Gnosticism, an ancient Greek perspective, values special, secret knowledge for the initiated. New Agers promote a similar form of insiders' knowledge. Paganism contributes its obsession with sacred objects like the sun and special places like Stonehenge. And the New Age movement mimics native American religions' allegiance to Mother Earth and other natural things.

The pantheistic philosophy underlying the New Age movement also has a history stretching back millennia. C. S. Lewis suggested that pantheism catches on precisely because, like an old shoe, it is so

11. Douglas Groothuis, "New Age or Ancient Error?" *Moody Monthly* (February 1985), pp. 20–22.
12. Robert Burrows, in *New Age Rage,* ed. Karen Hoyt (Old Tappan, N. J.: Fleming H. Revell, 1987), p. 31.

comfortable.[13] It tells us what we want to hear. We are good; we are gods. The pantheistic symphony of concepts on knowledge, reality, religious consciousness, and moral values has been heard before. Many New Age ideas are improvisations on ancient themes.

A Philosophical Response to the New Age

Though the roots of New Age thinking are ancient, the American consciousness of this Eastern alternative has arisen rapidly in the last few decades. Christian apologists have been caught unaware. Christians have become successful in defending their faith against Epicurean atheism, but they are relatively defenseless in the face of Stoic pantheism. For this reason, Christian apologists must turn their attention in a new direction by developing new arguments for this New Age. It is to this end that this book is dedicated.

Several different approaches to understanding these new cults and religions are possible. One important kind of analysis tracks the specific cultural manifestations of the New Age movement and its pantheistic expressions. This sociological approach considers pantheism's forms as they integrate with a new culture, shaping and being shaped by it. Other discussions take a psychological approach. These seek primarily to sort out the benefits of New Age forms of religion for the faithful or the psychological reasons why someone might espouse New Age religion. They also investigate the mind control techniques of some new religions.

The approach here is philosophical. Sympathetic acknowledgment of the theoretical insights and practical benefits of pantheistic religious viewpoints is important. But so is evaluating truth claims. Our philosophical method, therefore, emphasizes the ideas propounded by various forms of pantheism. What concepts do they claim describe reality, our knowing processes, and the meaning of life? How do these ideas constitute coherent world views? How adequate are these views to explain our experience of the world? Our philosophical discussion will focus on questions like these.

In order to accomplish our goal, we will seek to understand the teachings of the pantheistic world view, the soil in which the New Age movement grows. Our purpose is not to discuss the New Age movement directly, with all of its curious and bizarre cultural manifestations and ritualistic practices. Several excellent books do just this.[14] Instead, we will explore the basic world view of pantheism,

13. C. S. Lewis, *Miracles* (New York: Macmillan, 1947), p. 84.
14. Chandler, *Understanding the New Age*; Douglas Groothuis, *Unmasking the New Age* (Downers Grove: InterVarsity, 1986); Hoyt, ed. *New Age Rage*; Elliot Miller, *A Crash Course on the New Age* (Grand Rapids: Baker, 1989).

examining the views of its greatest defenders, East and West (part 1). This survey will reveal that the various patterns of pantheistic thought are similar, whether they come from the Orient or the West. And since New Age concepts reflect these repeating patterns of thought, we may infer that the New Age movement stands within a long tradition: it is not new.

Part 1 will describe five major examples of pantheism. The first three are Eastern. Chapter 1 discusses the Zen Buddhism of D. T. Suzuki (1870–1966), a *permeational pantheism* in which a oneness like a Life Force underlies and permeates all that is real. Chapter 2 presents the thought of the ancient Indian philosopher Shankara (c. 788–c. 820), who developed an *absolute pantheism* in which God alone is real and all else is unreal. Chapter 3 describes the philosophy of the modern Indian statesman Sarvepali Radhakrishnan (1888–1975), who reinterprets Shankara for the modern world. He defends a *multilevel pantheism* that holds that God is the ultimate reality and other things exist only at lower levels of reality.

The next two examples are Western. Chapter 4 lays out the thought of Plotinus (205?–270?), a late Greek philosopher and follower of Plato. His world view is *emanational pantheism*, which teaches that God's being overflows into the world as a flower grows from the bud. Chapter 5 describes the metaphysics of the modern rationalist Benedict de Spinoza (1632–1677). His *modal pantheism* treats the finite world as moments or 'modes' of God's infinite being.

After the historical examples are clarified, we will offer a response to these forms of pantheism from a Christian theistic perspective (part 2). We hope to demonstrate that there are good reasons why Christians choose not to accept pantheism. Christians resist pantheistic ideas not just because they are not Christian, but because they are not rationally convincing or plausible. The pantheistic philosophy promises a great deal philosophically and religiously, but in the end, it cannot deliver. It occasions a number of intractable conceptual difficulties. New Age advocates try to cover these shortcomings with mystical psychobabble, but the answers are deeply unsatisfying to the earnest questioner.

The first chapter of part 2—chapter 6—summarizes pantheism's common threads. It ties together similar themes in pantheism and shows how these ideas manifest themselves in the thought of typical New Age advocates. Chapter 7 criticizes pantheistic metaphysics, the New Age movement's view of reality. Chapter 8 scrutinizes pantheism's epistemology, its theory of knowledge and how we attain it. Chapter 9 evaluates the New Age perspective on religious experience. Chapter 10 analyzes the movement's understanding of good and evil and the implications of pantheism for suffering and morality. The Conclusion draws these themes together.

We present this volume because Westerners' understanding of pantheism is often minimal. Pantheism is a multiform world view that needs to be understood and evaluated. This is especially true in its New Age manifestations, which raise important questions. What are its roots and sources historically and philosophically? What forms does it take? How does it view God, the world, and human persons? What are its implications for life and ethics? In addition, pantheism needs to be evaluated philosophically. This volume, therefore, will address the conceptual adequacy of a world view that is apparently gaining the interest and attention of our culture.

The world view of pantheism presents itself to us in a variety of forms. In the shrinking world of the twentieth century, encounters between theism and pantheism are inevitable. The meetings occur not only in academic classrooms, but also in local movie theaters, corporate meeting rooms, and martial arts studios. In these marketplaces of ideas, pantheism's various types stand out prominently. They attract many adherents, who believe them to be psychologically helpful and spiritually enriching. Is pantheism philosophically adequate? Is it compatible with Christianity?

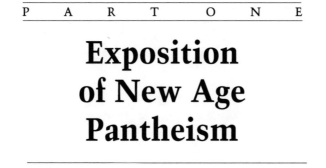

PART ONE

Exposition of New Age Pantheism

Suzuki
Permeational Pantheism

Don't do something; just stand there.—Alan Watts

The form of pantheism best known in the West is Zen Buddhism. Zen has its roots in India but usually is associated with Japan. Its world view may be called permeational pantheism. In this form, the pantheistic principle of unity is experienced as a oneness that underlies, penetrates, and infiltrates all reality. The confusing but fascinating world view of Zen Buddhism crystallizes "all the philosophy, religion, and life itself of the Far-Eastern people, especially of the Japanese."[1]

History of Zen

Zen is the most successful school of Buddhism in the West, particularly the U.S.[2] This is due largely to the impact of a diminutive Japanese scholar named D. T. Suzuki (1870–1966). Described by a

1. D. T. Suzuki, *An Introduction to Zen Buddhism* (New York: Grove, 1964), p. 37.
2. Ernst Benz, "Buddhism in the Western World," in *Buddhism in the Modern World*, ed. Heinrich Dumoulin, pp. 305–22 (New York: Macmillan, Collier Books, 1976), p. 308.

friend as the one "who taught me all that I don't know,"[3] Suzuki began introducing Zen to Western readers in 1927.[4] One observer wrote of him, "the only thing about him that suggests philosophical grandeur is a pair of ferocious eyebrows, which project from his forehead like the eyebrows of the angry demons who guard the entrances of Buddhist temples in Japan. These striking ornaments give him an added air of authority, perhaps, but the addition is unnecessary."[5]

Due to the effort of Suzuki and others, interest in Zen gained momentum in the West during the 1950s and 1960s. But Zen's roots go all the way back to Gautama Buddha (563?–483? B.C.). One day, according to tradition, an audience of students sat before the Buddha expecting an address. Instead of speaking, however, the Buddha silently held up a flower that had been given him and turned it in his hand. Most in attendance were puzzled. But one disciple, Kashyapa, apprehended the Enlightened One's meaning and smiled softly. In the Buddha's famous "Flower Sermon," says Suzuki, Zen was born.[6]

Zen is part of the variegated Mahayana or "Large Vehicle" branch of Buddhism. *Large* here refers to the greater degree of latitude in beliefs and practices tolerated in this branch. But Suzuki claims that Zen remains true to the spirit of the Buddha's experience of "enlightened subjectivity." Zen is therefore a legitimate extension of the Teacher's faith.[7]

Zen is a Japanese word corrupted from the Chinese *Ch'an*, which is in turn a corruption of the Sanskrit *dhyana* (meaning "meditation"). Though Zen's view of the purpose of meditation is different from yoga's, this etymology indicates Zen's roots in the meditative practices of Indian yoga. It also shows the route traveled by Zen through its history. With Mahayana Buddhism in general, Zen traveled north and east through China and Korea to Japan.

The monk revered for having brought what was to become Zen to China is Bodhidharma (Daruma in Japanese; A.D. 470–543). He crossed the mountains in 520 and became the first Chinese Patriarch of Zen. Soon after his arrival, he encountered Emperor Wu-ti, who claimed to have supported Buddhism lavishly.

"How great is the merit due to me?" asked the emperor.

"It is empty, no nobility whatsoever," replied the Indian monk.

3. R. H. Blyth, *Zen and Zen Classics: Selections from R.H. Blyth*, comp. Frederick Franck, 5 vols. (Japan: Hokuseido, 1960), vol. 1, p. xiii.

4. D. T. Suzuki, *Essays in Zen Buddhism*, series 1, was first published by Luzac in London in 1927.

5. Winthrop Sargeant, "Profiles: Dr. D. T. Suzuki," *The New Yorker* (August 31, 1957), p. 34.

6. Heinrich Dumoulin, trans., *Wu-men-kuan*, Series Monumenta Nipponica Monographs, no. 13 (Tokyo, 1953), pp. 17–18.

7. D. T. Suzuki, *Studies in Zen* (New York: Delta, 1955), p. 22.

"What is the First Principle of Buddhism?" the surprised Wu-ti pressed on.

"Vast Emptiness," stated the monk emphatically.

"Who is it then that is facing me?" The emperor was incredulous.

"I do not know, Sire," retorted Bodhidharma, and with that, it is said, he retired to a cave for nine years of uninterrupted meditation.[8]

This startling conversation is typical of Zen. Requesting a definition from a Zen master often elicits an answer calculated to confuse the intellect, for Zen is "round and rolling, slippery and slick, ungraspable and indescribable."[9] Suzuki does admit that Zen has a definite goal and purpose: "In spite of these endless complexities, all Zen masters strive to express that something in our life as we live it which gives us the key to the difficulties raised by the intellect and also stills the anxieties produced by our attachment to a world of relativities."[10] But an explicit statement like this is rare for Suzuki. The whole point of Zen's apparent madness is to force the student to experience its secrets firsthand.

On this point, the two sects of Zen that continue today agree. After a great persecution in 845, Zen developed into five sects. One that survives became known as Ts'ao-tung, a contraction of its founders' names, Tung-shan (807–869) and Ts'ao-shan (840–901). Better known today by its Japanese name, Soto, this sect emphasizes gradual enlightenment, quiet meditation, and the unobtrusive practice of everyday affairs. Transplanted to Japan in 1233 by the highly revered Dogen (1200–1253), Soto now boasts more adherents than its counterpart.

The second sect was founded by Lin-chi (Rinzai; d. 867). His unusual methods have become distinctive of the Rinzai sect, which depends on daring mental puzzles and seeks a lightning bolt of enlightenment. This bold approach plays down doctrines and ideas and emphasizes self-realization and insight. Eisai (1141–1215) officially established Rinzai Zen in Japan in 1191. Though fewer Japanese belong to the Rinzai sect, it is more important in the West since Rinzai is the influential Suzuki's brand of Zen.

Japanese culture has marked and been marked by Zen. But India and China also have made their contributions. All Buddhism, Zen included, feels the influence of the yogic meditation of India. The basic Buddhist creed (the Four Noble Truths, which explain the human predicament, and the Noble Eightfold Path, which provides

---

8. D. T. Suzuki, *Essays in Zen Buddhism,* series 1, ed. Christmas Humphreys (New York: Harper and Brothers, 1949), p. 187.

9. Peter Fingesten, "Beat and Buddhism," *Christian Century* (February 25, 1959), p. 226.

10. Suzuki, *Studies in Zen,* p. 201.

"salvation") has always been experienced through meditation. At the same time, the Buddha emphasized the Middle Way between self-indulgence and asceticism. Thus Buddhism rejects the punishment and purging of the body found in yoga.[11]

China, too, made its mark. One major force was Taoism, which taught that Tao (meaning "Absolute" or "Way") underlies all reality like a common thread of being tying all together. In this way the Tao became like the common divinity that unified all reality. Reality was viewed as a gestalt, a continuous whole, in which conceptual opposites like good and evil disappear.[12]

Taoism's moral ideal was found in its characteristic concept of nonaction or noninvolvement (wu-wei). To pursue nonaction, synchronize with the indescribable Absolute and Oneness that is Tao. Let Tao direct your actions. Do not dictate the course of events with personal desires. Let the pervasive essence of all life intuitively guide your behavior. What is—is! Let it be! This spirit is woven into the fabric of Zen.

We could enumerate influences other than those mentioned so briefly here. For example, the naturalism of Confucian thought deserves attention. However, Mahayana thought provides the major metaphysical background for Zen.

Metaphysics of Emptiness

Suzuki states with his usual daring that "Zen has no thought-system of its own; it liberally uses Mahayana terminology; it refuses to commit itself to any specified pattern of thinking."[13] Some see Zen as an "elimination of metaphysics," for Zen seems deliberately calculated to repudiate philosophical thought.[14] By consciously avoiding the intricacies of intellectual speculation, Zen captures the spirit of the Buddha himself. Metaphysical abstractions get in the way of the real goal of Zen meditation: firsthand experience of life itself.

Nonetheless, the philosophy of Mahayana Buddhism does form Zen's foundation. One commentator concludes that "Zen mysticism is rooted in the pantheistic or cosmotheistic metaphysics of the Mahayana sutras."[15] But the foundation is implicit, not explicit. Suzuki emphasizes that Zen does not think abstractly or intellectually about these doctrines. Zen experiences them in a straightforward, concrete manner.[16]

11. Heinrich Dumoulin, *A History of Zen Buddhism* (Boston: Beacon, 1969), p. 8.
12. Holmes Welch, *Taoism: The Parting of the Way* (Boston: Beacon, 1957), p. 57.
13. Suzuki, *Studies in Zen*, p. 61.
14. Harold McCarthy, "Zen and Some Comments on a Mondo," *Philosophy East and West* 17 (October 1967): 91.
15. Dumoulin, *History of Zen*, p. 271.
16. Suzuki, *Essays in Zen Buddhism*, series 3 (London: Rider, 1953), pp. 78–95.

A basic concept for Mahayana metaphysics is *tathata* ('suchness' or 'thusness'), "the ultimate idea of Buddhist philosophy."[17] While proponents of other world views debated the nature of the Ultimate, the Buddha deliberately shied away from such speculation. In his teaching, the Ultimate has no special qualities, no conditions, no fixed nature that could be grasped by the conceptualizing mind. Reality is neither this nor that. It has no 'sub-stance,' no positive something lying behind or beneath what appears. No thing-in-itself exists in addition to observable phenomena. Rather, things have 'thingness'; they just are what it appears they are.

An old Rinzai master named Bunan (1603–1676) expressed 'suchness' in this enigmatic manner:

> Once you have been greatly enlightened, there is no great enlightenment; when praying, there is no prayer; when rejoicing, there is no one to rejoice. Living, there is nothing living; dying, there is nothing that dies; there is nothing existent or nonexistent. . . .
> *While deluded,*
> *It is things that are things;*
> *When enlightened,*
> *You leave things to their thingness.* [18]

Though *tathata* is a central Mahayana concept, when Suzuki raises the question of metaphysics, he more usually discusses *sunyata* ('emptiness' or 'void'). Suzuki patiently explains that the emptiness of *sunyata* must not be misunderstood. It is not an absolute absence of reality such as the hair on a turtle's back. It is not extinction where something previously existing has somehow puffed out of existence like an extinguished flame. And it is not vacancy, lack of occupancy, like an empty room. These notions all operate in the realm of everyday knowledge dependent on observation and conceptualizing. *Sunyata* correctly understood is an absolute emptiness that transcends all dualities like God versus the world or subject versus object. "In Buddhist Emptiness there is no time, no space, no becoming, no-thing-ness; it is what makes all these things possible; it is a zero full of infinite possibilities[;] it is a void of inexhaustible contents."[19]

To grasp the relation between the two metaphysical ideas, think of *sunyata* (emptiness) as a negative expression of *tathata* (suchness).

---

17. Junjiro Takakusu, *The Essentials of Buddhist Philosophy*, ed. Wing Tsit Chan and Charles A. Moore (Honolulu: University of Hawaii, 1947), p. 47.

18. Bunan, "Sayings of Zen Master Bunan," in *The Original Face: An Anthology of Rinzai Zen*, trans. and ed. Thomas Cleary (New York: Grove, 1978), p. 103.

19. D. T. Suzuki, *Mysticism: Christian and Buddhist* (New York: Harper and Brothers, 1957), p. 28.

Tathata puts it positively: things exist in their mere appearance, in their mere 'thingness.' *Sunyata* puts it negatively: things are empty of substance.[20] What things are—*tathata*—is ultimately void of substance, so they can also be called *sunyata*. Thus *tathata* and *sunyata* may be experienced as one. Indeed Suzuki says, "*sunyata* becomes *tathata* . . . ; *tathata* is *sunyata* and *sunyata* is *tathata*."[21]

Sunyata also has epistemological connotations. The 'no-thing-ness' of reality entails a denial of the validity of the usual manner in which this world is perceived and conceived. This denial includes the data of the five senses as well as the intellectual process of interpreting these data by dividing the world into opposites. Thus merely conceptual knowledge is also "emptiness."[22] Only the highest dynamic, creative insight of enlightenment can rise above this illusion to real knowing.[23]

As all things are tied into the one reality of *sunyata*, this reality is essentially unified. Suzuki quotes a text attributed to Bodhidharma: "If you want to seek the Buddha, you ought to see into your own Nature, which is the Buddha himself. . . . This Nature is the Mind, and the Mind is the Buddha, and the Buddha is the Way, and the Way is Zen."[24] Here we find the basic teaching that all reality is one, for all possesses the Buddha-nature. Even the tiniest particles of dust can contain the whole of reality for the Buddha-nature interpenetrates all.[25]

A story about the Chinese monk Tao-sheng (Dosho in Japanese; d. 434) illustrates this point exactly. On the authority of his own experience, Tao-sheng taught that all rocks possess the Buddha-nature. But as there were no Indian scriptures to support this contention, other monks were skeptical and expelled Tao-sheng for heresy. Unperturbed, the monk began to preach to a collection of rocks in a field. It is said that the rocks were soon nodding their agreement with Tao-sheng's words.[26]

The Buddha-nature that infiltrates and penetrates all reality constitutes the heart of permeational pantheism. Because everything, even rocks and dust particles, is permeated by Buddha-nature, everything becomes its manifestation. The unity here is not unmitigated, for Zen continues to recognize the reality of the world around. There is no absolute absorption, for the plurality of things and persons remains.

20. Takakusu, *Essentials of Buddhist Philosophy*, p. 47.
21. Suzuki, *Studies in Zen*, p. 188.
22. Suzuki actually details eighteen forms of the Emptiness in *Essays in Zen*, series 3, pp. 248ff.
23. Suzuki, *Studies in Zen*, pp. 123–24.
24. Suzuki, *Essays in Zen*, series 1, pp. 232–33.
25. Ibid., series 3, p. 89.
26. Suzuki, *Studies in Zen*, p. 195.

In discussing the relation of human life to nature, Suzuki puts it this way: "The mountains are mountains and yet not mountains. I am I and you are you, and yet I am you and you are I. Nature as a world of manyness is not ignored, and Man as a subject facing the many remains conscious of himself."[27]

Though it recognizes manyness, Zen also teaches a fundamental intimacy with nature. This closeness with nature, based on the shared Buddha-nature, is illustrated by Suzuki's analysis of the contrast between Western and Zen views of nature. Westerners want to analyze and conquer nature. Japanese want to experience oneness with it. When Westerners climb a mountain, they conquer it; when Japanese climb it, they befriend it.[28]

Suzuki expresses his view of the existence of individual humans by using the usual Buddhist doctrine of 'no-self' or 'non-ego.' This doctrine denies any substantial existence to our individual egos. It means that human beings have no substantial reality that lies behind what is apparent. Although we inevitably cling to our egos as though they were permanent, they are in reality transient. They are 'no-thing-ness.' Since this clinging to our personal egos is rooted in ignorance, it can only lead to suffering. We suffer because we think that we can exist permanently and yet fear that we will not. This leads us to hope that we can exist forever, and so we perform religious rituals in hopes of achieving immortality.

The path toward overcoming this fear and sorrow lies through the realization of no-self, the intuitive recognition of the impermanence of our own egos. This knowledge comes only in the wisdom of enlightenment. Thus when we realize through enlightenment that there is no immortality, our anxiety over death can be quieted.[29] When we become aware through higher knowledge that there is no ego to cling to, we can let go of delusions and live in peace.[30] Knowing that we do not exist as a permanent ego takes the pressure off. We can relax and just live.

The doctrine of no-self denies substantiality, however, only to our relative and individual egos. The Absolute, the Cosmic Ego, is not impermanent, in Suzuki's view. Naturally, introducing the notion of an Absolute Self immediately raises the question of how no-self relates to the Absolute Self. The relative, conceptual intellect cannot answer. The question is resolved only by the higher wisdom of

27. Ibid., p. 188.

28. William R. Hoyt, "Zen Buddhism and Western Alienation from Nature," *Christian Century* (October 7, 1970), p. 1194.

29. "Everybody, everybody, in the eyes of illusion[,] though the body dies the spirit does not die—this is a great mistake." Ikkyu, "Skeletons by Zen Master Ikkyu," in *The Original Face*, ed. Cleary, p. 89.

30. Suzuki, *Mysticism: Christian and Buddhist*, pp. 40–45.

enlightenment, which leads you to experience and taste life itself: "the mystery is solved by living it."[31]

The traditional Buddhist view of the relation of the relative ego to the Absolute Ego implies a basic pantheism. Yet Suzuki claims that Zen is neither pantheistic nor theistic. Zen completely defies such categories. Critics are wrong in taking Zen's statements literally and logically. Its unusual statements are intended to explode all attempts to tie Zen down or to fix an unchanging definition for it. Conceptual descriptions inevitably distort the nature of Zen.[32]

Elsewhere Suzuki claims that Zen cannot be called pantheistic because Zen does not teach absorption or identity of the person with God or the Cosmos. Words like *absorption* and *identity* imply a prior, more basic duality between us and our surroundings, he argues. But Zen claims that this duality is part of the illusion. Since *pantheism* means two really distinct entities becoming one, and since Zen denies the substantiality of two distinct realities, it follows that Zen cannot be pantheistic.[33] Suzuki's logic here reveals its Mahayanistic roots: in his denial that Zen believes in two basically distinct realities Suzuki displays his essentially pantheistic notions.

At times, when he denies that Zen is pantheistic, Suzuki shows he is clearly thinking of pantheism in its most absolute form: "Mahayana Buddhism is . . . frequently and erroneously stamped as pantheistic, ignoring altogether a world of particulars."[34] But pantheism need not be unmitigated in the sense of denying completely the everyday world. Pantheism can have many forms. It is true that Suzuki does not hold to an absolute form of pantheism. But as Suzuki's Zen is grounded on the Mahayana Buddhist denial of two substantial realities, there can be no doubt that his concepts are pantheistic in the permeational sense.[35]

Mystical Wisdom

Suzuki makes it clear that one can apprehend the oneness of Zen's permeational pantheism only through a higher wisdom of enlightenment. This implies the 'two-truth theory' of knowledge that Suzuki spells out in detail.[36] The two kinds of knowledge are called *prajna* and *vijnana*. *Prajna* is intuition, the basic knowing principle that

31. Ibid., pp. 45–48.
32. Suzuki, *Introduction to Zen*, pp. 41, 78.
33. Suzuki, *Studies in Zen*, p. 81; Hoyt, "Zen Buddhism," p. 1194.
34. Suzuki, *Mysticism: Christian and Buddhist*, p. 11.
35. Dumoulin, *History of Zen*, p. 288.
36. Suzuki, "Reason and Intuition in Buddhist Philosophy," originally published in *Essays in East-West Philosophy*, ed. Charles A. Moore (Honolulu: University of Hawaii, 1951). It is reprinted in *Studies in Zen*, pp. 85–128.

makes possible a synthetic realization of something in its wholeness. *Vijnana* is rational or conceptual knowledge based on analysis and differentiation. Put another way, *prajna* is knowing directly; *vijnana* is knowing about.[37] That *prajna*, which can solve all philosophical problems, is central to Suzuki's thought should be clear when he ties it to *sunyata* (emptiness): "Epistemologically interpreted, reality is *prajna*; metaphysically interpreted, reality is *sunyata*. *Sunyata*, then, is *prajna*, and *prajna* is *sunyata*."[38]

Prajna cannot be defined intellectually, for definitions require that what is defined be treated as an idea, as an object in contrast to a subject. But *prajna* is pure experience that underlies all subject/object divisions. As such, *prajna* means precisely the overcoming of this division, and any attempted definition from the subject/object point of view will inevitably distort it. For this reason, *prajna* cannot really be called knowledge; it can only be designated 'unknown knowledge.' This complication, says Suzuki, means that the question of *prajna*, which constitutes the "essence of Buddhist philosophy," is "inexhaustible."[39]

But Suzuki does spell out several general characteristics of *prajna*. Perhaps the most important quality is its authority. One who possesses "unknowable knowledge" has an individual, private intuition that carries its own credentials. It brings an inherent sense of certainty and needs no external support from reason or argument. One would never have to ask, "Did I really experience that?" One who has experienced *prajna* can say with infallible assurance, "I am absolute knower."[40]

This sense of certainty comes from the immediacy that characterizes *prajna*. It is direct, not derived, inferred, or mediated. It contains no deliberating, no moving from one step to the next, no reasoning. It is pure experience. So *prajna* is more like a perception than the conclusion of an argument. For instance, one who sees a blue flower knows it is blue. No syllogism or conceptual discourse is necessary. Of course, *prajna* is unlike sense perception in that it is much deeper and more significant. But the point is that in sense perception, the blueness itself is perceived directly and immediately. So it is with *prajna*. [41]

In contrast to *prajna* stands *vijnana*. *Vijnana* is knowledge based on normal sense experience interpreted by the logical oppositions set up by the human reasoning process. While *prajna* is primitive, con-

37. Suzuki, *Studies in Zen*, pp. 85, 124, 146.
38. Ibid., pp. 111, 101.
39. Ibid., pp. 145, 107.
40. Ibid., pp. 146–47.
41. Ibid., pp. 147, 87, 94, 118.

crete, and irreducible, *vijnana* is derived, abstract, and reducible. *Prajna* is synthetic and functions by unifying and integrating, but *vijnana* depends on analysis and breaking apart. It goes without saying that in Suzuki's mind, *prajna* is quite clearly superior to *vijnana*.[42]

With all these contrasts, it might be expected that Suzuki would think of *prajna* and *vijnana* as utterly unrelated. Indeed, he says straight out that there is no relationship between "plunging into the silent valley of Absolute Emptiness" (*prajna*) and the "knowledge we highly value in the realm of relativity where our senses and intellect move" (*vijnana*).[43] But he also states that *vijnana* in its differentiation presupposes the more basic unity of *prajna*. And he recognizes the desire of a logical mind to understand the relationship. So he makes this concession: *prajna* is "not unity in multiplicity, nor multiplicity in unity; but unity is multiplicity and multiplicity is unity. In other words, *prajna* is *vijnana* and *vijnana* is *prajna*, only this is to be 'immediately' apprehended and not after a tedious and elaborate and complicated process of dialectic."[44]

The apparent contradiction does not faze Suzuki. If this seems incoherent to rational minds, it is because they tend to view the whole issue from the discriminating and bifurcating viewpoint of *vijnana*. What may seem like a "logic of contradiction" is really the dialectics of *prajna*.[45] Thus

> Zen would serenely go its own way without at all heeding . . . criticism [about contradictions]. Because Zen's first concern is about its experience and not its modes of expression. The latter allow a great deal of variation, including paradoxes, contradictions, and ambiguities. . . . Those who have a genuine Zen experience will at once recognize in spite of superficial discrepancies what is true and what is not.[46]

Indeed, Suzuki writes that no paradox exists in the experience of *prajna* itself. Contradiction arises only when we attempt to express the experience in *vijnana* terms. In a sense, *prajna* creates logical contradictions for *vijnana*.[47] From the higher point of view, so-called rational statements cannot adequately express the insight of *prajna*. Words can serve only to point the way to higher wisdom. Like scaffolding, they have a purpose, but must later be dismantled. Thus Zen's irrational statements, paradoxical question-and-answer dia-

42. Ibid., pp. 147, 85, 122, 100.
43. Suzuki, *Mysticism: Christian and Buddhist*, pp. 23–25.
44. Suzuki, *Studies in Zen*, pp. 93–95.
45. Suzuki, *Introduction to Zen*, pp. 32–33; *Essays in Zen*, series 3, p. 314.
46. Suzuki, *Mysticism: Christian and Buddhist*, p. 59.
47. Suzuki, *Studies in Zen*, pp. 124, 146.

logues (*mondo*), and mind-bending stories point toward *prajna* as a finger points to the moon. But words cannot describe it, and the finger should never be confused with the moon.[48]

All this means that Zen accepts a two-truth theory of knowledge. The following *mondo* and Suzuki's analysis illustrates this concept:

> Ungan Donjo (Yun-yen T'an-sheng, d. 841) . . . made this remark to the congregation: "There is a man for whom there is nothing he cannot answer if he is asked."
> Tozan questioned: "How large is his library?"
> The master said: "Not a book in his house."
> Tozan: "How could he be so learned?"
> The master: "Not a wink he sleeps day and night."
> Tozan: "May I ask him some special question?"
> The master: "His answer will be no answer."

Suzuki obliges us by rephrasing this cryptic story into *vijnana* language:

> We generally reason: "A" is "A" because "A" is "A"; or "A" is "A", therefore, "A" is "A". Zen agrees or accepts this way of reasoning, but Zen has its own way which is ordinarily not at all acceptable. Zen would say: "A" is "A" because "A" is not "A"; or "A" is not "A"; therefore, "A" is "A".[49]

What can all this mean? It seems like sheer nonsense. Perhaps this illustration will help. Many Christians believe their faith should be conceptualized without the familiar division between secular and sacred. All of life is sacred, for God is as concerned with the mundane details of everyday life as with the majesty of worship in the cathedral. So the Christian may say that secular is sacred and sacred is secular. And this may seem like a contradiction.

But the apparent contradiction is real only if the Christian means to say that the concept of sacredness is equivalent to the concept of secularity. Of course, he is not saying this at all. The Christian is really saying that the so-called secular dimensions of life equal the so-called sacred aspects of life simply because the categories of secular and sacred do not adequately interpret life as he understands it. His point has nothing to do with the logical contradictoriness of reality. It has everything to do with the inappropriateness of the categories.

Something like this is Suzuki's point. Logical thought takes conceptual opposites (black versus white, good versus evil, heaven versus

---

48. Suzuki, *Introduction to Zen*, pp. 33, 59, 63, 74; *Studies in Zen*, pp. 109, 165.
49. Suzuki, *Studies in Zen*, p. 152.

hell, you versus me) with final seriousness. Such thinking contributes to suffering by fostering the illusion that our egos really exist separate from the world. We experience fear because we want to protect the safety and well-being of these false egos. But concepts just limit life. They are as unnecessary as "adding legs to a snake."

Zen concedes that words symbolize things. Yet Zen emphasizes that symbols should never be confused with the things themselves. Zen despises intellectualism and ultimately seeks to rise above mere concepts to find life itself. You will gain life not through thinking, but through experience. If you understand Zen (cognitively), says Suzuki, then you do not (really) understand it.[50] Zen "does not like the odour of abstraction which oozes out from even such terms as 'Transcendence'." As soon as intellection begins, life itself slips out the side door.[51] The only answer is to let go of *vijnana* and to find enlightenment though *prajna*.

Religious Enlightenment

Zen's path to *prajna* is called *satori* (translated *enlightenment*). Not unexpectedly, Suzuki states that *satori* is inexplicable to the one who has never experienced it—like trying to explain the sunset to someone blind from birth. "A *satori* turned into a concept ceases to be itself; and there will no more be a Zen experience."[52] But having issued his warning, Suzuki again accedes to the human desire for definition: *satori* is "an intuitive looking into the nature of things in contradistinction to the analytical or logical understanding of it."[53] In the *prajna* that *satori* brings, no particular object exists. *Satori* can mean intuiting a blade of grass, a stick belonging to the master, or nothing in particular. *Satori* is perception of Reality itself in its wholeness and thus has no specific content.[54]

Historical records indicate that *satori* is always sudden. Suzuki describes it as a "sudden flashing," a "mental catastrophe" in which the conceptual framework of the mind breaks like a dam exploding from the force of a tidal wave. When someone asks if enlightenment is gradual, Suzuki uses the illustration of a man walking north whose steps suddenly turn south. Certainly the abrupt conversion is in the midst of a larger process, but the walker cannot help but be aware of the entirely new perspective that this complete reversal in direction

50. Suzuki, *Essays in Zen*, series 3, p. 319; *Studies in Zen*, pp. 150, 76, 59; *The Zen Doctrine of No-Mind* (London: Rider, 1949), p. 14.
51. Suzuki, *Studies in Zen*, p. 201.
52. Suzuki, *Introduction to Zen*, pp. 33, 92.
53. Suzuki, *Essays in Zen*, series 1, p. 228.
54. Suzuki, *Studies in Zen*, p. 89; *Introduction to Zen*, p. 93.

brings. No matter how we look at it, the change of perspective is instantaneous.[55]

This revolution in one's point of view affects how ego is viewed. The isolated ego that had been so vociferously defended "becomes loosened somehow from its tightening grip and melts away into something indescribable." As a child who is dreaming she is sick needs simply to wake up to be cured, so the person suffering from illusion needs this new view of life. When it happens and there is realization of no-self, life's problems take care of themselves. The enlightened one can relax and let what is simply be! Zen's raison d'etre is this liberation—without *satori* Zen is pointless.[56]

Many Zen stories make it clear that enlightenment can be achieved without recourse to a superior being. One master named Tai-chu (Daishu; d. 814) told his disciples, "'I do not understand Zen, nor is there any special teaching to give out for your sake. Therefore, there is no need for you to be standing here for so long. It is best for you to get the matter settled with yourselves.'"[57]

Zen abounds with statements of this sort. Sacred books, ancient traditions, and even the teachings of Buddha and Bodhidharma are subjected to scorn. One of Zen's cherished ideals is the wordless "Zen creed," which Suzuki quotes with approval:

A special transmission outside the scriptures;
No dependence upon words and letters;
Direct pointing at the soul of man;
Seeing into one's nature and the attainment of Buddhahood.[58]

This iconoclasm reinforces the notion that *satori* must be a first-hand experience not based on doctrine or rational knowledge. To insure this principle, a master named Feng (Seppo; 822–908) is said to have declared, "'The [Buddha] is a bull-headed jail-keeper, and the Patriarchs are horse-faced old maids.'"[59] And Suzuki reports that Tan-hsia (Tanka; 738–824) is well-known for having burned images of the Buddha to keep warm. Several Zen artists have depicted Tan-hsia warming his posterior and smiling brightly as the fire cheerily consumes the images![60]

55. Suzuki, *Introduction to Zen*, p. 95; D. T. Suzuki, *Studies in the Lankavatara Sutra* (London, 1930), p. 207.
56. D. T. Suzuki, *Essays in Zen Buddhism*, series 2 (London: Rider, 1950), pp. 28–34; Bassui, "The Sermon of Zen Master Bassui," in *The Original Face*, ed. Cleary, p. 95; Suzuki, *Introduction to Zen*, p. 95.
57. Suzuki, *Essays in Zen*, series 3, p. 43.
58. Ibid., series 1, p. 174.
59. Ibid., series 3, p. 373.
60. Ibid., series 1, pp. 328–29.

Such unusual stories reflect a basic dilemma felt within Zen teaching. Its repudiation of words and concepts is so strong that we wonder what Suzuki means when he uses words to say that words say nothing. Like other Zen masters who circumvent the problem by uttering sheer nonsense, Suzuki knows well what he is doing and the problems it causes: "To say 'empty' is already denying itself. But you cannot remain silent. How to communicate the silence without going out of it is the crux. It is for this reason that Zen avoids as much as possible resorting to linguistics and strives to make us go underneath words, as it were to dig out what is there."[61]

At times Suzuki apologizes for uttering the unutterable, calling his philosophical works "my sins." Zen "despises those who indulge in word- or idea-mongering," says Suzuki, admitting his infractions will send him straight to hell.[62] At other times he argues resolutely that both speaking and non-speaking fall short. The only solution is a higher form of statement where eloquence and silence merge.[63]

If word-mongering will not elicit *satori*, what will? The Zen answer is twofold, the *koan* and *zazen*. Suzuki calls these techniques the handmaidens of Zen. *Koan* is the eye, and *zazen* is the foot.[64] In Suzuki's Rinzai Zen, the *koan* gets more attention. *Zazen* (meaning "sitting meditation") plays a role in Rinzai, but is more dominant in Soto Zen.

The *koan* (literally meaning "public document" or "judicial case") is an absurd dialogue, question and answer, or anecdote which opens a novice's experience to *satori* without using direct teaching.[65] The *koan* is not just an entertaining diversion. Its purpose is to build pressure on the conceptual mind like flood tides rising behind an earthen dam. As tension and frustration build, the structural integrity of the dam of logical thinking begins to break down. When the pressure is too great, the dam suddenly breaks, and striving for conceptual understanding ceases. At that moment, *satori* rushes in to fill the vacuum. The lightning bolt of enlightenment strikes, and the world is perceived with the eye of *prajna*.[66]

Though all are not still in use, about seventeen hundred *koan* exist. Along with their "orthodox" answers, these have become codified over the years. Suzuki believes the *koan*, despite their rigidity, have kept Zen alive through the centuries.[67] As many examples could

61. Suzuki, *Mysticism: Christian and Buddhist*, p. 29; *Studies in Zen*, p. 193.
62. Sargeant, "Profiles: Dr. D. T. Suzuki," p. 36; Suzuki, *Studies in Zen*, p. 142.
63. Suzuki, *Introduction to Zen*, p. 70.
64. Ibid., p. 101.
65. Suzuki, *Studies in Zen*, p. 27; *Introduction to Zen*, p. 102.
66. Suzuki, *Introduction to Zen*, pp. 108–9; *Essays in Zen*, series 2, p. 66.
67. Suzuki, *Essays in Zen*, series 2, pp. 83–84; *Introduction to Zen*, pp. 110, 113.

attest, the *koan* embody Zen's irreverent attitude toward doctrines, concepts, scriptures, and tradition.

For instance, perhaps the most famous *koan* is attributed to Hakuin (1686–1769), the father of modern Rinzai Zen. "When both hands are clapped a sound is produced: listen to the sound of one hand." Another illustration: "Last night a wooden horse neighed and a stone man cut capers."[68] The purpose here is none other than to grind logical thought to a standstill and open the path to *satori*. Suzuki quotes with approval the descriptive comment of Yuan-wu (Engo; 1063–1135): "there is no crack in it to insert [your] intellectual teeth."[69]

Suzuki says that the religious experience of Zen is historically unique. While this is a broad claim, he is correct in one respect. In many cases, mystics of other religions believe that the mystical experience of God comes only when God is pleased to send it. Encounter with God, in other words, is a gift of grace that cannot be manipulated. But the distinctive religious experience of Zen, unlike some others, comes as a result of practices specifically designed to elicit it. *Satori* is not left to chance.[70] Rather, Zen admits straightforwardly that *satori* comes from within, not from without. When *satori* helps one realize *sunyata* (emptiness), striving for more ceases, and the *koan* has accomplished its purpose.

Zen's esthetic taste and art forms express the enlightened outlook. The *dō* (literally *ways*) aid one in developing sensitivity, naturalness, simplicity, emptiness, and spontaneity. Especially well known is the tea ceremony, which captures the Japanese soul. An ancient proverb says, "Zen and tea are one." Other *dō* include *kendo* (ceremonial sword fighting), judo or *jujitsu*, archery, poetry, ink painting, and *ikebana* (flower arranging). These can exemplify unity with nature, as when an ink painter becomes one with her brush or an archer with his bow.

Zen art can capture the madness as well. In judging several monks' efforts to produce the best portrait of himself, one master gave first prize to the monk who did a somersault and left the room. Zen art tells us to relax, to be at one with our surroundings, to refuse analysis, and to embrace first-hand experience.[71] Art is expressly manipulated to develop the life of enlightenment.

Zen Lifestyle

But if what is, just is, what becomes of ethics? When things appear evil, does any moral principle oblige one to change them? In theory, it

68. Suzuki, *Introduction to Zen*, p. 59.
69. Suzuki, *Essays in Zen*, series 2, p. 89.
70. Suzuki, *Introduction to Zen*, pp. 110–11.
71. D. T. Suzuki, *Zen and Japanese Culture* (New York: Pantheon, 1959), pp. 150ff., 227ff.; *No-Mind*, p. 86.

would seem that Suzuki should answer in the negative. Theoretically, all conceptual opposites, including good versus evil and virtue versus depravity, are transcended in *prajna*. Such distinctions should belong to *vijnana*. You would expect Suzuki to agree with R. H. Blyth, who tells the story of Tao-shan (Yakusan; 758–834). It seems the monk shouted to his disciples, "'The Hall's falling down.'" The disciples completely misunderstood, for they tried to prop up the hall, where-upon Yakusan unceremoniously died. Blyth comments, "When some famous work of art or monument of culture is destroyed, when a moth is burnt in a flame, when five million Jews are slaughtered, let us do what Yakusan did,—yell, and die."[72]

This point of view seems to find support in the Zen idea that in *prajna* one just lives. Suzuki tells this story: One of the monks of Tai-chu (Daishu, d. 814), working in the field, heard the dinner drum. With a laugh, he went to dinner. The master thought this indicated great insight and inquired what the monk had learned. "Nothing much, Master," came the reply. "As I heard the dinner drum go, I went back and had my meal."[73]

In this spirit, Suzuki frequently repeats that the enlightened one simply accepts what is, seeking oneness with the spirit that animates life.[74] Illustrating this enlightened attitude, Suzuki quotes the Chinese master Yun-men (Ummon; 862/4–949) discussing the nature of his stick: "As regards Zen followers, when they see a staff, they simply call it a staff. If they want to walk, they just walk; if they want to sit, they just sit. They should not in all circumstances be ruffled and distracted."[75]

Zen expresses this attitude in its penchant for manual labor. Sweeping, cooking, farming, and begging keep the monks' minds focused on the concrete. The master not only states but also demonstrates that meditation has everything to do with the ordinary events of life. Menial work overcomes the artificial division between thought and life that precludes the student's enlightenment. This emphasis on the ordinary reinforces the sense that life *is* Zen![76]

Zen's celebration of the everyday infuses the culture of Japan with a distinctive flavor. The *haiku* is a special form of Japanese poetry always containing seventeen syllables (at least in Japanese). The writers of *haiku* seek to capture this commonness of life. For example:

72. Blyth, *Zen and Zen Classics*, vol. 2, p. 53; Dumoulin, *History of Zen*, p. 81.
73. Suzuki, *No-Mind*, p. 104.
74. Suzuki, *Introduction to Zen*, pp. 71, 111; *Studies in Zen*, pp. 28, 157, 181.
75. Suzuki, *Essays in Zen*, series 3, p. 280.
76. Suzuki, *Essays in Zen*, series 1, pp. 312–17; *Studies in Zen*, p. 156; *Introduction to Zen*, p. 119.

> *On the temple bell*
> *Perching, sleeps*
> *The butterfly, Oh!*[77]

Zen wants nothing of the extraordinary or the other-worldly. As Chao-chou (Joshu; 778–897) once said, "Zen is your everyday thought."[78]

The ethical implications of all this might seem to be antinomianism, that is, rejection of the moral law. Reality simply is what it is. What guidelines for improved behavior would be possible? The *koan* seeks to break down thought and tradition, including the moral teachings of Buddhism. What motivation would there be for virtuous living? The whole point is to get beyond traditions, scriptures, even Zen itself.

But Suzuki forcefully rejects any thought that Zen implies antinomianism. History tells of many masters who went into ascetic retirement for a time of moral development. This implies the subjugation of moral impurities and temptations: "many serpents and adders are waiting at the porch, and if one fails to trample them down effectively they raise their heads again." Zen advocates a simple lifestyle with efficient use of resources, self-restraint, and a reverential attitude toward life.

In addition, Suzuki writes that Zen admires the "secret virtue," the "deed without merit": a "child is drowning; I get into the water, and the child is saved." One simply does what needs to be done, walking away and giving it not a second thought. There is no God to keep track, no praise to win, no condemnation to avoid. No thought of future reward enters the heart and mind of the enlightened one.[79]

In Suzuki's view, Zen affirms everyday life, and this includes its moral dimension. Zen's primary concern lies behind the phenomena of life with the realization of *sunyata* as the nature of the real. But this does not imply absolute negation of everyday ethical concerns. "As to what relates to our worldly lives [Zen] leaves all this where it properly belongs."[80] Acknowledging the legitimacy of the everyday moral sphere is just part of realizing that what is, simply is.

This approach reveals the great influence on Zen of the Mahayana concept of the *bodhisattva*. The *bodhisattva* is one who has attained enlightenment but postpones entrance into this state to keep a vow to assist all life to achieve salvation. The *bodhisattva* in popular Buddhism has become a magic-working semi-god whose compassion

77. Suzuki, *Zen and Japanese Culture*, p. 248.
78. Suzuki, *Introduction to Zen*, p. 97.
79. Ibid., pp. 130–31.
80. Suzuki, *Studies in Zen*, p. 79.

knows no bounds. Throughout their lives, Zen disciples repeat the vows of the *bodhisattva*, promising to save all sentient beings and to master the truth of Buddhism. Compassion, the highest virtue, requires giving up possessions and instead seeking tasks that reinforce humility and meekness. In this spirit, the Zen monk acts only for the good of others. Never would self-interest or self-desire motivate a *bodhisattva*.[81]

But how could the *bodhisattva* ideal be squared with Zen's view of life? If all beings are *sunyata*, why save them? Would saving them be better than not saving them? Is there any difference between 'better' and 'worse'? Indeed, who or what is there to save? Suzuki recognizes this problem and states that its solution is a mystery. Logic cannot explain the relation of *prajna* and compassion, for it only produces paradox. If one searches for a metaphysical basis for compassion, Suzuki offers this analogy: "It is . . . like the shooting of one arrow after another into the air by a man whose mastery of archery has attained a very high degree. He is able to keep all the arrows in the air making each arrow support the one immediately preceding. He does this as long as he wishes."[82] If that does not help, consider that "fire is something that burns; water is something that wets; a buddha is someone who practices compassion."[83] Once again, what is, simply is!

Conclusion

Since the 1950s, Zen's nomenclature has been infiltrating our vocabulary. Consider the gag, How many Zen Buddhists does it take to screw in a light bulb? The answer? Two—one to screw it in, and one not to screw it in. Today's Americans know enough about Zen *koans* to get the joke.

Western society has absorbed more than jokes, however. The Zen ideas planted in the West during the last fifty years have born fruit in the New Age movement. Zen propounds a philosophy of life that fits these times. For example, without the moral constraints of *bodhisattva* vows or the discipline of the master in the temple, Zen can degenerate into a rationalization for self-centered living. If Suzuki protests this antinomian heresy, his voice is not always heard. Misunderstood, Zen gives life a moral imprimatur. What is, just is! I'm O.K., you're O.K., and the world is O.K. All of us should "do our own thing" and "get in touch with ourselves."

Zen in this form is too much in tune with the prevailing cultural

81. Suzuki, *Introduction to Zen*, pp. 120, 126.
82. Suzuki, *Essays in Zen*, series 3, p. 299.
83. Bunan, "Sayings of Bunan," in *The Original Face*, ed. Cleary, p. 102.

permissiveness. Zen master Frederick "Rama" Lenz funded a massive advertising campaign costing $850,000 to boost his tour of meditation sessions until former students exposed his morally bankrupt activities. Of course, traditional Zen masters did not endorse his work.[84] But this does not change the perception of many who believe, on the authority of masters like Lenz, that we all have the right to develop our own standards of morality.

In another vein, the Zen world view finds connections with the scientific perspective. Some physicists are highlighting what they perceive to be parallels between their discipline and Zen philosophy. Fritjof Capra, whose *Tao of Physics* is a favorite among New Age connoisseurs, writes, "The basic elements of the Eastern world view are also those of the world view emerging from modern physics. . . . The further we penetrate into the submicroscopic world, the more we shall realize how the modern physicist, like the Eastern Mystic, has come to see the world as a system of inseparable, interacting, and ever-moving components with man being an integral part of this system."[85]

Today we find the ancient religion of pantheism defended both in the sophisticated lectures of Capra and in the naive philosophizing of movie starlets who are "into metaphysics." Various themes have been ingested by the New Age. They add bright colors to a swirling kaleidoscope we now recognize as New Age philosophy.

84. Russell Chandler, *Understanding the New Age* (Waco: Word, 1988), pp. 65–66.
85. Fritjof Capra, *The Tao of Physics* (Berkeley, Calif.: Shambhala, 1975), p. 25.

Shankara
Absolute Pantheism

Brahman is eternal, all-knowing, absolutely self-sufficient, ever pure, intelligent and free, pure knowledge, absolute bliss.—Shankara

Of the many forms of pantheism, perhaps the purest example is the philosophy of the medieval Hindu Shankara (c. 788–c. 820). His world view ascribes less reality to the world of everyday life than perhaps any other Eastern philosophy. Most pantheisms acknowledge that objects in the world have some sort of limited secondary reality as either modes or aspects or levels of the pantheistic one. But the sophisticated philosophy of the Indian sage Shankara gives us a good example of a pantheism that approaches an absolute form.

History of Hinduism

The background for understanding Shankara's Hindu pantheism begins with the confluence of two societies, the native Dravidians of India and the migrating Aryans from the northwest. The Aryans, Indo-European relatives of the Greeks, Romans, and Iranians (note *Aryan* and *Iran*), appeared in India during the second millennium before Christ. They brought with them a polytheism that bore family resemblances to the Greco-Roman pantheon. For example, the Hindu god of heaven, Varuna, may well be related to the Greek god Ouranos (Uranus in Latin). The name of the Hindu fire god, Agni, is etymologically related to the Latin *ignis*, from which we get ignition.[1]

These polytheistic worshipers produced the earliest Indo-European literary milestone, the Vedas (meaning "knowledge"), dating from perhaps 1500 to 1000 B.C. The oldest of four Vedas, the Rig Veda, contains more than one thousand hymns to various gods. The three other Vedas contain sacrificial formulas, liturgical hymns, and various magical incantations and spells.[2]

The polytheism of the Vedas only hints at the unified concept of God that would develop later into a full pantheism when theistic and pantheistic strains appear in the Hindu scriptures. In certain passages, the god addressed is treated as supreme. For example, Section 10 of the Rig Veda (thought by some to be a later insertion into an earlier Vedic writing) contains many monistic ideas. It includes a "Hymn of Creation" that identifies the creator as the One. Then it asks,

> But was the One above or was it under [creation]? . . .
> Who knows for certain? Who shall here declare it?
> Whence was it born, and whence came this creation?
> The gods were born after this world's creation:
> Then who can know from whence it has arisen?[3]

Quite clearly, the writer wonders whether someone or something is beyond the gods.

In another place, it is said of this transcendent reality, "To what is one, sages give many a title: they call it Agni, Yama, Matarisvan."[4] Religious teachers throughout Indian religious history used this very famous maneuver to solve the problem of the multiplicity of gods. It matters not what symbols are used; everyone worships the one and only Ultimate Reality.

In the centuries after 1000 B.C., religious writers added to the four Vedas over 200 (traditionally, 108) Upanishads. The Upanishadic writers attempted to explain the essence of true religion that lay beneath the formal rituals and practices that had developed. This corpus of essential Hindu sacred literature, four Vedas plus the Upanishads, is

---

1. Ninian Smart, *The Religious Experience of Mankind* (New York: Charles Scribner's Sons, 1969), pp. 59–60.

2. Sarvepali Radhakrishnan and Charles A. Moore, eds., *A Sourcebook in Indian Philosophy* (Princeton: Princeton University Press, 1957), pp. 3–5.

3. Rig Veda, 10.129.5, 6, quoted in *Sourcebook*, ed. Radhakrishnan and Moore, p. 23.

4. Rig Veda, 1.164.46, quoted in *Sourcebook*, ed. Radhakrishnan and Moore, p. 21.

sometimes collectively called the Veda. The Veda is the Hindu scripture.

The monism that the four Vedas occasionally prefigure becomes explicit in the Upanishads. The distinctive doctrine is Brahman. ("Brahmin" [the priestly class] is a related word.) *Brahman* originally meant the power inherent in sacrificial ritual, but later it came to mean the mysterious One out of which all action proceeds. The intuitions of the Upanishadic writers led them to affirm that Brahman is within the human soul. In this fundamental doctrine lies the genius of the Upanishads.

The classical era of Hinduism (roughly 450 B.C. to A.D. 600) saw the rise of yogic meditation and of various cults emphasizing devotion to personal gods. (This personal devotion, called *bhakti*, is practiced by the so-called Hare Krishna devotees, among others.) In addition, the period saw the development of other religions like Jainism and Buddhism as well as the writing of more Hindu religious literature. This Hindu literature took the form of commentary on the Veda and technically did not possess the authority of the Veda. One exception to this, the well-loved *Bhagavad Gita*, is informally accorded the authority theoretically reserved only for their scripture.

The *Gita* is based on Upanishadic philosophy, but it develops the personal side of Brahman as incarnated in the god Krishna. In the *Gita*, personal worship and devotion are elevated to equal status with both knowledge and works as means to union with God. Typical Hindu tolerance of various paths to the Supreme has made the *Gita* acceptable in India, and this piece of literature has become an international favorite.

Into this context came the commentators of medieval Hinduism which began around A.D. 600. Six traditional schools had developed, the most important being Vedanta ("end of the Veda"). Vedanta expresses certain philosophical and religious speculations on the Upanishads. A group of 555 *sutras*, two- or three-word statements, systematize the teachings of the Upanishads. These are called the *Vedanta-sutras*. The *sutras*, however, are very enigmatic; they are in fact unintelligible without commentary. Therefore, prominent commentators interpreted the *Vedanta-sutras* according to their philosophical perspectives. In later centuries, others wrote commentaries on commentaries and even commentaries on commentaries on commentaries.

Three whose commentaries on these *sutras* are most important include Ramanuja (1017–1137), Madhva (1197–1276), and, of course, Shankara (or Samkara or Sankara). Shankara did not found Vedantic philosophy, but his commentary shines as its most influential expression. It has been called "the fulcrum on which most of the subsequent development of classical Indian philosophy turned."[5]

Reality as Nonduality

Shankara's philosophy is best described by the term *Advaita*, meaning "non-duality." To distinguish his form of Vedanta philosophy from Ramanuja and Madhva, his thought has been called *Advaita Vedanta*. This name indicates the centrality of the *Advaita* concept for Shankara's thought. According to the principle of nonduality, all Reality is considered to be a single, inclusive whole not subject to any distinctions. Shankara expresses this basic doctrine in these words: "In the same way as those parts of ethereal space which are limited by jars and waterpots are not really different from the universal ethereal space, . . . so this manifold world with its objects of enjoyment, enjoyers and so on has no existence apart from Brahman."[6]

This empirical world may seem to be brute reality, but this appearance arises from a wrong view of things. As the dream seems real to the dreamer, everyday reality seems real to one who does not have the ultimate vision of oneness. But when the dreamer awakens, he understands from the higher perspective that his dream is unreal. In an analogous way, when the person who had placed full confidence in everyday experience realizes the absolute unity of Brahman, the true nature of Brahman and the illusion of the everyday can be understood.[7]

This doctrine of nonduality implies that the cause of the universe is not different from the effect—the universe itself is in a sense both cause and effect. Shankara tells us that the effect, this world, and its cause, Brahman, are in reality "non-different." Thus he has no place for the idea of creation in the theistic sense, for God does not create a world that is distinct from himself. To put it another way, the world depends so completely on Brahman for its existence that it is Brahman.[8] The universe is not in the final analysis really different from God.

To emphasize the ultimacy and absoluteness of Brahman, Shankara says that Brahman has no being. This may seem to imply that Brahman does not exist. But his statement must be understood as an attempt to deny limitation of Brahman. Brahman is entirely unlimit-

5. Stuart C. Hackett, *Oriental Philosophy: A Westerner's Guide to Eastern Thought* (Madison: University of Wisconsin Press, 1979), p. 147.

6. Shankara, *The Vedānta Sūtras of Bādarāyaṇa with the Commentary by Śaṅkara,* trans. George Thibaut, 2 parts (New York: Dover, 1962), 2.1.14.

7. Ibid.

8. Ibid.

ed. 'Non-being' does not denote absolute non-existence. Rather, since 'being' indicates differentiation by names and forms, Brahman is prior to and beyond 'being,' that is, it must be 'non-being.' Calling something "A" implies that it is not "not-A," and this is a limitation. 'Form,' he says in one place, belongs to individual selves, but not to the Absolute Self. The river abides by forms, the banks, which limit its flow; the ocean into which the river flows does not have such forms. Alternatively, he suggests that Brahman has form in connection with the world, but it has no form in itself. Consequently, Shankara says only that "Brahman is distinctly denied to be Non-existing, defined to be that which is."[9]

By introducing the distinction between Brahman in itself and Brahman in connection to the world, Shankara alludes to a distinction between Unqualified Brahman (Brahman not described by concepts) and Qualified Brahman (Brahman to whom qualities are ascribed). The Sanskrit term *guna* means quality or attribute. Nirguna (Unqualified) Brahman is the Ultimate conceived without qualities; Saguna (Qualified) Brahman is the Ultimate conceived to possess many attributes. Nirguna Brahman is the unqualified, absolute reality. Saguna Brahman, also known by the name of the personal god, Īśvara, is the lord of this world. This double nature of Brahman depends on whether it is viewed from the perspective of knowledge or ignorance. As the object of true knowledge, Brahman has no qualities. When one views Brahman from a lower point of view, attributes can be ascribed to it.

By using this distinction, Shankara can freely attribute various qualities to Brahman. It is eternal, imperishable, omniscient, omnipotent, omnipresent, pure, blissful, immutable, and absolutely self-sufficient.[10] Those who believe that Orientals do not use logic will be interested to know that Shankara refuses to apply logically contradictory attributes to Brahman. The qualities of mutability and immutability, for example, cannot both be attributed to Brahman.[11]

Indeed, seeking the attributes of Brahman is a wrongheaded procedure from the beginning. From the ultimate perspective, the whole enterprise of finding the attributes of Brahman is mired in ignorance, even though it is true and helpful from the lower point of view. To the devotee who meditates on and worships a personal god, qualified Brahman is useful. From the phenomenal, everyday point of view, ascribing attributes to Brahman is proper. But from the perspective of ultimate reality, the denial of attributes is true. Shankara illustrates this with one of his favorite examples: universal space limited by

9. Ibid., 1.4.15, 21; 3.2.15.
10. Ibid., 1.1.4; 2.1.14.
11. Ibid., 2.1.14.

glass jars is different from universal space from one point of view, but ultimately the space within the glass is one with space outside the glass.[12] Brahman is *advaita*, nonduality.

This illustration raises questions about the creation of the world. At certain points, Shankara claims that the origin and continuation of the world process depend on an omniscient, omnipotent deity. In this context he denies that a nonintelligent principle could explain the existence of the world.[13] But at other times he denies a conscious, free, premeditated creation by God. The creative process is like breathing, he tells us, entirely unplanned. Like play, it is entirely unserious. Breathing and playing occur without any specific goal in mind. They are simply processes that result from the nature of things.[14]

In this way, the world comes from Brahman and so depends completely upon it. Even a world that arises from earlier worlds depends finally upon Brahman, for the previous worlds were themselves the result of Brahman breathing and playing.[15] For moral reasons, Shankara holds that these worlds must follow one after another. If this world came into being from nothing, the inequities humans suffer in this life could not be explained as the result of virtuous and sinful acts performed in previous lives. This, of course, is the principle of *karma*. So this world did arise from a previous world. In reality, both depend on the creative activity of Brahman. Brahman is the only cause of the entire chain of successive universes.[16]

When Shankara says that the world depends on Brahman, he means that it does so in every way. Brahman is both the stuff of the world and the form that shapes the stuff: "If there were admitted a guiding principle different from the material cause, it would follow that everything cannot be known through one thing. . . . [Brahman] is thus the operative cause, because there is no other ruling principle, and the material cause because there is no other substance from which the world could originate."[17] Brahman does not in any way depend on the world, however, for Brahman is utterly unaffected by the world. The dreamer is not changed by mere dreams; the magician is not influenced by illusions. So Brahman is entirely the causer and never at all affected.[18]

It is important to see that Shankara does not deny the existence of the world entirely. The lower form of thinking, the dream-like illu-

12. Ibid.
13. Ibid.
14. Ibid., 2.1.33.
15. Ibid., 1.4.3.
16. Ibid., 2.1.36; 1.1.2.
17. Ibid., 1.4.23.
18. Ibid., 2.1.9.

sion of everyday experience, is not completely unreal. He preserves the reality of the world while speaking simultaneously of its dependence on Brahman. As some scholars argue, Shankara's sense of empirical reality is so strong that it prevents him from accepting the Buddhist theory that the objects of the world are simply elements in the minds of individuals.[19]

Shankara uses clay to illustrate his point. If you really know the nature of clay, then you also know the true nature of any object made of clay, whether pot, jar, or dish. For each object's true nature is clayness, not pot-ness or jar-ness. We use different words to differentiate these things, but in reality they are not different from each other, for they share a common substance. In the same way, the objects of our world are not different from Brahman, even though we have different words to describe them.[20]

What is true of objects is true of persons. The individual self (called *anatman*), the person who lives each day in the world, is in fact part of the Cosmic Self, Atman (which is also Brahman). Of course, we are not literally *part* of Atman, Shankara reminds us, for Atman has no parts. But the two are one, according to a basic theme of the Upanishads: "the individual self and the highest Self differ in name only, it being a settled matter that perfect knowledge has for its object the absolute oneness of the two."[21]

The central doctrine that identifies the individual self (*anatman*) with the Cosmic Self (Atman) is called "that art thou" (in Sanskrit, *tat tvam asi*). This is one of the most fundamental principles of Hindu thought. The union of individual self with Cosmic Self is not something we need to establish, seek, or achieve. It is, says Shankara, "self-established," not "accomplished by endeavour." It is already a reality whether we try to make it so or not. It is true whether we think we know Atman or not. In a sense, we all know Cosmic Self because we all know our inner selves. To deny that I am Atman would be to deny that I exist. But none of us ever says, "I am not."[22]

The reality with which we are all one, the Cosmic Self, is Brahman. Shankara tells us that Brahman manifests itself in a series of beings that exist at various levels of reality, even though Brahman itself is eternally immutable. Paradoxically, Shankara can also say that Atman is not the individual self. Cosmic Self is not in its own being in contact with anything in the empirical world. The whole notion that individual selves could be different from Brahman at all is the result of erroneous thought.

19. Hackett, *Oriental Philosophy*, p. 149.
20. Shankara, *Vedānta Sūtras*, 2.1.14.
21. Ibid., 2.3.43; 1.4.22.
22. Ibid., 2.1.14; 1.1.

To illustrate this point, Shankara tells us that Brahman differs from the individual self in the same way a real juggler differs from a juggler who climbs up a rope to the sky with sword and shield in hand. Presumably, a juggler who climbs a rope with one hand cannot exist. So it is with the individual soul who lives in the world we know. Brahman's alter ego, the isolated individual, that which depends on the "fictitious limiting conditions" of human thought, is not the real nature of Brahman. That these should be identified can only be a sign of ignorance.[23] To sum up, Shankara is telling us that an individual self finds its true nature in the Cosmic Self. But Cosmic Self cannot be identified with empirical selves. From the ultimate point of view, only Cosmic Self is real.

Knowledge of the Cosmic Self

Why are we so systematically confused, we may wonder? Shankara says that the ignorance that plagues us arises from 'superimposition,' the ascription of attributes of one thing to something different. When we confuse mother of pearl and silver, we apply wrong qualities to an object. When we mistake a coiled rope for a snake, we commit the fallacy of superimposition. Sometimes, in comparing two objects, we wrongly suppose that things that are similar in one way are similar in all ways.[24]

These common flaws of thought may create problems in everyday living. But they become even more serious when they cause us to believe that the distinction between empirical selves and Self is ultimately real. In order to avoid this ignorance and its disastrous consequences, therefore, Shankara begins his inquiry into the nature of the *Vedanta-sutras*.

The senses can perceive only external things. Our senses connect us with the external world, which is only the effect of Brahman. Brahman itself is not knowable by the senses, in Shankara's view, since it is not the sort of object that the senses could detect. (Brahman, of course, is not a thing "out there.") And since Brahman cannot be perceived, it could never be learned through the senses that Brahman is the cause of that world. Shankara does tell us that we should not accept theories that contradict our observations, but this warning applies only to observations in this world. When Shankara gives us this warning, he is speaking of the current state of the empirical world as compared with its original state. Ultimately, sense knowledge and its little rules are limited to the sense world, the

23. Ibid., 1.1.2; 1.1.11, 17; 1.3.19.
24. Ibid., 1.1; 3.2.20.

world of everyday living and thinking, the world that exists dependently.[25]

Logic, too, is useful and necessary in the everyday view of things. For one thing, Shankara says the sheer multiplicity of viewpoints, not all of which can be correct according to logic, underlines the need to study the nature of Brahman. Additionally, Shankara argues that the existence of this diversity of opinion also proves that depending on reason alone leads to error.[26] Of course, the false-minded man, bound by the apparent reality of the phenomenal world, cannot be as correct as the true-minded man who has found unity. Now to call one man's views false is to imply a basic contradiction between two sets of views and to reject one set because it is incoherent with the other. This sort of thinking assumes that rational tests possess at least some rudimentary validity.[27]

Similarly, Shankara assumes logic's validity in his rejection of Buddhist doctrine. Because the Buddha holds "three mutually contradictory systems" of thought, his teachings are "incoherent assertions" and "absurd doctrines" that confuse his listeners. Such Buddhist doctrines should be "entirely disregarded by all those who have a regard for their own happiness."[28]

The scriptures are consistent, says Shankara, and this confirms their truth. In fact, the point of many of Shankara's discussions is precisely to show the coherence of various teachings of the sacred scriptures. For example, he considers the objection that scripture should be considered true within its own sphere but correctable by other, higher means of right knowledge. In response, Shankara maintains that the two elements of truth operate at different levels. For example, the critic of Hindu scripture may point out that sensuous experience teaches a distinction between enjoyer and object of enjoyment, an idea that contradicts the Veda. But Shankara resolves this logical problem by assigning the empirical data, not the scriptural teaching, to the lower level of knowledge and thought.[29]

As he develops the notion of two levels of thinking, the pattern we observed in metaphysics repeats itself in epistemology. By distinguishing the ultimate from the phenomenal, Shankara is able to explain the apparent contradictions that pepper the Vedas. Similarly, the concept of two levels serves an epistemological function by resolving logical paradoxes. The Vedanta texts state that both fire and ether are the source of the creation. Shankara notes that these state-

25. Ibid., 1.1.2; 1.4.15.
26. Ibid., 1.1.1; 2.1.11.
27. Ibid., 2.1.14.
28. Ibid., 2.2.32.
29. Ibid., 2.1.13.

ments conflict. Promising to reconcile the problem later, he writes, "a conflict of statements [in the Vedanta-texts] regarding the world would not even matter greatly, since the creation of the world and similar topics are not at all what Scripture wishes to teach. . . . The passages about the creation and the like form only subordinate members of passages treating of Brahman."[30]

In this way, when Shankara uses mechanisms to avoid apparent contradictions, he demonstrates an interest in making ideas consistent. This procedure shows the relevance of logic to his thinking and philosophy—at least at the lower level of everyday thinking and experiencing.

These factors do not imply that the lower perspective is entirely wrong. The everyday world is not ultimately real, but it is not on that account unreal. In just this way, the lower perspective of everyday knowledge, based on the senses and on logical inferences from sense experience, possesses its own validity. In Shankara's words, "In every act of perception we are conscious of some external thing corresponding to the idea . . . and that of which we are conscious cannot but exist. . . . The things of which we are conscious in a dream are negated by our waking consciousness. . . . Those things, on the other hand, of which we are conscious in our waking state, such as posts and the like, are never negated in any state."[31] As the illustration implies, empirical knowledge (the dream) is real in its own way, although it is negated by the ultimate knowledge (wakefulness) that could never be negated by a dream.

Logical distinctions and arguments are also applied to Brahman. At times Shankara says that Brahman possesses one attribute and not its opposite. For example, Brahman is not broken into parts. To think that Brahman has parts is as ignorant as to think that two moons exist merely because you happen to look at the moon and "see double."[32] With respect to the immutability of Brahman, he says, "to the one Brahman the two qualities of being subject to modification and of being free from it cannot both be ascribed." Shankara's point, of course, is that these two qualities necessarily contradict each other.

Someone might object that these qualities could be appropriately ascribed at different times just as one body can at different times be in motion and be at rest. But Shankara anticipates this possibility. He answers that absolute immutability precludes this. The changeless reality called Brahman cannot be subject to changing qualities.[33]

Ultimately, that Brahman is actually changeless and eternal is

30. Ibid., 1.4.14.
31. Ibid., 2.2.28, 29.
32. Ibid., 2.1.27.
33. Ibid., 2.1.14.

known as the result of the denial of all attributes. This sounds self-defeating: the attributes of eternality and changelessness follow "on account of the negation of all attributes."[34] For this reason Shankara's solution may not seem entirely satisfactory. But in his teaching, the dilemma simply exemplifies the truth that Nirguna (Unqualified) Brahman (which is a truer vision than Saguna [Qualified] Brahman) is beyond description. This reflects an essential Upanishadic doctrine, *neti, neti,* "not this, not that." Nirguna Brahman has no attributes either positive or negative. It can be described neither as A nor as non-A. The best that can be done is to deny every attribute of Brahman.

It is for this reason that *Advaita Vedanta* has its name. It is not dualistic. But it is not monistic either. It is nondualistic. Calling Shankara's thought nondualism, *advaita,* is different from calling it monism precisely because of the problem of positive attributes for Brahman. Calling reality monistic implies that it is not dualistic. But to call it nondualism makes no implications about monism or dualistic. It merely points to the truth that in the ultimate perspective, Brahman is beyond logical distinctions. Language cannot touch Brahman. Brahman is not this and not that.

This doctrine, "not this, not that," denies the plurality of the world, but it does not negate Brahman: "Brahman is that whose nature is permanent purity, intelligence, and freedom; it . . . constitutes the inward Self of all. Of this Brahman our text denies all plurality of forms; but Brahman itself it leaves untouched. . . . The clause, 'Not so, not so!' negatives [sic] not absolutely everything, but only everything but Brahman."[35]

Shankara is careful, therefore, to protect the reality of Brahman despite the "not this, not that" doctrine. He explicitly denies that it leads to the Buddhist conception of the ultimate Void.[36] But in that he affirms the continued existence of Brahman, he infers from the doctrine simply the inadequacy of logic and language for describing from the ultimate perspective. The Self of all possesses the character of intelligence, but it lacks any distinctions and transcends all language. Thus it can be described only negatively, by the denial of attributes.[37] *Neti, neti* is consequently not primarily metaphysical in its significance. For Shankara the importance lies in the realm of epistemology. It is not the being of Brahman but the language we use to describe Brahman that is inadequate.

Naturally, the distinctions of language and logic are true from the

34. Ibid.
35. Ibid., 3.2.22.
36. Ibid.
37. Ibid., 3.2.18.

sensuous perspective. Again the two-levels-of-truth idea comes to our rescue. Indeed, the "entire complex of phenomenal existence is considered as true as long as the knowledge of the Brahman being the Self of all has not arisen."[38] These distinctions differentiate Brahman, Atman, and individual selves.[39] They also account for the difference between Nirguna Brahman and Saguna Brahman. In this way these distinctions also give rise to the various types of religious devotion. Some forms of religious expression lead to "exaltation," some to "gradual emancipation," and some to "success in works." Each is acceptable in its own way and at its own level.[40]

Since knowledge that uses concepts is not ultimately true, a non-logical, nonconceptual knowledge must be more basic than inferential thinking. Shankara exhibits this common pantheistic tendency toward intuitive knowledge when he says, "Is Brahman known or not known (previously to the enquiry into its nature)? If it is known we need not enter on an enquiry concerning it; if it is not known we can not enter on such an enquiry. We reply that Brahman is known."[41] At the same time, Shankara makes it clear that logical thinking is legitimate, but not when it is "bare" or "independent." Rather, conceptual thought is "a subordinate auxiliary" to the more basic, intuitive kind of knowledge.[42]

The direct kind of knowing that must precede reason is knowledge of the Self within. Based on the metaphysical view that my empirical self is the Cosmic Self or Atman, which is in turn Brahman, Shankara claims that the necessary intuition of this identity comes from an awareness of what is within. The connection between Cosmic Self and empirical self is the ground for the teaching of scriptures that knowledge of one implies knowledge of the other. In the introduction to his commentary, Shankara tells us that we know the Self because it is present to us in immediate intuition.[43] Or, as he says explicitly elsewhere, we know Brahman because it is the ground of our very being.[44]

The knowledge of Brahman does not admit of higher or lower degrees, for there are no qualities to be added to or subtracted from this knowledge of oneness. The absolute knowledge that comes from awareness of Brahman leads to a knowledge of all. To reach that qualityless awareness is to see that everything in this phenomenal world is non-existent. This is the ultimate knowledge of one who knows

38. Ibid., 2.1.14.
39. Ibid., 1.3.19.
40. Ibid., 1.1.11.
41. Ibid., 1.1.1.
42. Ibid., 2.1.6.
43. Ibid., 1.4.20; 1.1.
44. Ibid., 1.1.1.

that everything exists in the Absolute Self. This perspective is not just one of several views, limited to certain states of mind. It is the absolute view of the true-minded one.[45]

> Before the knowledge of the unity of the Self has been reached[,] the whole real-unreal course of ordinary life, worldly as well as religious, goes on unimpeded, [as] we have already explained. However, when final authority having intimated the unity of the Self, the entire course of the world which was founded on the previous distinction is sublated, then there is no longer any opportunity for assuming a Brahman comprising in itself various elements.[46]

Shankara affirms the final truth of the view of reality that comes through the unifying vision. But he also recognizes another important source of truth that leads to an understanding of the oneness of reality. It is the Vedanta scriptural texts. The scriptures have Brahman as their source, says Shankara, and this implies their entire truthfulness. The study of these texts brings an understanding both of the absolute unity of Brahman and of the liberation that this knowledge alone can bring. In fact, the real nature of Brahman and the world, the nature of right and wrong, cannot be known or even thought of without the scriptures. Perception and inference are both decidedly inadequate for this ultimate form of knowledge.[47]

Yet, Shankara can say that a true understanding of Hindu scripture *is* the most reasonable position. In one place, he comments that those who insist on distinguishing logically between individual persons and Brahman are mistaken in that they both deny the Veda and commit logical errors.[48] Indeed, though logic is not to be followed when it contradicts Vedantic scripture, "inference also, being an instrument of right knowledge in so far as it does not contradict the Vedanta-texts, is not to be excluded as a means of confirming the meaning ascertained. Scripture itself, moreover, allows argumentation; for [certain] passages . . . declare that human understanding assists Scripture."[49]

Shankara asserts that the Hindu scriptures are all equally authoritative.[50] This raises questions for those who observe that the Vedas sometimes seem to contradict Shankara's nondualism. Some might suppose that these scriptures are right with respect to religious matters only, while perception and inference are the true guides in other

45. Ibid., 3.4.52; 1.4.23; 2.1.14.
46. Ibid., 2.1.14.
47. Ibid., 1.1.3; 1.1; 2.1.11; 3.1.25.
48. Ibid., 1.4.22.
49. Ibid., 1.1.2.
50. Ibid., 3.2.15.

areas. Ordinary reasoning leads us to believe that everyday distinctions (e.g., the difference between one who enjoys and the object of enjoyment) are possible. But scripture teaches the oneness of all in Brahman.

Now, these two truths could be assigned to different areas so that Vedantic scripture would not contradict in other areas what is revealed by the other right means to truth. But Shankara explicitly denies this solution to the problem. There is a sense in which, from the everyday point of view, reason is right in distinguishing between enjoyer and what is enjoyed. But ultimately the Vedas are right in affirming the unity of all. The waves, bubbles, and foam on the sea are, from a limited point of view, different from the sea. At the same time, they are, from a higher point of view, not different. Thus, both viewpoints are in one sense correct, although, of course, from the ultimate perspective (viz., that of scripture), only one is really true.[51] Once again, Shankara posits two levels of truth, only one of which is ultimately sound. It may seem initially that the scriptures are contradicted by empirical knowledge, but in the final analysis they are not.

Salvation Through Knowledge

The goal of Shankara's epistemology is never pure knowledge for its own sake. Its goal is always religious. The Vedantic teaching that ignorance is the source of evil is important because it is the first step to solving the human dilemmas of suffering. That the Cosmic Self, Brahman, becomes embodied in individual selves with all the miseries that this implies is due to ignorance: "As . . . the application of the conception of the Ego to the body on the part of those who affirm the existence of a Self different from the body is simply false, not figurative, it follows that the embodiedness of the Self is (not real but) caused by wrong conception."[52]

Ignorance of our oneness with Brahman causes transmigration, the state so greatly dreaded by Hindus. Reincarnation simply perpetuates the experience of suffering. The American press has reported that some Western celebrities have found the idea of reincarnation fascinating. They seem to enjoy discovering the activities of their earlier lives. Shirley MacLaine is sure she was a court jester whose life ended when she was "personally decapitated by Louis XV for telling impertinent jokes." Sylvester Stallone feels sure he was beheaded in the French Revolution. Loretta Lynn, Glenn Ford, and Anne Francis also have tales to tell.[53]

51. Ibid., 2.1.13.
52. Ibid., 1.1.4.
53. "I Was Beheaded in the 1700's," *Time* (September 10, 1984), p. 68.

The reincarnation that is the talk of Hollywood cocktail parties, however, is vastly different from the transmigration of Hindu religious philosophy. For Hinduism in general and Shankara in particular, to be reincarnated is to be caught in a cycle of despair, in life after life of misery and suffering. After you toil under backbreaking conditions for your allotted seventy years, your reward is to face another seventy pain-filled years, and another seventy, and another, and on and on. Reincarnation is the evil above which every Hindu believer hopes to rise.

Shankara taught that the grip of this cycle of transmigration can be broken through knowledge. Since ignorance mires me in the cycle of reincarnation, it is knowledge that gets me out. Once I understand that Brahman is All and Brahman is Atman or Cosmic Self, then I can rise above this transmigratory world. But if a person fails to escape the cycle of reincarnation, it is because he has not yet grasped the unity of Brahman and the Cosmic Self.[54]

That knowledge is the road to salvation from the curse of reincarnation is perhaps one of Shankara's most consistent themes. By disregarding sensuous observation and rational knowledge, the saved one arrives at knowledge through scripture. This knowledge is not part of this empirical world, but is "the True, the Real, the Self, whose nature is pure intelligence." Then the saved one acquires "unchangeable, eternal cognition," and rises to union with Brahman, which is itself characterized by eternal intellection.[55]

Some might hope to achieve salvation through good works. The *Gita*, which contains the well-known story about the personal lord Krishna, allows, like some elements of the Hindu scriptures, salvation through good works. But Shankara explicitly says that actions cannot save. Actions are nothing, he says, and nothing gives rise to nothing.[56] All works, whether good or evil, must be extinguished, for both kinds of action—even good action—cause bondage to the cycle of reincarnation. For the one who comes to knowledge, works no longer seem attractive and in the end are destroyed. Ultimately, only through knowledge, at death, does release come.[57]

On the other hand, Shankara does acknowledge the initial benefits of works. But the path of works is a preliminary stage only. In commenting on the *Gita*, Shankara argues that good works will improve one's place in society in the next incarnation. From the higher position of being "born again in a good family," gained through good works, a spiritual person may then attain the knowledge that leads to

54. Shankara, *Vedānta Sūtras*, 1.1.4; 3.2.26.
55. Ibid., 1.3.19; 1.1.4; 2.1.14; 4.4.22.
56. Ibid., 3.2.38.
57. Ibid., 4.1.14.

emancipation.[58] Shankara's way of salvation through knowledge, therefore, does not absolutely repudiate other avenues by which to gain release from suffering. Thus, the scriptures that advocate these other means to salvation do not contradict those that hold up knowledge as the path to salvation. The way of knowledge can benefit from other ways in the earlier stages, but once knowledge has been attained, these other paths become useless and fall away.[59]

One special kind of action, religious ritual, is likewise rejected by Shankara as a means to release. Ceremonial cleansing may purify the empirical self, but it has no connection with the true Self. The thought that we could remove blemishes from the pure Self, which has no defects and to which no excellence could be added, is absurd. The only thing that could be purified is the self that is under the influence of ignorance. Thus, religious ceremonies like ritualistic cleansing may, from one point of view, seem to contribute to the release true knowledge brings.[60] But their benefits for achieving knowledge are minimal.

Another kind of religious activity, meditation, also possesses some benefit in preparing for release. Meditation on Brahman, even Qualified Brahman with its various attributes, can contribute to final release.[61] The release to which this meditation leads is an enlightenment, a coming to realization. *Enlightenment* refers not to knowledge gained by someone who does not have it, but to knowledge gained through rediscovery. Someone who comes to awareness of release suddenly realizes that he had knowledge all along; in reality he never was in bondage. It is like suddenly remembering where you put your lost car keys. The knowledge was always there; it was simply covered up, waiting to be rediscovered. This apprehension of what has always been true is the ultimate goal of life in this world. Knowledge of Brahman, because it completely destroys ignorance, is the noblest goal of human existence.[62]

The Sanskrit word for this release or freedom is *mokṣa. Mokṣa* possesses certain characteristics that distinguish it from ordinary consciousness. For one thing, it does not have higher or lower degrees. It is absolute, for degrees are possible only where there are qualities and attributes. The ultimate release, of course, has no qualities: it is eternal, omnipresent, immutable, and entirely self-sufficient.[63]

58. Ibid., 3.4.51.
59. Ibid., 3.4.26.
60. Ibid., 1.1.4.
61. Ibid.
62. Ibid., 3.4.52; 1.1.1.
63. Ibid., 3.4.52; 1.1.4.

Because *mokṣa* is Brahman, it is easy to see that Shankara's concept of salvation depends intimately on his pantheistic doctrine. Shankara was convinced that if the identity of the individual with the All were not true, those who seek *mokṣa* would not find true knowledge and the question of knowledge would never be resolved.[64] Since the scriptures do teach this oneness, however, the sense of absolute identity with Brahman can lead appropriately to release. And this has the religious purpose that is central to Shankara's philosophy. When the mystic achieves blissful identity with Brahman, then the fear of reincarnation into another life of pain is overcome.[65] This is Shankara's view of salvation.

If the world perspective is false, what happens to the world when one achieves enlightenment? Shankara says that the world does not change. It is our ignorance that is shattered. The covering of ignorance that lay over our fundamental knowledge is stripped away, and knowledge (*vidya* in Sanskrit) replaces ignorance (*avidya*). Our view of the world changes when the false perspective is dissolved. But the world does not entirely disappear; it is suddenly understood to be what it was all along. It is *maya*, an illusory appearance of Brahman.[66]

At death, the one who has finally achieved true knowledge ceases to know in the ordinary sense. The self is absorbed in the ultimate Self, Brahman, and is no longer associated with the senses that gave rise to ignorance. Of course, this does not mean that the Self ceases to exist or to know absolutely. Only the finite self, born of ignorance and suffering in the cycle of reincarnation, ceases to be. As soon as death comes, the enlightened one experiences final release from the suffering of transmigration.[67]

The Role of Morality

In achieving this release, morality serves a preliminary function. Shankara mentions four prerequisites for the inquiry into Brahman: discerning the difference between the eternal and the temporal; renouncing the desire to enjoy the benefits of one's good deeds; developing tranquility and restraint; and longing for release from the cycle of reincarnation.[68] Setting forth these preconditions is consistent with Shankara's claim that knowledge of Brahman does not necessarily destroy all means to salvation. Although other good deeds are

64. Ibid., 1.4.22.
65. Ibid., 1.1.19.
66. For an evaluation of the teaching about reincarnation, see Norman L. Geisler and J. Yutaka Amano, *The Reincarnation Sensation* (Wheaton: Tyndale House, 1986), chap. 10.
67. Shankara, *Vedānta Sūtras*, 1.4.22; 4.1.14.
68. Ibid., 1.1.1.

extinguished by knowledge, the initial value of those actions that lead to the realization of Brahman is not negated by absolute knowledge.[69]

Indeed, Shankara uses the works one does in this life to explain the various positions people hold in society. This is the law of *karma*, the law of merit and demerit. *Karma* teaches that every person receives in this life the rewards or punishments for actions in previous lives. If I inhabit a very low station in life, I cannot complain. My plight is due to my own sins in a former life. If I happen to be born in an upper-class family, I am being rewarded for good deeds in a past life. *Karma*, then, is the law of cause and effect: those who suffer most are being punished while those who have every conceivable advantage are being rewarded. Do not blame Brahman, therefore, for misfortune. God is not the creator of evil. Each person shapes his or her own life.[70]

From the ultimate perspective, in fact, Brahman is not subject to any moral categories. If Nirguna Brahman has no attributes, then it does not relate to the distinctions between good and evil, or pleasure and pain. Brahman is neither good nor evil because it is beyond all such distinctions. Embodied or empirical selves experience these categories, but the highest Self is of an opposite character altogether, for Brahman is free from all good and evil.[71]

It follows from this metaphysical claim that the evil experienced in this life is not part of the ultimate scheme of things. Even the sins that cause suffering and pain (through the law of *karma*) are part of the illusion of this world. Thus, Shankara claims that the pain we experience is imaginary, not real. It is caused by the failure to distinguish Brahman from the body, senses, and other limiting concepts. These concepts, of course, arise out of ignorance.[72] The pain of injuries and disease comes from our ignorance of the fact that they are not real. If we understood that they are part of the illusion of the senses, we could avoid pain. In a word, Shankara's solution to individual events of pain and suffering in this world is identical to his response to the great dilemma of reincarnation: come to the realization of oneness with Brahman and you will see the problems of this life for what they really are. They are nothingness.

Understanding the basic reality of oneness with Brahman, that central doctrine of "that art thou" (*tat tvam asi*), means that we will have no more desires. If nothing exists, there is no self to do any

69. Ibid., 4.1.15, 19.
70. Ibid., 2.1.34, 36.
71. Ibid., 1.2.8.
72. Ibid., 2.3.46.

desiring and there are no things to desire. If there is nothing to desire, there can be no frustration of desire and therefore no pain and suffering. The solution to evil is the realization that there is no such thing as evil.[73]

The same holds for moral injunctions. From the everyday point of view, they have some reality. But they are possible in that ordinary perspective only because of the connection of individual selves with individual bodies. But "to him who has obtained the highest aim no obligation can apply."[74]

Conclusion

In the religious philosophy of Shankara we find a pantheism of the strongest kind. All is one in Brahman; all else is, from the ultimate perspective, illusion. Certainly the medieval Hindu admitted some reality to the perspective of individual selves that we experience each day. But the phenomenal perspective is true only from that limited point of view. A dream is true as long as you are having it. When you awaken, the dream can be identified for what it really is.

If this seems unrealistic to hard-nosed Western rationalists, consider the potential benefits of such a world view. The strain and stress of competition, whether in business, education, or athletics, could be eliminated if we would realize the fictitious nature of this world. The competition for attention and affection, competition we enter in hopes of soothing bruised egos, can be seen for what it is—nothing. Crushing defeats, in whatever field of endeavor, will lose their sting if we can recognize their transitory nature. This world view has more to offer the pragmatic West than might be evident at first.

Benefits like these attract Westerners to the New Age manifestations of Shankara's classic position. Promises of soothing meditation through TM, inducements to the true inner peace available through contact with the divine within, and advertisements for stress-reducing seminars for business executives entice our frazzled society in ways that were unanticipated a generation ago. Shankara is not so far out of step with the uptown group in today's Western culture.

No doubt some people consider the Vedantic form of Hinduism a viable philosophy of life. It is, in fact, the strain of Hinduism that has the greatest influence in the modern world. In the next chapter, we will discuss the reinterpretation of Vedanta by a modern Hindu, Sarvepalli Radhakrishnan. Radhakrishnan believed that this philoso-

73. Ibid., 2.1.14.
74. Ibid., 2.3.48.

phy would offer something of benefit to those harried by the rush of a technocratic society. If Radhakrishnan has something positive to offer, it is partly because of the richness of the thought of one of India's most significant philosophers, the medieval commentator Shankara.

Radhakrishnan
Multilevel Pantheism

*God . . . is the innermost Being of one's own self, wrapped up,
so to say, in so many covers or layers.—Sarvepali Radhakrishnan*

The multilevel pantheism of Sarvepali Radhakrishnan (1888–1975)
ascribes a greater reality to the world than does Shankara's philosophy. Yet multilevel pantheism grows directly from the root of
Vedanta philosophy. In Radhakrishnan's system, the Absolute is
found at many levels or grades of reality. These levels form a hierarchy of being and thus possess greater or lesser degrees of reality
depending on where they stand in that hierarchy. Radhakrishnan's
philosophy also may be called manifestational pantheism because the
unity of the Supreme is manifested or expressed in and through the
lower orders of being.

Historical Background

Radhakrishnan sought to develop a sophisticated interpretation of
Hinduism directed specifically toward the English-speaking world
with its peculiar interests and beliefs. One author's description of

Radhakrishnan as a "propagandist" is probably too strong.[1] Yet the multilevel pantheism that finds clearest expression in his voluminous writings is undoubtedly one of this century's most persuasive Hindu perspectives.

Radhakrishnan spent his early career as a scholar and professor. He taught philosophy at several Indian universities before becoming a professor at Oxford in 1936. After his retirement from Oxford in 1952, his interests turned to the practical matters of government. A friend of Mahatma Gandhi, Radhakrishnan served India as ambassador to the Soviet Union, as vice president, and as its second president from 1962 to 1967. His writings in this period indicate a longing for world peace and a just democracy. Interestingly, he based these aspirations specifically on his pantheistic belief that God is manifest in each person.

This belief finds its roots in the ancient religious traditions of India. The medieval era witnessed the development of great commentaries on the Hindu tradition. Classical schools, developed in earlier centuries and traditionally thought to be six in number, became the subject of philosophical debate and speculation. One of these, the Vedanta ("end of the Veda"), is of particular importance because three dominant medieval writers all developed extensive interpretations of Vedanta. These three include, of course, Shankara, the greatest of the medieval commentators, and the authors of competing systems of thought, Ramanuja (1017–1137) and Madhva (1197–1276).

The variegated character of the Upanishads and the cryptic nature of the *Vedanta-sutras* meant that the three commentators could develop rather different philosophies despite their common sources. Madhva's dualism and Ramanuja's qualified nondualism both ascribed a greater degree of reality to the everyday world than did Shankara's nondualism. This fits their emphasis on the personal union and worship of *bhakti*, the path to salvation through devotion to a personal god.

In his commentary on the *Vedanta-sutras*, Shankara developed most fully the pantheistic elements of the Upanishads. His *Advaita Vedanta* is important not only in its own right, but also as background for this chapter because Radhakrishnan's philosophy depends on it heavily. Radhakrishnan described his thought as an independent development of Vedanta, a contemporary reinterpretation of Shankara for the modern world.[2]

The last century has witnessed a reawakening of interest and pride among Hindus in their own religious traditions. Radhakrishnan is

1. Robert C. Zaehner, *Hinduism* (London: Oxford University Press, 1966), p. 187.

2. Sarvepali Radhakrishnan, "Reply to Critics," in *The Philosophy of Sarvepali Radhakrishnan*, ed. Paul A. Schilpp (New York: Tudor, 1952), p. 820.

among those who have spearheaded this movement. Another is Ramakrishna, the nineteenth-century *bhakti* enthusiast whose disciple Swami Vivekananda made a historic appearance at the Congress of Religions in 1893 in Chicago. At this meeting, Swami Vivekananda dynamically presented Hinduism as a viable religious option for the modern world. The response was enthusiastic and positive. The audience accepted his faith as on a par with their own Western religious beliefs. In so doing they implicitly abandoned the traditional view that Hinduism is a primitive religion that Christian missionaries should seek to supplant with Christianity. This tolerance marked a change in attitude of historic significance. Others who have contributed to the rebirth of Hinduism include Ram Mohan Roy, who worked to reform Hinduism, and Mahatma Gandhi, who led India to political freedom.

These modern Hindus have various philosophies and beliefs. But they hold in common two themes that may be traced through the history of Hindu literature. They share the belief that Hinduism should tolerate various doctrines and practices within its wide-reaching arms. And they believe in one way or another that there is a oneness of reality that expresses itself in the plurality of everyday things and events. Interpreting this oneness is the major task of Radhakrishnan's metaphysics.

The Oneness of Brahman

The basic reality is Brahman, which Radhakrishnan often calls God or the Lord. This name, derived from *brh*, "to grow, to burst forth," implies a living, growing, dynamic reality. Brahman is not a static abstraction. It is the "timeless reality of all things in time." It is both immanent and transcendent; it both indwells the world and lies behind all that exists. Yet it cannot be equated with the world process. It is a "living unity of essence and existence, of the ideal and real, of knowledge, love and beauty."[3]

Brahman totally explains this world. The Real in itself is exempt from change. But it is illogical, to use Radhakrishnan's own word, to think that nature could ever evolve without the impetus of the Supreme. The Absolute is both the efficient cause and the final cause of the universe. It brings the world into being and lures the world toward its intended purpose. No other reality need be posited to

3. Sarvepali Radhakrishnan, *The Principal Upanishads* (London: Allen and Unwin, 1953), p. 52; *Indian Philosophy*, 2d ed., 2 vols. (London: Allen and Unwin, 1929), vol. 1, pp. 172–73, 194–95; "The Religion of the Spirit and the World's Need: Fragments of a Confession," in *Philosophy of Sarvepali Radhakrishnan*, ed. Schilpp, pp. 38–39; Sarvepali Radhakrishnan, *An Idealist View of Life* (London: Allen and Unwin, 1932), p. 106.

account for what is. The Upanishads teach that our world with all its plurality can be reduced, without any residue, to Brahman alone.[4]

The Supreme in no way depends on anything else, for Brahman is utterly self-sufficient. This is the fundamental metaphysical truth. The universe of nature is dependent on the Absolute as its necessary ground, but Brahman is independent. Nature must pass away, but neither its existence nor its passing could affect the Absolute.[5] In fact, Brahman contains the potential for all possible worlds. Whether or not we realize it, God is the principle that lies behind all possible realities. At the same time, God is immanent in the world: "God is *in* the world," Radhakrishnan tells us, "though not *as* the world."[6]

This raises a critical question: How exactly do the world and the Absolute relate? Radhakrishnan believes that in the final analysis, this question is unanswerable. Trying to use logic to solve the puzzle transforms Brahman into a philosophic system. But the Upanishads do not push the insight of unity toward systematization. The Upanishads leave the question of the Absolute's relation to the world deliberately unexplained, and Radhakrishnan agrees. He admits that Shankara allows the use of metaphors to describe the relation of Brahman to the universe. But due to the shortcomings of the human mind, Radhakrishnan advocates "a wise agnosticism." With respect to observations about the everyday world, "they are there, and there is an end of it. We do not know and cannot know why. It is all a contradiction, and yet it is actual."[7]

Because Radhakrishnan's tradition willingly leaves this question open, it is called *Advaita*, "not-twoness" or "nonduality," rather than pure monism. In Radhakrishnan's view, *Advaita Vedanta*, the tradition of the Upanishads and Shankara, admits real plurality. It affirms that "perfect being is real; unreal becoming is actual, though, we do not know why."[8] In contrast, pure monism follows the unifying tendency of the mind toward an unmitigated oneness. Dogmatic views that accept the ultimacy of logic are driven to pure monism, Radhakrishnan tells us. But why accept the absoluteness of conceptual thought? Far wiser, he believes, to leave the question open than to commit oneself to the ultimacy of logically oriented thinking.[9]

4. Sarvepali Radhakrishnan, *The Hindu View of Life* (London: Allen and Unwin, 1927), pp. 46, 88; *Indian Philosophy*, vol. 1, pp. 181–83, 195.

5. Radhakrishnan, *Indian Philosophy*, vol. 1, pp. 185–86, 194–95; "Fragments of a Confession," pp. 44–46.

6. Radhakrishnan, "Fragments of a Confession," p. 46; *Indian Philosophy*, vol. 1, pp. 175, 184; *Hindu View of Life*, pp. 51, 88.

7. Radhakrishnan, *Indian Philosophy*, vol. 1, pp. 180–86; *Hindu View of Life*, p. 50; *Indian Philosophy*, vol. 1, p. 35.

8. Radhakrishnan, *Indian Philosophy*, vol. 1, pp. 40, 187, 190.

9. Ibid., p. 39.

In this distinction between *Advaita Vedanta* and pure monism lies the basis for one of Radhakrishnan's most consistent themes. Westerners are wrong, he says, to criticize Hinduism for its alleged failure to recognize the reality of the everyday world.[10] That Brahman is ultimately real does not imply that the world is not real. From the reality of the One we should not deduce the unreality of the many. Rather, he concludes, we should infer that the many reveal the One.[11]

In Radhakrishnan's view, neither the Upanishads nor Shankara teach the world to be non-existent. Other Hindu thinkers have claimed that objects in the world are mind dependent. When someone thinks them, they exist; when that person ceases to think them, they puff out of existence. But Vedanta philosophy teaches that things control thinking, not vice versa. The world of everyday life is reinterpreted to be sure, but Vedanta does not deny that it is what it is.[12]

Vedanta Hinduism answers the question of the world's reality by the doctrine of *maya. Maya* literally means "illusion" or "appearance." While Shankara's meaning may be debated, Radhakrishnan clearly defends himself and his mentor against the charge of complete illusionism. *Maya* does not imply solipsism or non-existence. The world does not have the status of the horns of a hare, as the saying goes.[13] Two famous similes describe the world as a rope mistaken for a snake or as mother of pearl mistaken for silver. But these illustrations imply the dependency of the world, not its non-existence. *Maya* explains both our inability to understand the world and its contingent, fragile nature. How can we account for this world? What metaphysical status does it possess? The answer in both cases is *maya*.[14]

An ancient story aptly illustrates *maya*. The famous Indian emperor Akbar built a large and beautiful city. Over the gate of the city his artisans carved this message: "Said Jesus, may his name be blessed, 'This world is a bridge, pass over it, but build no house upon it.'" According to the legend, Akbar illustrated this truth by deserting the city as soon as he finished it.[15]

The world, then, is not nothingness. It is not denied; it is reinterpreted. Because Brahman is the basis of the world, the world is an expression or a manifestation of God. Our world of everyday events reveals the presence of the Absolute. Without Brahman as its ground,

10. Radhakrishnan, "Fragments of a Confession," p. 41; *Eastern Religions and Western Thought*, 2d ed. (London: Oxford University Press, 1940, 1975), pp. 30–31; "Reply to Critics," p. 800; *Indian Philosophy*, vol. 1, pp. 186–98.

11. Radhakrishnan, *Idealist View of Life*, p. 110.

12. Radhakrishnan, *Hindu View of Life*, pp. 45–48.

13. Radhakrishnan, *Eastern Religions and Western Thought*, pp. 86–88.

14. Ibid., p. 27; "Reply to Critics," pp. 801–2; *Hindu View of Life*, p. 48; *Indian Philosophy*, vol. 1, p. 34.

15. Radhakrishnan, "Fragments of a Confession," p. 50.

the material universe would not exist.[16] This implies that God does not bring the world into being. God did not suddenly decide, after existing alone for a while, to have some company. In fact, Brahman did not temporally precede the world at all. The world is not a creation, but a self-limitation or self-expression of Brahman. It is best to say that the world of becoming reveals the being of the One.[17]

The Absolute expresses itself differently at each of several levels. Brahman is not manifested evenly, but to greater or lesser degrees. The levels possess different grades or phases of reality. Though this is intelligible only from the finite point of view, it is helpful to think of Brahman as manifested to a greater degree in the organic, for example, than in the inorganic.[18]

Since Brahman is revealed in everything that is personal and organic, it is not surprising that Radhakrishnan affirms that Jesus was typical, not exceptional. We all have the divinity to which Jesus was sensitive. If we knew what he knew, we would realize that we, too, are different from the Supreme not in kind but only in degree.[19] Jesus' example shows that various levels of reality meet within each person. The true selfhood of each individual, therefore, is the Absolute Self.

The example of Jesus reveals the nature of all persons. We can think of ourselves from two points of view. From one perspective, our finite, material, everyday self is real. But from a higher vantage point, we are really part of the Cosmic Self. Those who assume that the apparent self is identical with the true self are deluded. This misconception is an instance of *maya*. To put it in the form of an illustration, each individual leaf on a tree may believe it has its own existence apart from the other leaves. In truth, however, all the leaves share the life of the tree. They are dependent on and supported by a reality they may not even recognize.[20]

In a sense, therefore, we are amphibians, for we live in both the material and the spiritual worlds, in both time and eternity. Though our conscious, everyday selves, our personalities, fade in and out of consciousness, our real selves do not pass out of existence with physical death. These persisting selves, incapable of proof or, better, self-proven, are eternal. They continue beyond death as choosing selves. In the final analysis, our individual souls are aspects of the transcen-

16. Radhakrishnan, *Hindu View of Life*, p. 48; *Eastern Religions and Western Thought*, p. 31; *The Principal Upanishads*, pp. 80–83; *Idealist View of Life*, p. 109.

17. Radhakrishnan, *Indian Philosophy*, vol. 1, pp. 184–85.

18. Ibid., vol. 1, pp. 184, 197–200.

19. Radhakrishnan, *Indian Philosophy*, vol. 1, p. 230; *Idealist View of Life*, p. 104.

20. Radhakrishnan, *Indian Philosophy*, vol. 1, p. 192, 204–5; *Eastern Religions and Western Thought*, pp. 28, 81, 83.

dent ground of reality. Thus, when we are liberated from temporal limitations, we return to oneness with Brahman, who is our truest self.[21]

This distinction between two selves is grounded in the fundamental Hindu concept *tat tvam asi* ("that art thou"), so central to Shankara's thought. This essential doctrine identifies the human ego (*anatman*) as a manifestation of the Cosmic Self, Atman. Atman, in turn, is Brahman and Brahman is Atman. This doctrine expresses the fundamental pantheism undergirding Hindu thought. In Radhakrishnan's view, even popular Hinduism, with its belief in the existence of distinct personal gods, is interpreted in light of this tolerant but fundamentally true oneness.[22]

The concept of the levels of reality solves the riddle of how personal theisms and polytheisms could relate to monistic underpinnings. The Supreme appears in four important levels of reality: Brahman, the Absolute; Īśvara, the Creative Spirit; Hiranya-garbha, the World-Spirit; and Viraj, the world itself.[23] These levels or phases of being are simultaneous. Since there is no separation or temporal succession, they are to be distinguished only logically.[24] Of course, the Absolute alone is ultimately and finally real. For example, Īśvara, the personal deity, is to Brahman what an idol is to the true God. But it is still correct to say that the other levels of being are expressions of Brahman.[25]

The Absolute, which is beyond personality and impersonality, and Īśvara, the personal god, are distinct only in our logical point of view, not in their essence. We may distinguish "God as he is and God as he seems to us," but at root they are one. Therefore, when theists worship a personal god, they worship Brahman. When devoteés of a personal God like Krishna pray to their god, they are, in reality, approaching Brahman. In Radhakrishnan's view, there can be no final contradiction between god as spirit and god as person.[26]

Īśvara, the personal god, is creative spirit, the "Causal God." Because of his personality, Īśvara is the god of personal devotion. For this reason, those who criticize Hinduism for having no place for worship are incorrect.[27] Īśvara is the guide, the director of the world process. Īśvara is the explanation for this particular world, for the

21. Radhakrishnan, *Eastern Religions and Western Thought*, pp. 84, 26; *Recovery of Faith* (London: Allen and Unwin, 1956), pp. 112–13; "Reply to Critics," pp. 799, 800; "Fragments of a Confession," p. 43; *The Principal Upanishads*, pp. 117–18.

22. Radhakrishnan, *Hindu View of Life*, p. 30.

23. Radhakrishnan, "Fragments of a Confession," p. 41.

24. Radhakrishnan, "Fragments of a Confession," p. 41; "Reply to Critics," p. 797.

25. Radhakrishnan, *Indian Philosophy*, vol. 1, p. 234.

26. Radhakrishnan, *Idealist View of Life*, pp. 107–8; "Reply to Critics," p. 805.

27. Radhakrishnan, *Indian Philosophy*, vol. 1, pp. 171, 235–36.

actualization of this possible universe as opposed to others. Our world exists as it does because Iśvara is at work.[28]

The third level of being is World-Soul, Hiranya-garbha. Like Iśvara, of course, Hiranya-garbha differs from Brahman only from a certain point of view. They are logically distinct, but not actually so. Hiranya-garbha is the activity of spirit in the universe. If Iśvara is Brahman viewed as a personal God who creates, sustains, and protects the universe, Hiranya-garbha is Brahman viewed as an omnipresent spiritual power.[29]

Finally, the world, Viraj, is the last level of being. Again, it is not illusion; it is reality, even though it is of a different level from Brahman. Because it is an expression of God, Viraj is dependent and contingent. Like the other levels, Viraj is another manifestation of Brahman. In Radhakrishnan's multilevel pantheism, all that exists expresses at its own level and to its own degree the being of the Absolute.[30]

The Primacy of Intuitive Knowledge

In coming to know these levels of reality, three kinds of knowledge can be distinguished: intuitive, conceptual, perceptual. Intuition is the highest form of knowledge, though the others have their places. Intuition brings contact with being itself; it is the highest thought humanly possible, for it is more insightful than logical thinking. It necessarily has a religious dimension, for knowledge is not simply logical and empirical cognition. Where perceptual and conceptual knowledge break down, feeling reveals reality with a fullness not achieved through thought alone. In the final analysis, we can resolve intuitively those riddles that intellect cannot solve.[31]

The primacy of intuitive experience leads Radhakrishnan to distinguish fact from interpretation. Although he admits that there is no pure, raw experience, he also says that the individual in contact with the power of the Absolute is the basic fact. Interpretations of this basic fact take various forms when the Absolute is identified with Krishna, Christ, or Buddha. Radhakrishnan believes that everyone experiences Brahman. But different people unconsciously and variously interpret the experience in the religious categories with which they are familiar. Any doctrine, then, is interpretive.[32]

28. Radhakrishnan, *The Principal Upanishads*, pp. 63–64; *Eastern Religions and Western Thought*, p. 92; "Fragments of a Confession," pp. 39–40.

29. Radhakrishnan, *The Principal Upanishads*, p. 71.

30. Radhakrishnan, "Fragments of a Confession," pp. 41–42.

31. Radhakrishnan, "Fragments of a Confession," p. 60; *Idealist View of Life*, pp. 128, 134; *Indian Philosophy*, vol. 1, pp. 165–66, 43, 176.

32. Radhakrishnan, *Idealist View of Life*, p. 98–99; *Eastern Religions and Western Thought*, p. 23; *Hindu View of Life*, p. 19.

Because of the primacy of experience, Radhakrishnan believes that the Vedas do not possess inherent truth or authority. Instead, he considers them "transcripts from life," not "dogmatic dicta." What authority they have is derivative, for it depends on the spiritual lives of their authors. The Vedas are acknowledged authorities because they record the intuitive experiences of religious geniuses.[33]

Though we might expect him to say that the intuitive experiences provide their own certainty, Radhakrishnan surprisingly argues that intuition, or "spiritual perception," is susceptible to error just as other kinds of knowing are. Logic, therefore, plays an essential confirming and testing role even for spiritual experience. Although the intuitive insight is primary, the logical test of coherence applies in the Orient as much as anywhere. For example, one cannot simultaneously affirm and deny the reality of God. As in other areas, religious truth is discovered by insight, but tested by logic.[34]

Radhakrishnan acknowledges that he is building not a "dogmatic theology" but a philosophy to interpret reality. As such he must use logical tests and conceptual language.[35] Of course, he also affirms that conceptual and perceptual forms of knowledge never will fully explain Brahman. Though intellect, which must function conceptually, often succeeds at the relative level, it cannot resolve the complexities of the Absolute or capture its fullness. Radhakrishnan writes vividly, "reality is never so clear-cut in its differences as the rubrics under which we dismember it for neat handling." Supposing that our categories could contain the divine is like thinking that the child at the seashore could contain the ocean in one of its shells.[36]

But the inadequacy of human concepts does not negate eternal truth. The truth that issues from the Supreme cannot be squeezed into finite categories. The divine revelation always comes within the framework of human prejudices. Therefore, the reception of truth occurs in an imperfect, incomplete way. In his view, "no knowledge is entirely false, though none is entirely true."[37]

Of course, the same may be said of conflicting religious doctrines. No dogma is entirely false. As "ugliness is halfway to beauty," so "error is a stage on the road to truth." At the same time, Radhakrishnan implies that some concepts are truer than others. He complains that many Hindus admit too freely the complete legitimacy of

33. Radhakrishnan, *Idealist View of Life,* p. 90; *Hindu View of Life,* pp. 14–15.
34. Radhakrishnan, *Hindu View of Life,* p. 14; "Reply to Critics," pp. 794, 825; *Idealist View of Life,* pp. 177–78; "Fragments of a Confession," p. 77.
35. Radhakrishnan, "Reply to Critics," p. 820; *Idealist View of Life,* p. 98.
36. Radhakrishnan, *Indian Philosophy,* vol. 1, pp. 34, 43, 174–79; *Eastern Religions and Western Thought,* p. 110; *Hindu View of Life,* p. 27.
37. Radhakrishnan, "Reply to Critics," p. 810; "Fragments of a Confession," pp. 60–61; *Hindu View of Life,* p. 19; *Indian Philosophy,* vol. 1, p. 175.

crude, popular concepts of the divine. His vision for "a spiritual religion, that is universally valid, vital, clear-cut, [possessing] an understanding of the fresh sense of truth and [an] awakened social passion" depends on judgments of truer and not-so-true if not on true and false. Since theological expressions will vary, we ought to recognize a graduated scale of truer and less true doctrines.[38]

This graduated scale allows Radhakrishnan to conceptualize Hindu thought as moving forward in a dialectical, evolutionary way. Hinduism is not static, but dynamic and growing; it is a river, not a pond. In new times, old doctrines become false. But the river moves forward, expelling what is extraneous or false and developing philosophical underpinnings for what is true. "Hinduism is a movement, not a position; a process, not a result; a growing tradition, not a fixed revelation," he says. If we petrify the bark that protects the growing tree, we will strangle the tree's growth. The bark of doctrine must expand to allow for the growth of the tree of life.[39]

No belief, in his view, is absolutely wrong. The particularities of doctrinal formulations differ as do languages. No one believes that one language is right and the others wrong. Each is legitimate in that it enables people to communicate. Similarly, even the crudest of concepts can be tolerated if they bring good results. The beauty of the lily justifies the muddy waters from which it grows.[40]

This metaphor suggests the pragmatic test as the primary criterion for judging truth and dealing with doctrinal disagreement. Doctrines are good if they support personal growth or evoke spiritual life. Even animistic beliefs are legitimate if they help believers overcome egoism and individualism. A religion has validity, Radhakrishnan writes, in that "only through it have its followers become what they are. They have grown up with it and it has become a part of their being." Any religion is to be accepted as "long as it creates for those who use it a true path for spiritual life."[41]

This view of doctrine coheres with the claim that the Absolute cannot be described positively. Because the divine is ineffable, only negative[42] or symbolic[43] descriptions are possible. That God is person

---

38. Radhakrishnan, "Fragments of a Confession," pp. 25–26; Hindu View of Life, pp. 24–25, 88–89.

39. Radhakrishnan, Indian Philosophy, vol. 1, pp. 25–26; Hindu View of Life, pp. 24, 31, 91.

40. Radhakrishnan, Eastern Religions and Western Thought, pp. 335, 318; Hindu View of Life, p. 43.

41. Radhakrishnan, Eastern Religions and Western Thought, pp. 316–27; cf. Hindu View of Life, p. 32.

42. Radhakrishnan, Indian Philosophy, vol. 1, p. 178; Idealist View of Life, pp. 101–2.

43. Radhakrishnan, Eastern Religions and Western Thought, p. 317; Idealist View of Life, pp. 96–97.

is a symbolic description. It is a parable that the imagination uses to express its convictions about Brahman. To take this symbol literally as the final way to speak of Brahman is misleading. Any myth will change and consequently must be reinterpreted in light of new needs. Brahman is always far greater than any human language. God, like light, illuminates everything else, but remains invisible himself.[44]

This analysis provides the basis for a major theme in Radhakrishnan's thought. Since he assumes that all doctrines are legitimate in varying degrees, he infers that all religious people worship the same God. All doctrines, despite variety, point to the same ultimate Reality.[45] Within all religious traditions, Christianity included, variety of expression is tolerated. Indeed, all religions incorporate doctrinal elements from other traditions. Thus, the real issue is not Christianity or some other religion as opposed to Hinduism. It is religion as opposed to self-sufficient humanism.[46] Metaphorically stated, there is one religious mountain, but there are many paths to the top. There is one religious ocean to which various streams flow.[47]

On this foundation, Radhakrishnan builds an argument for toleration among religions. This has been part of the Hindu tradition for millennia. Hinduism always has accepted doctrinal variety on the ground that truth has many sides. A Hindu teacher, for example, would never ask a Christian to give up allegiance to Christ, but would ask only that Christ be recognized as one of several expressions of the Ultimate.[48] To love your own sect best is selfishness, a type of spiritual chauvinism. Proselytizing must give way to cooperation. Missions must concentrate on helping all persons live up to their own best principles.[49]

This tolerance seems to imply a relative view of truth: there is no final truth; any view is acceptable; just be true to your own convictions. But Radhakrishnan claims that this is not his view. Hinduism does not stand on skepticism. It is confident of its own truth, yet tolerant of other views. But tolerance cannot be taken to imply indifference. It means only that some doctrines are better than others, that some views approximate the real more closely. For Radhakrishnan,

44. Radhakrishnan, *Hindu View of Life*, p. 21; *Idealist View of Life*, pp. 108, 96.

45. Radhakrishnan, *The Creative Life* (New Delhi: Orient Paperbacks, 1975), pp. 28–29; *Hindu View of Life*, pp. 20–22.

46. Radhakrishnan, *Indian Philosophy*, vol. 1, p. 168; *Eastern Religions and Western Thought*, pp. 165, 343, 26, 75.

47. Radhakrishnan, *The Creative Life*, p. 10; *Hindu View of Life*, p. 35.

48. Radhakrishnan, *The Creative Life*, pp. 135–36; *Indian Philosophy*, vol. 1, p. 49; *Hindu View of Life*, pp. 16, 30, 49.

49. Radhakrishnan, *Hindu View of Life*, pp. 38, 42; "Fragments of a Confession," pp. 73–74.

the most fundamental fact is that all views contain some truth and so must be respected.[50]

The Intuitive Experience of Brahman

The apprehension of the Absolute, the spiritual intuition that forms the basis of Radhakrishnan's epistemology, is fundamentally religious in character. It breaks down the artificial wall separating Atman, my true self, from my empirical self. Knowledge is no longer based on a division of subject from object. Radhakrishnan claims that Hinduism, like every religion, emphasizes the experience of the inner life. It is essentially personal transformation. It is rebirth, regeneration. "It is to become new, [to] reach a higher level of understanding."[51]

Radhakrishnan argues that intuitive knowledge must be grounded in a form of self-awareness. Since Atman is Brahman, we must say with Socrates, "Know thyself." Radhakrishnan states repeatedly that knowledge is being; the knower is the known.[52] Such knowledge is more than a function of mind; it requires inward change and realization. The knower is not a spectator but a participant in reality. With the whole of our being, not just with our abstract, isolated minds, we must experience "knowledge by coincidence."[53]

Like sight, which apprehends its object directly, intuition is always immediate and non-inferential. The possibility of this directness rests on the presupposition that the Absolute is within. If Brahman and the person were not one, no knowledge of God— whether intuitive, conceptual, or perceptual—would be possible. Thus, argues Radhakrishnan, some form of pantheism is necessary to explain the direct experience of the divine to which all religious traditions attest.[54]

Not unexpectedly, Radhakrishnan claims that this immediate apprehension is ineffable: "silence is more significant than speech regarding the depths of the divine. . . . The mystery of the divine reality eludes the machinery of speech and symbol." Neither Brahman in itself nor our experience of Brahman can be communicated any more than the sunset can be explained to a man who is blind

---

50. Radhakrishnan, *Eastern Religions and Western Thought*, p. 314; *Hindu View of Life*, p. 36.

51. Radhakrishnan, *Eastern Religions and Western Thought*, p. 50; *Recovery of Faith*, p. 112; *Idealist View of Life*, p. 112.

52. Radhakrishnan, *Indian Philosophy*, vol. 1, pp. 45, 165, 194; "Fragments of a Confession," pp. 60–61; "Reply to Critics," p. 792; *Idealist View of Life*, p. 102.

53. Radhakrishnan, "Fragments of a Confession," p. 61; *Indian Philosophy*, vol. 1, p. 228; "Reply to Critics," p. 792.

54. Radhakrishnan, *Indian Philosophy*, vol. 1, p. 177; *Recovery of Faith*, pp. 103–7; *Idealist View of Life*, p. 103.

from birth. So essential is this principle that India chose a white background for its flag to symbolize the ineffability of the divine.[55]

Generally, pantheists ascribe a special status to these immediate encounters with the divine. Of course, Radhakrishnan does employ logic to confirm what intuition reveals. While intuition reveals truth, logic tests it. However, he also emphasizes that insight gives the experiencer a sense of complete certainty. The experience of intuiting the divine is self-certifying: "it carries its own credentials."[56]

The claim of self-authentication does not square easily with the assertion of logical tests for truth. The resolution of this apparent conflict comes in Radhakrishnan's claim that religious sages use logic only to confirm truth to others. The wise one will appropriate the logic typically used by his contemporaries to justify his experiences to them. Yet though others may not accept truth without arguments, the seer still believes without the supportive work of intellect. Faith in this true sense is trust based not on external authority but on the experience itself. The basic intuition is the beginning and the end of any intellectual effort. Thus, though Hinduism has no fear of intellection and no reason to avoid it, the religious insight is self-certifying for the person who has it.[57]

The soul in union with the Absolute experiences a sense of freedom, joy, and peace. Temporary refuge from the doubts and fears of everyday life can be found in substitute forms of happiness. But only when we realize the seed of divinity that lies within us, hidden by our carnal nature, does lasting joy result. Those who achieve this enlightenment no longer feel isolated from the world. Instead they realize their fundamental union with God and in this way are saved from selfishness, pain, and despondency.[58]

In a beautiful and revealing passage, Radhakrishnan describes his view of the ultimate experience of identification with the Supreme:

> Tasting nothing, comprehending nothing in particular, holding itself in emptiness, the soul finds itself as having all. A lightning flash, a sudden flame of incandescence, throws a momentary but eternal gleam on life in time. A strange quietness enters the soul; a great peace invades its being. The vision, the spark, the supreme moment of unification or conscious realization, sets the whole being ablaze with perfect purpose. The supreme awareness, the intimately felt presence, brings with it a

55. Radhakrishnan, *Hindu View of Life*, p. 20; *Eastern Religions and Western Thought*, p. 317; *The Principal Upanishads*, p. 67; *Indian Philosophy*, vol. 1, p. 178; *Idealist View of Life*, pp. 95–97; *The Creative Life*, p. 10.

56. Radhakrishnan, *Hindu View of Life*, p. 13; *Idealist View of Life*, pp. 92–94.

57. Radhakrishnan, *Hindu View of Life*, p. 14.

58. Radhakrishnan, *Recovery of Faith*, pp. 108–9; *Idealist View of Life*, p. 93; *Eastern Religions and Western Thought*, pp. 44–45.

rapture beyond joy, a knowledge beyond reason, a sensation more intense than that of life itself, infinite in peace and harmony.[59]

As this passage implies, the union with God is not only the basis of knowledge but also the stuff of religious salvation. Indian philosophy, both Hindu and Buddhist, identifies ignorance as the cause of the basic human predicament. We suffer because we are unaware of our true selves. The false identification of our empirical selves as our true selves leads to the illusion of a loss of unity with the Absolute, the fear of isolation, and the dread of death.[60]

Hindu thought agrees that liberation (moksa in Sanskrit) is the solution to this predicament. This liberation is release from the burden of the cycles of death and rebirth, the long-awaited triumph over temporal life and all its sorrow. It comes when we transcend our desire for ego-fulfillment and ego-gratification. When we have the spiritual realization that we are part of the All, desire is extinguished and fear and pain vanish. Since intuitive knowledge leads to liberation, in a very real sense "knowledge is power."[61]

Does this mean that we fade into nothingness? The Upanishads do affirm the "disintegration of individuality," says Radhakrishnan, but this does not mean annihilation. The individual self continues a life of full and free activity. If it were really describable, perhaps we could describe it best as the experience of divine life. Our separated and isolated being may cease, but "the self is not annihilated any more than the ray of the sun is lost in the sun, the wave of the sea in the ocean, the notes of music in the one harmony."[62]

In this experience of the divine, the sage reaches the goal of the spiritual life. The human soul is reintegrated with the source of its being. "God in [us] realises itself." Radhakrishnan writes that in this experience we may strip ourselves of the "outer sheaths of consciousness, penetrate to the nerve and quick of . . . life . . . until [we are] alone in the white radiance of a central and unique ecstasy. This is the fulfillment of man. This is to be with God. This is to be God."[63]

This experience, in one form or another, is the common property of every religious faith. The experiential, not the doctrinal, theoretical, or philosophical, forms the ground for fellowship among religions. Every act of worship is accepted by the divine regardless of the theo-

59. Radhakrishnan, *Eastern Religions and Western Thought*, p. 50; cf. "Fragments of a Confession," p. 63.

60. Radhakrishnan, *Eastern Religions and Western Thought*, pp. 43–44.

61. Radhakrishnan, *Indian Philosophy*, vol. 1, pp. 241–42; "Fragments of a Confession," p. 48; *The Principal Upanishads*, p. 127; *Idealist View of Life*, p. 128.

62. Radhakrishnan, *Indian Philosophy*, vol. 1, pp. 236, 241.

63. Radhakrishnan, *Eastern Religions and Western Thought*, p. 44; *Indian Philosophy*, vol. 1, pp. 206–7; "Fragments of a Confession," pp. 53, 63.

logical cloak in which it is hidden. Since all persons possess divinity within, all deserve the love of the Supreme.[64] Based on this, Radhakrishnan affirms universalism unequivocally: "there is no hell." But, of course, neither is there individual salvation. The final redemption of the human race finds consummation in an ultimate "transfiguration of the world" in union with the Absolute.[65]

The Significance of Moral Discipline

If all of us ought to seek this union with the divine, what is the significance of ethical concerns for this life? Radhakrishnan does affirm that union with Brahman takes us beyond good and evil. Moral distinctions belong to this world, while the Real is beyond ethical categories. The goal for us is to pass from mere symbols to reality. When we succeed in achieving a realization of Brahman, therefore, we move beyond good and evil. In the life of spirit, all symbolism is overcome.[66]

Yet Radhakrishnan also affirms the importance of ethics in this life. Because Hindu pantheism calls good and evil ultimately unreal, Westerners infer that Hinduism has no use for ethics whatever. But he vehemently rejects this inference. Of relationships in this world he writes, "to behave as if they do not exist simply because they do not persist is to court disaster."[67]

Radhakrishnan states that his multilevel pantheism provides the metaphysical basis necessary for ethics. "As we think ultimate reality to be, so we behave. Vision and action go together. If we believe absurdities, we shall commit atrocities."[68] Rather than negating ethics, our common grounding in the divine being gives all of us the potential for good. Since each person is divine, we must bear one another's burdens.[69] When Hinduism teaches us to rise above the world of *maya*, it does not destroy this world and its personal relationships or treat them as illusions. It only recognizes that the world of *maya* is not ultimate.[70]

Moral duty, therefore, must rest on truth. Morality must grow out

64. Radhakrishnan, *Recovery of Faith*, p. 110; "Fragments of a Confession," p. 75; *Eastern Religions and Western Thought*, pp. 116, 320.

65. Radhakrishnan, *Hindu View of Life*, pp. 32, 88; *Idealist View of Life*, p. 125; "Fragments of a Confession," p. 64.

66. Radhakrishnan, *Eastern Religions and Western Thought*, pp. 104–5.

67. Radhakrishnan, *Hindu View of Life*, p. 57; *Eastern Religions and Western Thought*, p. 32.

68. Radhakrishnan, *Eastern Religions and Western Thought*, p. 80.

69. Radhakrishnan, *Eastern Religions and Western Thought*, pp. 83, 101–2; *Indian Philosophy*, vol. 1, pp. 209–10.

70. Radhakrishnan, *Indian Philosophy*, vol. 1, pp. 208–9; *Eastern Religions and Western Thought*, p. 47.

of an awareness of reality as it is.[71] The desire, sin, and rebellion we experience in this life come from a basic ignorance of our divine nature. Overcoming evil begins when unawareness and ignorance are replaced by awareness and wisdom. This means that we are obligated first and foremost to seek union with the Supreme, the ultimate self-realization of divinization. All else is secondary.[72]

Radhakrishnan ties ethics intimately to this experience of salvation. But he views ethics not as the result of salvation, as in the Christian view, but as a contributing cause. Mere intellectual awareness alone cannot bring salvation. We must practice ascetic training to purge away what is unnatural and earthly while developing goodness, humility, and holiness.[73] In Radhakrishnan's view, the ethical life is the practice of ascetic discipline that leads to the realization of Brahman. Morality is a means to salvation, not its result.[74]

The ethical dimensions of salvation mean that those who would be saved are called to great personal striving. Radhakrishnan rejects "cheap grace." The realization of Brahman is difficult and costly; it requires great self-sacrifice and self-discipline. An important corollary of this claim is that salvation is defined as personal transformation of being, not as placation of a god. Radhakrishnan is opposed, therefore, to the biblical idea that guilt may be transferred to a substitute who could mercifully bear our sins for us. We must earn our own salvation.[75]

With no one else to take away sins, the spiritual one must work diligently to renounce selfish desires. Ignorance leads us to believe that our egos are ultimate. This individualism creates the world's problems. But spiritual wisdom means realizing that the "ego sense" should be renounced through a disciplined process of purifying the self. It does not mean the world is put aside. Virtuous people have desires, but they do not have selfish desires. They simply give themselves in selfless devotion to God and others.[76]

At the same time, Radhakrishnan acknowledges the legitimacy of Hinduism's traditional four stages of life. After the initial stages of trainee and householder, the third stage is retreat, and the fourth,

71. Radhakrishnan, *Recovery of Faith*, p. 103; *The Creative Life*, p. 9; *Indian Philosophy*, vol. 1, pp. 211–13.

72. Radhakrishnan, *Indian Philosophy*, vol. 1, pp. 208–10, 226; *Eastern Religions and Western Thought*, p. 37; *Idealist View of Life*, p. 123.

73. Radhakrishnan, *Indian Philosophy*, vol. 1, pp. 221–24; *Eastern Religions and Western Thought*, pp. 51, 94.

74. Radhakrishnan, *Indian Philosophy*, vol. 1, p. 41; *Hindu View of Life*, p. 48.

75. Radhakrishnan, *Indian Philosophy*, vol. 1, p. 243; *Idealist View of Life*, pp. 112–13, 122–23; *Hindu View of Life*, p. 54.

76. Radhakrishnan, *Eastern Religions and Western Thought*, pp. 113, 53; *Indian Philosophy*, vol. 1, pp. 242, 212–15.

renunciation.[77] The emphasis is clearly not on bearing one another's burdens for the sake of others. Yet these stages are active and ethical, even if the inner life is primarily in view. While outward action is put aside, its opposite is inward action, not complete inaction. Thus, dedicated moral effort is helpful in achieving inner transformation, even if outward results seem negligible. Through this inner renewal our nature is changed, and its basic divinity shines through. This is the "mandate of religion."[78]

This inner change can lift us from the cycle of rebirth, the dilemma of reincarnation. Though we may not be conscious of our past lives, our personal identity and the moral values (or dysvalues) of our lives are connected intimately with those previous lives. What we are today is largely the result of who we were before. Reincarnation implies that the ascent to realization of the divine is gradual, not rapid. But though the series of lives may seem endless, we can eventually develop into our divine selfhood.[79]

In their ascent toward the divine, our lives follow the law of karma. Karma means that I reap what I sow—no more, no less. In one place, Radhakrishnan says karma is an attribute, an immutable embodiment of the Absolute. Like *Rta*, the ancient Hindu principle of moral law pervading the universe, karma is blind and unyielding. Although it is part of the created order, not even Brahman can change karma, for it expresses God's ultimate will.[80]

Many misunderstand karma to mean fatalism or determinism. Radhakrishnan emphatically rejects this interpretation. Those who fail to realize that their actions determine their future karma may have their destiny taken out of their hands.[81] But if we know the law of karma, we can be mightier than karma; it cannot usurp our freedom. Karma deals us a hand of cards, but we must play them; thus, there is no fatalism or inevitability. Indeed, karma brings a brighter future. Only with the confidence that good is rewarded and evil punished can we have assurance that our efforts will pay off. Karma brings not despair but hope.[82]

We are free, and the law of karma does not alter this fact, says Radhakrishnan. Neither karma nor the will of God prearranges life.

77. Radhakrishnan, *Hindu View of Life*, pp. 59–64.

78. Radhakrishnan, *Eastern Religions and Western Thought*, p. 107; *Recovery of Faith*, p. 102; "Fragments of a Confession," pp. 80, 71.

79. Radhakrishnan, *Indian Philosophy*, vol. 1, pp. 249–51; *Idealist View of Life*, p. 122.

80. Radhakrishnan, *Hindu View of Life*, p. 53; *Indian Philosophy*, vol. 1, pp. 244–49; "Fragments of a Confession," p. 42.

81. Radhakrishnan, *Hindu View of Life*, pp. 54–55; *Recovery of Faith*, pp. 102, 111.

82. Radhakrishnan, *Hindu View of Life*, pp. 52–54; *Indian Philosophy*, vol. 1, pp. 246–49.

We have no sin nature to pull us down. Only failure to realize our divine nature can stop us. If we live for self in isolation from our environment, we will sin and cause discord and evil. But with self-discipline and training, we can achieve creativity and goodness. The future is in our hands.[83]

In sum, the primary emphasis in Radhakrishnan's ethics is on the contribution of moral discipline to the realization, upon which salvation depends, of oneness with God. Ethical service is only secondarily related to helping others for their sake; my ethical striving is primarily for my sake. Yet Radhakrishnan is sensitive to the Western ideal of service to others and therefore maintains that this is a legitimate dimension of ethical life. Charles Moore summarizes it this way: "*Dharma*, the essence of morality, is essentially a combination of ethics and religion. The goal is the 'double object' of happiness on earth and salvation."[84]

Conclusion

Various forms of Hinduism have come to the West in recent years, and most of them have fed the New Age movement. Some of these forms are authentically Indian. Many, in the minds of true Hindus, are not. They are plastic-packaged versions of the true faith served up to wealthy Westerners. But Hinduism traditionally tolerates such diversity. All doctrines, including the New Age formulations that borrow so freely from Hinduism, reflect the Supreme. The important thing is not thinking correctly, but acting rightly.

This is the basic Hindu principle of *dharma*, right action. To follow *dharma* is to live according to the "truth of things."[85] Since the truth of things, in Radhakrishnan's view, is the multilevel pantheism of his *Advaita Vedanta* philosophy, virtue is to live freely in harmony with the world so conceived. This means to experience the good life now as well as ultimate liberation from the curse of rebirth later. Ethics is religion and religion is ethics. The good life is union with the Supreme.

83. Radhakrishnan, "Fragments of a Confession," pp. 42, 50–51; *Hindu View of Life*, pp. 52–55.

84. Charles A. Moore, "Metaphysics and Ethics in Radhakrishnan's Philosophy," in *The Philosophy of Sarvepali Radhakrishnan*, ed. Schilpp, p. 285.

85. Radhakrishnan, *Hindu View of Life*, p. 56.

Plotinus
Emanational Pantheism

The One cannot be any existing thing, but is prior to all exis-
tents.—Plotinus

The Academy, the school founded by the great Greek philosopher
Plato, lasted for almost a millennium. Those who followed Plato,
however, did not simply repeat the master's words. Platonic philosophy developed in several directions. The teachings of the last great
Greek philosopher, Plotinus (A.D. 205–270), exemplifies one of these
directions. Plotinus, a neo-platonic thinker, developed what can be
called emanational pantheism.

This philosophy posits an ultimate Source, the One, that lies
behind everything that exists. The world as we know it is an emanation, a radiance, or an overflow of this One. The ancients thought the
sun could shine forth its light without reducing its own reality. In the
same way, the One overflows as the world but is not reduced in any
way by this emanation.[1] The world, therefore, can be thought of as a
reflection of the One. Although few today hold his views in their original form, the emanational pantheism of Plotinus did play a surprisingly important role in medieval thought and continues to exert an
influence today.

1. Plotinus, *The Six Enneads*, trans. Stephen MacKenna and B. S. Page, 6 vols.
(Chicago and London: Encyclopaedia Britannica, 1952), 1.7 [1].

Historical Context

Times were hard. Political unrest pervaded a decaying Roman Empire. The army routinely sold the title of emperor to the highest bidder, only to assassinate its client to make way for another sale. Taxes ran rampant while the wealthy ran from the tax collectors. Sturdy warriors from Asia and Europe plundered Roman territory. But as Bertrand Russell points out, not a trace of these events can be found in the writings of Plotinus. Plotinus, whom Russell called a "melancholy optimist," found a true land of happiness in another realm: mystical union with the One.[2]

Plotinus grew up in Egypt and studied under various teachers in Alexandria, a hotbed of Greek philosophical thinking. He finally found a mentor who suited him when, at age twenty-eight, he sat at the feet of Ammonius Saccas. This teacher is often thought to be the initiator of the form of Plato's thought that came to be called neo-Platonism. The pupil, Plotinus, has the distinction of becoming neo-Platonism's greatest expositor. (Plotinus's tutor also taught Origen, a man who became an influential but unorthodox Christian theologian and proponent of the allegorical method of Bible interpretation. As the peculiar twists of history would have it, Ammonius Saccas came to influence Christian thought through both of his celebrated students.)

At thirty-nine, Plotinus joined the army of Emperor Gordian III as it marched toward Persia, hoping thereby to learn about Eastern philosophy. But the army, true to its normal pattern, murdered the young emperor, leaving Plotinus stranded in the East and in danger of captivity. Only with great difficulty did he escape and return to Rome. Because of this trip, some have sought an Indian or Eastern connection in the development of his philosophy.[3] Emile Brehier argues, "What relates Plotinus to Indian thought is his decided preference for contemplation, from which he derives the only true reality, his scorn for the practical moral life, and finally, the egoistic and universal character of the spiritual life as he conceived it."[4]

This question of Plotinus's sources has several sides. While we cannot resolve it here, several factors seem significant. First and most important, Plotinus himself claimed that his concepts of the One and its overflow into lower levels of being are to be found in Plato.[5]

2. Bertrand Russell, *A History of Western Philosophy* (New York: Simon and Schuster, 1945), pp. 284–86.

3. Sarvepali Radhakrishnan, *Eastern Religions and Western Thought,* 2d ed. (London: Oxford University Press, 1940, 1975), pp. 207–15.

4. Emile Brehier, *The Philosophy of Plotinus,* trans. Joseph Thomas (Chicago: University of Chicago Press, 1958), p. 132.

5. Plotinus, *Enneads,* 5.1 [8]; A. H. Armstrong, *Plotinus* (London: Allen and Unwin, 1953), pp. 16–25.

Second, Plotinus stayed in the East only a very short time and then under trying circumstances. He hardly had time to study philosophy while fleeing for his life. Third, the neo-Platonic ideas that Plotinus developed had been taught in Alexandria for centuries. It seems best, therefore, to hold that Plotinus's sources were primarily Greek. Similarities or parallels in thinking do not prove direct influence of one philosophy on another.

Upon his return to Rome, Plotinus spent nine years teaching in the capital. He attracted an elite clientele that included Emperor Gallienus, who possessed skill in oratory, poetry, gardening, cooking, and "several curious but useless sciences" but who, as an emperor, was incompetent: "when the great emergencies of state required his presence and attention, he was engaged in conversation with the philosopher Plotinus, wasting his time in trifling or licentious pleasures, preparing his initiation to the Grecian mysteries, or soliciting a place in the Areopagus of Athens."[6]

Plotinus, for his part, almost convinced Gallienus to permit the founding of a new city, Platonopolis. He planned to organize this community according to Plato's plans in the *Republic.* But the vacillating emperor withdrew his support, and the city was never built. Other plans came to fruition, however, for in 253, Plotinus began to write. During the next decade, considered his first period, Plotinus produced a number of disjointed works.

When Plotinus was about fifty-eight, a student named Porphyry came to study under him. Porphyry's stay (263–268) constitutes the second period of Plotinus's literary career. Porphyry later wrote a biography of his beloved mentor, but his most important contribution was to organize Plotinus's writings. In contrast to his skilled speech, the master's writings proved difficult to follow. The thick style was only partly due to poor eyesight, which prevented him from making corrections. Porphyry dutifully compiled the writings into six books of nine chapters each. These are the *Enneads,* the word meaning groups or sets of nine.

Plotinus lived his final days, the third period (268–270), with many friends and no enemies. Though he was in failing health, his literary output continued at a high level, and he acted as a sort of spiritual guide to many who sought his advice. Having sent Porphyry to Sicily in 268 to recover from some depression, he died a couple of years later while his biographer was away. Plotinus uttered his last words to a trusted friend and physician, Eustochius. The doctor, who had traveled some distance to be with Plotinus, reported that his dying words reflected his fundamental belief in the all-embracing One: "I was

6. Edward Gibbon, *The Decline and Fall of the Roman Empire,* vol. 1, new ed. (New York: Peter Fenelon Collier, 1899), pp. 328–29.

waiting for you, before that which is divine in me departs to unite itself with the Divine in the universe."[7]

While Plotinus's sources were Greek philosophy, Christian theology felt the effects of his work. Several avenues of influence account for this. The great Christian thinker and writer Augustine, in his intellectual journey, traveled through Plotinus's writings. A dualistic religion called Manicheism had proved intellectually unsatisfying to Augustine. In the wake of that experience, Plotinus's philosophy opened Augustine's eyes to the possibility of a spiritual realm and helped him resolve his intellectual struggles with the problem of evil. Later Augustine wrote (with too much enthusiasm) that Plotinus, if he had lived a few years later, could have "changed a few words and phrases and become a Christian."

The other pipeline of influence runs through the four treatises of an unknown monk, possibly of Syrian origin, known as Pseudo-Dionysius the Areopagite. This name reflects the claim that these works were written by Paul's convert in Athens, the Dionysius mentioned in Acts 17:34. The treatises cannot be authentic, however, for they reflect the philosophy of a later neo-Platonic writer named Proclus (c. 410–485). Proclus, last of the great platonists, agreed in many important respects with Plotinus. Since the works of Pseudo-Dionysius were thought by medieval writers to be the work of Paul's associate, they were accorded a special place of authority. Consequently, certain important elements of Plotinus's thought found their way through Proclus and Pseudo-Dionysius into many medieval Christian works of theology and devotion.[8]

Four Levels of Reality

Plotinus's metaphysical system consists of four levels. The first (the One) is beyond being, the next two (Mind and World Soul) are within being. The next level (matter) is almost nothing, and the last (non-being) is absolutely nothing. Everything begins at the top (the One) and flows downward toward nothing. It begins at absolute Unity and splits up into greater and greater multiplicity.

Plotinus's fundamental metaphysical concept is what he calls the One. The One is the Source of all reality. In fact, Plotinus thought it necessary to posit the One in order to account for the rest of reality. The One is a "necessity prior to all necessities." It did not just happen as the result of mere chance, nor can its character be ascribed to

7. Frederick Copleston, *A History of Philosophy*, vol. 1, *Greece and Rome* (Garden City, N. Y.: Doubleday, Image Books, 1963), pt. 2, p. 208.

8. Philip Merlan, "Plotinus," in *The Encyclopedia of Philosophy*, ed. Paul Edwards, 8 vols. (New York and London: Macmillan, 1967), vol. 6, pp. 351–59.

chance. It must be; it must be what it is; and what it must be is what is best.[9]

Plotinus gives several arguments to show that the One is necessary. For example, he asserts that nothing could exist were it not for a prior unity, for unity precedes everything as its source. It would be no more possible to have plurality without unity than to have a book without an author. Oneness is more basic than manyness, for plurality must presuppose unity both in the realm of being and in the attainment of knowledge. Nothing could exist or be known without the prior unity of the One.[10]

As pure unity, the One neither possesses nor experiences plurality. It is entirely undifferentiated.[11] Precisely because the One is the Source of all, it must itself be above all. Therefore, Plotinus tells us, the One is beyond being. In order for finite existing things to come into being, there must be a generator of being. But finite things cannot create. So an infinite reality beyond existence must be posited as the generator of all finite beings. Because the One does not "exist," it is in a position to bring other things into existence.[12]

To understand his point, we must grasp what Plotinus means by the words *being* and *exist*. For Plotinian metaphysics, the word *being* refers to something that can be defined or that possesses a definite form.[13] To *exist* would be to have a definite limit. But to be "definite" is to be finite, and to "de-limit" is to limit. Since the One can be neither finite nor limited, it cannot "exist" or "have being." It must be beyond form and definition. It is important to understand that while the One is "no being" and "beyond being," it is not unreal. It must be omnipresent and completely transcendent. In describing the union of the soul with the One, Plotinus tells us that the soul "is not in nothingness but in itself; . . . it is no longer in the order of being; it is in the Supreme."[14] When the human soul becomes one with the One, it is beyond being, but it is not in nothingness.

Since to describe something is to use language that divides things conceptually, the One cannot really be described. At least this is what Plotinus says. When we receive a quality of our being from the One, we are tempted to assign that quality to the Source. But this ought not to be done. The One cannot possess the characteristic. It simply "subsists in itself." When we affirm that the One is our generator, for example, we are really speaking about ourselves, not about the One.

9. Plotinus, *Enneads*, 6.8 [8, 9, 18].
10. Ibid., 6.9 [1]; 3.8 [9]; 6.6 [13]; 5.3 [15].
11. Ibid., 5.4 [1]; 6.9 [3].
12. Ibid., 5.2 [1].
13. Ibid., 5.1 [7]; 6.9 [3]; see also Joseph Owens, *A History of Ancient Western Philosophy* (New York: Appleton-Century-Crofts, 1959), p. 405.
14. Plotinus, *Enneads*, 6.9 [11].

When we try to describe the One, we "hover" around it; sometimes
we get close to a description, but usually we are lost in a fog of mystery. In a word, since the One possesses no characteristics, it cannot
be described. The best thing to say, as the Indian sages advised, is that
the One is not this, not that.[15]

Any positive description will create distorted images, for conceptual language treats things as though they have parts. Negative language
is better: the One is "neither thing nor quantity nor intellect nor soul;
not in motion, not at rest, not in place, not in time; it is the self-
defined, unique in form or, better, formless, existing before Form
was."[16] Clearly, these qualities cannot be predicated of the One. But
this does not entail that the One is lacking in something. The problem lies not in the One itself, but in the inappropriateness of the
descriptions, which necessarily limit the One. The One is not less
than what language can say; it is far more. And so only negative
descriptions are even close to accurate. The One can "neither be spoken nor written of." Language can only point toward the path of experience, which is the only way to apprehend the One.[17]

The names given to the One, therefore, ought to be negative. But
Plotinus uses many positive names to describe the One. The One is
Beauty, Supreme, and the Good; it is an Entity, a Cause, the First, and
the First Principle. It is also free and all-powerful.[18] Yet the negative
names clearly have priority; Plotinus qualifies any positive statements. For example, he explains that the One does not actually possess the quality of goodness; it is "The Good" itself. To be consistent,
he also explains that while the One is "The Good," this does not
imply that the One possesses being.[19] When he ascribes beauty to the
One, Plotinus often calls it "beyond Beauty" (reminiscent of his
description of the One as "beyond being"). In fact, he denies that we
can really call the One "good" or "intellect." He says that it has no
power and even that the word *first* does not really apply. In these
ways, Plotinus quickly qualifies his statements, even though he
sometimes uses positive language. Language at best gives a fuzzy picture; indeed, it distorts the One. The One can have no positive
name.[20]

Because knowledge divides things into conceptual opposites,
Plotinus forcefully and repeatedly denies that the One can have
knowledge. Although he sometimes concedes a minimal self-aware-

15. Ibid., 6.9 [3].
16. Ibid.
17. Ibid., 6.9 [4].
18. Ibid., 1.6 [6]; 6.8 [13, 14, 18]; 6.9 [4]; 5.4 [1]; 5.6 [6]; 6.2 [17].
19. Ibid., 6.7 [38].
20. Ibid., 6.7 [32, 33, 40]; 5.3 [13]; 3.8 [11]; 2.9 [1].

ness in the Ultimate, his usual argument is that knowing involves duality which never can be found in the One. Since knowing implies the twoness of knower and known, and since the One is beyond all duality, the One must be beyond knowledge. The One has no self-knowing, for no twoness resides in it.[21] However, to deny that the One has knowledge is not to ascribe a defect or a limitation to the One. Plotinus explains that although the One does not know, it does not need to know.[22]

The One is also the Source of all reality; it generates all. The highest thing is absolutely unified; all duality derives from the basic unity. But the One is not simply the sum of all. As the cause of all, the One is distinct from everything else.[23] There is some tension on the question of whether the One possesses what it produces. At times Plotinus seems to say that the One does in some sense contain its effects. But more fundamentally, his view is that the qualityless One produces finite things with definite qualities that delimit their nature. But according to that basic principle of Plotinian metaphysics, since these qualities are definite, they are also finite; because they delimit, they also limit. The One is neither finite nor limited. Thus only things in the world possess form. No qualities can be found in the One.[24]

For this reason, there is some debate about whether Plotinus is really a pantheist. Reality as we know it does not exist absolutely in the One. Frederick Copleston warns that calling Plotinus's system pantheistic without proper qualification could lead to misunderstanding. The metaphysical ultimate, the One, remains transcendent and undiminished in the creative process. It does not empty itself fully into the world. Yet with proper qualification, we can describe the system as a "dynamic pantheism" if not an absolute monism.[25] There is a Unity beneath all that exists—although of course that Unity is not to be identified with existing things.

The means by which being derives from the One is called 'emanation.' The metaphor of emanation is closely associated with Plotinus and plays a central role in his thought. But it is somewhat ambiguous. 'Emanation' refers to something radiating, like light rays emitted from a source of light. For Plotinus, it pictures an overflow, a radiance, or an issuing forth by the God who is beyond being into the levels of being, or existence, below.

Plotinus's use of this metaphor guards against several misconcep-

---

21. Ibid., 6.6 [6]; cf. 3.9 [9].
22. Ibid., 5.4 [2]; 5.3 [10, 12].
23. Ibid., 6.9 [3].
24. Ibid., 5.1 [6]; 6.7 [15].
25. Copleston, *History*, vol. 1, pt. 2, 211; Merlan, "Plotinus," in *Encylopedia of Philosophy*, ed. Edwards, vol. 6, p. 354.

tions. For one, emanation is not the result of a free decision by a conscious God. It is rather a necessary process. Plotinus describes emanation as involuntary. For example, a woman whose baby is due does not decide whether to deliver. The baby just comes. What is mature must give birth. What is full must overflow. In his later writing, Plotinus tries to say that freedom and necessity coalesce in the One.[26] But he generally understands 'creation' in terms quite different from those normally employed by monotheists. Things overflow because they must.

The idea of emanation also guards against the view that 'creation' somehow diminishes the One. The One remains entirely unmoved and unaffected by the overflow into being. The metaphor of emanation expresses this well, for a source of light emits its rays without itself being diminished. Today, of course, we know that stars like our sun do lose energy when they give off light. To the ancients, however, nothing could be more obvious than the constancy of the sun. So Plotinus refers to the sun to illustrate that the One is entirely unchanged by the overflow into being.[27] Another illustration of emanation is the center of a circle and its radii. As the radii move out from the center, the center is unmoved. So the many issue from the One, but the One remains unaffected. The sun warms and lights the planets, but it never changes. The radii radiate from the center, but it never moves. The One emanates but is immovable.[28]

The process of emanation is not a single act that completes for all time the generation of the world. Because the One abides, it is rather a timeless, eternal event.[29] The One is absolute simplicity, but at the same time it contains the potential for multiplicity in that it is the Source of all. On the principle that what is caused is more complex than the causer, Plotinus infers that the universe cannot be the simplest, most fundamental cause. Instead, as a stream is traced to its source and the sap in a tree to its root, so everything is traced back to the One.[30]

Beneath the primary reality, the One, lies the secondary reality that Plotinus calls *Nous*. Variously and somewhat imprecisely translated Mind, Intelligence, Spirit, or Intellectual Principle, *Nous* (which we will call Mind) refers to highest being. It carries a "model" of the One and may be called its "offspring."[31] Mind is like the Source; it is an "image" of that ultimate Reality. But Mind cannot be equated

26. Plotinus, *Enneads*, 5.4 [1]; 5.1 [6]; 5.2 [1].
27. Ibid., 5.1 [6].
28. Ibid., 6.8 [18].
29. Ibid., 1.7 [1]; 5.1 [6].
30. Ibid., 3.8 [10].
31. Ibid., 5.5 [5]; 5.1 [6].

with the One. Mind reflects the One as the sun's rays reflect the sun. But despite this similarity, Mind, unlike the One, contains duality.[32]

Generally, Plotinus does not say that the One produces Mind. At times he states that Mind comes from a self-reflection—as the One looks at itself, its own vision is Mind. But at times he also denies that the One has self-awareness, because self-consciousness in the One would imply the duality of knower and known. In any case, Plotinus also says that Mind must reflect upon itself. Only in this self-contemplation of Mind is its own creation complete.[33]

The self-vision of Mind introduces into the system for the first time an actual multiplicity. Mind is one in its own essence, yet it contemplates both the One and itself. Thus Plotinus calls Mind the One-Many. It is neither purely unified like the One (because it has knowledge and the duality of knower and known that this entails), nor completely many like the world (because it is in itself unified). It is halfway between. In this position, it also contains all ideas of the lower rungs of the emanational ladder. While it is itself unified, its ideas involve it in multiplicity.[34]

At several points, Plotinus struggles to explain how Mind, which is one, can also have ideas about the many existents in the world. Mind is one, he says, yet it exists in every individual's mind. He tells us that unextended (non-spatial) Mind is omnipresent in the extended realm below it. In this way it can contain all ideas of the beings below. In one illustration, Plotinus compares Mind in its relation to individual minds, with the universal concept Human in its relation to individual human beings.[35]

As the One overflows into being, it emanates into several levels of being. Mind is the highest of these levels and is called the highest being: "When a thing is a Being, it is also [a Mind], when it is [a Mind] it is Being; intellection and Being are co-existents."[36] Mind is superior to all things other than the One. It contains not only ideas, but matter as well. Mind, therefore, is generated by the One, and in turn then produces those beings below it on the ladder of existence. First, it contemplates the One and constitutes itself. Next, it looks within and creates ideas. Finally, looking outward, it emits the next level of reality.[37]

Plotinus calls the third level of reality World Soul. As the emanation continues, this universal Soul flows out from its own source, Mind, as Mind does from the One. Soul, like Mind, contemplates

32. Ibid., 5.1 [7].
33. Ibid., 5.1 [5, 6, 7]; 5.2 [1]; 3.9 [9].
34. Ibid., 5.7 [1].
35. Ibid., 6.5 [2–6]; 6.2 [22].
36. Ibid., 5.6 [6].
37. Ibid., 5.1 [6, 7]; 6.2 [22].

itself and in this way constitutes its own being.[38] As the third member of Plotinus's 'trinity,' Soul is a connecting link between Mind above and the world below. It consists of a higher aspect that connects it to Mind and a lower aspect through which it contacts the world. As Mind contains all minds, so Soul is the cosmic depository for all individual souls. To use a modern comparison, Soul is something like Jung's collective unconscious. In other words, individual souls collectively form a whole living organism. In fact, says Plotinus, because individual souls all find unity in Soul, they can communicate with each other by a kind of extrasensory telepathy.[39]

Individual souls are actually instances of Soul. They are nonphysical, substantial, eternal realities. They indwell not only humans, but also animals and even plants, accounting for their physical life. And, since souls are eternal and immortal, Plotinus defends reincarnation. The soul indwelling an animal in this life could theoretically come back in another life to indwell a plant or a person.[40]

From the overflow of Soul comes the physical universe that is called matter. The material world in its wholeness is necessary as the destination of the overflow. Here emanation reaches its conclusion. Matter is pure stuff without structure. We may think of matter as bodies from which all form or structure is abstracted or removed. For example, imagine a dress on a mannequin. If we vaporize the mannequin, which gives form or shape to the dress, then what is left over, the dress in an unformed pile, would be like matter. Matter is the stuff that has no determinate shape or nature, the lump of clay without a mold. It is a pure potential that cannot in itself become anything. Only when shaped by Soul does matter become the physical universe.[41]

Because it is completely indeterminate, with no structure or form, matter is ironically both the opposite of the One and like the One. Matter is the lowest limit, the farthest extension, of emanation and so exists at the opposite end of the overflow from the One. If emanation were to proceed beyond matter, it would move into sheer nothingness or absolute nonbeing. Yet despite its distance from the One, paradoxically, matter is also similar to the One. Since neither has a fixed nature, both are without form and entirely elude concepts.[42]

In summary, the complex metaphysic of Plotinus consists of four levels of reality, the One, Mind, Soul, and matter. Plotinus believed he had shown, "as far as it is possible to demonstrate about things of

38. Ibid., 5.1 [6]; 5.2 [1].
39. Ibid., 4.3 [11]; 4.9 [2, 3].
40. Ibid., 4.8 [6]; 3.9 [3]; 4.7 [1, 9–14].
41. Ibid., 3.9 [3]; 2.5 [4, 5]; 1.8 [9].
42. Ibid., 2.4 [15].

this kind," that these form a hierarchy of what is real. The One, the top rung of the ladder, is beyond being. The three rungs below it have decreasing amounts of being. Below matter, the lowest rung, could only be nonbeing—absolute nothingness. The levels are tied together by the metaphor of emanation, the overflow of being. As Plato taught, each level generates the one below.[43] We could think of the system as a series of four pools of water with each pool (except the first) receiving the overflow of water from the one above it. Of course, the problem with this picture is that the top pool eventually will run dry. In Plotinus's thought, however, the One overflows into being without ever being depleted. The One is the absolute, eternal, unchanging Source of all.

Ascent to Knowledge

The material world represents the extreme to which emanation flows. As emanation flows down the ladder of being it becomes more multiple and less real. The light that the One produces gradually diminishes as it radiates farther and farther from its source. Beyond matter, the fading of light ends, and complete darkness, pure nothingness, completely envelops the light.[44]

But we are not left without recourse. In the darkness are little signposts pointing back to the Source. After the descent down the ladder, these signals call us to retrace our steps back to the higher. For example, we might see beauty in material objects. But we realize this beauty is not worth pursuing, for physical things are "copies, vestiges, shadows" of the One. Instead, says our guide, "let us flee . . . to the beloved Fatherland," that is, the One.[45] This we do in a mystical ascent leading out of the mire of multiplicity and back to union with the One.

Though it also has religious implications, this ascent is essentially Plotinus's concept of epistemology. Matter is indefinite and unformed. As we perceive matter via the five senses, we find the signposts that point us toward the One. Then we begin the ascent from the realm of the senses, and escape from the lower to the higher. With a sense of passion and love fostered by the One, we feel compelled to climb. Abandoning the outer reaches of emanation, we head upward toward the Source. In this way the individual soul abandons the "realm of deceit and falsity, and pastures the Soul in the 'Meadows of Truth.'"[46]

43. Ibid., 5.1 [8].
44. Ibid., 2.4; 6.3 [7].
45. Ibid., 1.6 [1–9].
46. Ibid., 6.9 [3]; 1.3 [4].

From the realm of the senses, we must rise to the level of intellect, where we contemplate Mind. Here, taking only that aspect of our being that is suited to such rarefied flight (that is, our minds), we reach up to the realm of Mind. In this way we rise above the multiplicity of matter and the senses. Yet knowledge at the level of Mind is still necessarily characterized by duality, the twoness of knower and known. And so we must push higher, to the land where there is no multiplicity at all.

As we move above Mind, we reach a state where we do not 'know' objects in a dualistic way. There, with the One, we pass beyond all twoness. In this state, a "man is changed, no longer himself nor self-belonging; he is merged with the Supreme, sunken into it, one with it; centre coincides with centre."[47] We pass the entrance, in other words, into a level of intuition that is the highest knowing—a union with the One. To see God we become God; to find beauty we become Beauty; to apprehend oneness we become the One. To reach this state of union we move beyond being and essence to where God is; in a sense we are God. Variously Plotinus describes this experience as "simplicity," "touching," and "self-surrender." In a well-known phrase that Porphyry places at the end of the *Enneads*, Plotinus calls this the union of the alone with the Alone.[48]

Absolute union with the One, the climax of the ascent, is the highest knowledge. In this union, the twoness of conceptual knowledge entirely passes away. The oneness cannot even be described as a vision, for even this word preserves a sense of twoness. Calling it 'union' expresses the absolute oneness of the experience.

This union means we cannot really *know* the One in the everyday sense of that word. Knowledge as we usually think of it is limited to duality, but the One is beyond duality. Because of this, Plotinus not surprisingly says that knowledge of the One is ineffable: "we must be patient with language; we are forced to apply to the Supreme terms which strictly are ruled out; everywhere we must read 'So to speak.'" To describe the One would be to make it one thing among other things, to give it definition (which implies finitude). Of course this always means distortion. So while no name can identify the One exactly, we "try to indicate, in our own feeble way, something concerning it."[49]

According to Porphyry's count, Plotinus himself experienced mystical union on four occasions in the six-year stretch of the biographer's stay.[50] Obviously, Plotinus thought it could occur repeatedly.

47. Ibid., 5.3 [4]; 6.9 [10].
48. Ibid., 1.6 [9]; 6.9 [11].
49. Ibid., 6.9 [3, 10, 11]; 5.3 [13]; 6.8 [12, 13].
50. Copleston, *History*, vol. 1, pt. 2, p. 208.

In this life, any experience of oneness is brief and ecstatic. Plotinus describes it as a sudden seizure, an illumination. From any union we achieve in this life we fall back into everyday experience. Thus, we wait for the time when, through virtue and wisdom, the experience is made eternal and complete. In the famous final paragraph, Plotinus calls this "the life of gods and of the godlike and blessed among men." It is the life of absolute oneness with God.[51]

Naturally, after the sudden seizure is over, we can in a sense know something of the One. After warnings against divulging this knowledge to the uninitiated, Plotinus says that a person who has experienced unity is marked by that experience; such a person carries the image of the One.[52] This is possible only because there exists a real connection between the One and its offspring. He does warn that "the One is all things and not one of them; the source of all things is not all things." On the other hand, the One is all things in a transcendent sense. There is something in us that is like the One, and this is the basis for our intuition of that which transcends all intelligence. We find in our beings faint traces of the One, signposts that enable us to experience mystical union.[53]

It is difficult to determine exactly how Plotinus thinks the union of which he speaks takes place. Is it a union of being, an ontological union, in which the one who experiences ecstatic union ceases to exist as a distinct person? Or is it a psychological union in which the person retains a separate identity? There are some passages that seem to support the first of these interpretations.[54] But Plotinus also states that the individual does not become extinct when it merges with Soul. And he also implies that in this life, union with the One is temporary.[55] Either way, it is clear that knowledge, for Plotinus, is ultimately found not through the senses or even in the mind. Knowledge of the One is found in the final, absolute union with the One.

Religious Dimensions of Union

Plotinus is unusual in Western philosophy in the way he gives his epistemology heavily religious overtones. There is no clear demarcation between his concept of epistemology and his view of religious experience. For Plotinus, the ascent from the world of sense to the ultimate union with the One is both knowledge and salvation. As Copleston says, "Philosophy now includes, not only logic, cosmology, psychology, metaphysics and ethics, but also the theory of religion

51. Plotinus, *Enneads*, 5.3 [17]; 6.9 [11].
52. Ibid., 6.9 [11].
53. Ibid., 5.2 [1]; 3.8 [9].
54. Ibid., 5.3 [4]; 5.5 [6].
55. Ibid., 6.4 [16]; 6.7 [34].

and mysticism . . . philosophy tends to pass into religion . . . [It is] the intellectualist reply to the contemporary yearning for personal salvation. . . . "[56]

To interpret this yearning, Plotinus pictures the soul as unsatisfied with its earthly situation. Being is unhappy with multiplicity and recoils back toward unity. Though it takes effort to rise above the world, we feel motivated to experience the One. We become "homesick" for the "Fatherland" of goodness and light. An inner urge for the divine compels us to rise to our Source. To motivate us to hurry back to God, Plotinus encourages us to be indignant about our position far from the One.[57]

In the culmination of the *Enneads*, Plotinus teaches that liberation from the world and its mundane pleasures leads to true happiness. The person who lives in the body may not experience true happiness. But the true person, who rises above matter, finds happiness in contemplation. Here human existence finds comfort in its original Source. The wanderer can come home.[58]

When this return is accomplished, does the soul thereby entirely lose its individual existence? On the one hand, Plotinus does not completely deny personal immortality. In fact, like the Eastern pantheists, he assumes that the soul of a human being can be reincarnated in an animal or a plant. Yet on the other hand, we always desire the One. When we join the One, we have a new life in our true home: "Our being is the fuller for our turning Thither; this is our prosperity. . . . Here is the soul's peace. . . . Here is living, the true; that of today, all living apart from Him, is but a shadow, a mimicry. . . . Life here, with the things of earth, is a sinking, a defeat, a failing of the wing."[59] It appears that ultimately, our life here is a dream, and our true reality is found when we return to become merged with the One.

As inspiring as this thought may be, Plotinus also shows a willingness to accept religious ideas that seem far less noble. For example, his concept of mutual sympathy among souls gives grounding to his belief in extrasensory perception. He also teaches prayer, which might seem to imply the continued existence of personal identity. Prayer, after all, demands two persons. You cannot pray to yourself. Prayer is a kind of interpersonal communication that requires the reality of two persons.

But Plotinus explains that prayer is possible not because there is a loving deity whose will it is to answer but because of the interaction

56. Copleston, *History*, vol. 1, pt. 2, pp. 215–16.
57. Plotinus, *Enneads*, 6.9 [9]; 4.8 [4].
58. Ibid., 6.9 [9, 11].
59. Ibid., 4.3 [5]; 3.4 [2]; 6.9 [9].

of the parts of reality in an organic whole. In discussing why the One overflows in emanation, he alludes to prayer as something that is possible because we aspire to be one with the One. Prayer is rooted in the sympathetic feeling of connection between all the parts of reality. Prayer is like an intrabodily communication of the human nervous system, not an interpersonal communication between individual humans.[60]

Ultimately, the religion of Plotinus is not one of personal relation to God. It is essentially a mystical union with the One, with God. This union is experienced by those who turn from the world, which weighs us down. But throwing off this weight is the function of ethics. If we would lighten our load so that we may ascend to God, we must practice ethical living.

The Role of Virtue

Speaking of his belief that Plotinus was influenced by Eastern sources, Brehier cites as evidence "his scorn for the practical moral life."[61] Ethics does, however, play an important role in the Plotinian religious philosophy. The ascent to God begins in the senses, where we live every day. Yet we must find the light of God in God, not in some lower source. Thus the ascent to God must be accomplished by ruthlessly pruning away everything that smacks of the material. We are to rise to the One by purifying ourselves of the weight of the world. When we cast it off, we achieve unity with the One.[62]

The psychology Plotinus develops follows a common Greek division into three parts. The highest part lives in the intellectual realm of Mind and is not contaminated with matter. The lowest part is the body. In between, there resides a "composite" where the mind exists in real union with the body.[63] Salvation begins when the higher rules the lower. In beginning his discussion of virtue, Plotinus quotes Plato to prove that we escape this world by becoming godlike through developing virtue. This means living by wisdom, holiness, and justice. In this way, the ascent to God begins; we become like God and begin to enjoy salvation.

We achieve the first stage in the salvation process when we overcome the body and the senses through the four cardinal virtues. When the soul refuses to be mired in the body and follows intellect instead, it finds wisdom. If it acts upon the body rather than being passive, it develops self-control. When it does not fear separation from the body, it achieves courage. If it follows reason, it possesses justice. Through

60. Ibid., 6.4 [30–40]; 6.1 [6].
61. Brehier, *Philosophy of Plotinus*, p. 132.
62. Plotinus, *Enneads*, 5.3 [17]; 6.9 [3].
63. Ibid., 4.8 [8].

these virtues, the worldly, the sensuous, and the physical are cast off, and the ascent toward the One begins.[64]

We reach a second stage in our ascent toward the One when we move toward Mind and pursue intellectual activities of science and philosophy. A third stage, however, moves above these intellectual pursuits into a realm beyond logical and discursive thought. Here we experience union with Mind. But the union is still a two-in-one union where self-consciousness continues and self-identity is maintained.[65]

These phases prepare us for the final stage, the indescribable, ecstatic experience of the truly virtuous and wise person—"splendour, brimmed with the Intellectual light, become that very light, pure, buoyant, unburdened, raised to Godhood or, better, knowing its Godhood, all aflame." Here the cultivation of virtue bears mature fruit. The domination of intellect over the lower parts of the body yields its reward. As we struggle upward, "we awaken the virtue within . . . once more we are lightened of the burden and move by virtue towards Intellectual-Principle and through the Wisdom in That to the Supreme." On this path we find union with the One.[66]

That this ethical ascent should be necessary poses something of a problem for Plotinus. The morally good ascent of ethics and intellect leading to salvation implies a morally evil fall into the mire of matter. If there is a need for moral and intellectual purification, then emanation must have involved a contamination with evil. But the downward emanation of the One into the hierarchy of being is not the free choice of a moral being but a necessary overflow of the One. If there is no free choice to fall into evil, why is purification necessary? Because the descent is not chosen but necessary, it seems odd that Plotinus should consider it evil. Plotinus walks a tightrope on this question; at one point he even says that the descent is in some sense neither free nor necessary: "The Souls go forth neither under compulsion nor of freewill."[67]

Although he basically denies freedom, Plotinus does at times describe the process of emanation toward matter in moral terms. He calls emanation a "fall," an "apostasy." Mind breaks away from the One because it desires independence. Soul turns from Mind because it wants to be alone and because it desires what is crude and base.[68] There is an aspect of Plotinus's thought, therefore, that describes emanation in terms of sin, guilt, and moral responsibility.

64. Ibid., 1.2 [1, 3].
65. Ibid., 1.3 [4].
66. Ibid., 6.9 [9, 11].
67. Ibid., 4.3 [12, 13].
68. Ibid., 5.2 [1]; 5.1 [6, 7]; 3.9 [3]; cf. Armstrong, *Plotinus*, p. 29.

Many ancient philosophies and religions accepted a dualistic answer to the problem of evil. In this view, soul is essentially good, while matter is inherently evil. As Br'er Rabbit tries to save himself by extricating his limbs from the Tar-Baby, the soul that is stuck in matter finds salvation by disentangling itself from inherently evil matter by some moral, ritual, or intellectual means. Manicheism, the Persian religion from which Saint Augustine escaped, saw evil as inherent in matter. Plotinus borders on this answer at times,[69] but it is essentially at odds with his system, for he claims that matter is not evil but the last remnant of good, or, better, the mere capacity for good.

Several factors mitigate this tension in Plotinus. One is the notion that evil is not a positive thing, but a lack, a privation. Evil is not a bad cookie, but a good cookie from which someone has taken a bite. The bite mark, the gap, is the evil. What exists of the cookie is still good. In Plotinus's explanation, the evil in matter is due to the fact that it "possesses nothing and so is in destitution." It is evil because it has no specific nature; it is evil not positively, but negatively—it lacks good.[70]

Here Plotinus is reflecting his belief that the degree of being possessed by the various levels of reality decreases as we move down the ladder toward chaotic matter. When matter is reached, being is almost gone. So, in a sense, matter is almost nothing. The cookie is almost gone. Such matter, because it almost lacks being and is "in destitution," is as evil as it is possible to be without being completely evil. It is as close to absolute nonbeing, pure nothingness, as it can get. In fact, matter possesses no actual good (since it has no "specific character"), but only the capacity for good. It is the place on the ladder of being where good nearly peters out. Below matter is only nothingness.[71]

A second factor Plotinus mentions is that the evil of the part is sometimes necessary to the good of the whole. This argument finds its roots in Plato and the Stoics. It shows that the broad picture can be good even if segments of the whole are not. A painting must have dark areas to contrast the light. The dark colors in themselves may be evil, but as part of the whole, they contribute to the beauty of the larger painting. Similarly, reality itself cannot be good in every detail.

69. Ibid., 1.8 [4].
70. Ibid., 2.4 [16].
71. At times, however, Plotinus complicates this by saying that there are two kinds of matter. In addition to the chaotic matter at the bottom rung of the ladder of being, he speaks of a kind of "intelligible matter" or "divine matter" that exists in connection with Mind. Divine matter, says Plotinus, has life; world matter is a corpse. *Enneads*, 2.4 [2, 3, 5, 11, 14].

From the ultimate perspective, evil contributes to order and beauty, and it is therefore good.[72]

Plotinus uses a third picture to explain the evil of the soul. As the soul descends through emanation, it picks up parts that weigh it down. These need to be cast off if the soul is to ascend again to the One. The soul itself, in other words, does not need inner purification. It needs to shake off these clinging parts.[73] In this analysis, the human soul, including the three component parts of mind, the composite, and even the body, can be considered good. The soul is splattered with mud that does not penetrate. In the ethical ascent, the soul must be washed of this external contamination.[74]

These three themes enable Plotinus to develop his view of the fundamental role of ethics. In none of them is evil caused by personal rebellion or what theists call sin. Evil is not a metaphysically positive reality, but a negative one, a lack of being. Understanding evil as a lack of being preserves the fundamental goodness of reality. Evil is not internal, but essentially external to the soul. Since evil is not a powerful, positive force, as the dualists believe, the soul through virtue has the power to gain salvation. Through moral perseverance, the soul rises to salvation. The soul has the power to achieve the delight of oneness with the One. It can ascend to be alone with the Alone.

Conclusion

The Plotinian understanding of God and the world was very influential in the medieval period. Plotinus influenced the Western church to accept many of his themes. Negative language about God and the doctrines of the ascent to God, and of evil as a lack or privation, are examples of language and ideas reflecting Plotinian philosophy. Although the New Age movement today does not derive directly from Plotinian thought, it is a close relative that displays many of the character traits of its ancient cousin.

These traits suggest that the thinking of pantheists follows a logical sequence that is shaped not only by cultural and religious traditions but also by the inner logic of the thrust for union with God inherent in pantheism. The commitment to pantheism, in other words, generates a typical pattern of thought, a common web of beliefs. Thinkers who spring from the soils of medieval India, modern Japan, and the ancient Mediterranean share many of the elements of this recurring pattern of thought. Pantheism is not an exclusively Eastern phenomenon.

72. Ibid., 1.8 [8–15]; 3.2 [3, 5]; 3.3 [7].
73. Ibid., 1.1 [12].
74. Ibid., 5.5 [12].

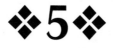

Spinoza
Modal Pantheism

God or Nature.—Spinoza

Albert Einstein is famous for his statement that "God does not play dice" with the universe. However, when asked by a rabbi about God, Einstein replied: "I believe in Spinoza's God, who reveals himself in the orderly harmony of all that exists." For Einstein, God as "a spirit is manifest in the laws of the Universe—a spirit vastly superior to that of a man."[1] In brief, the God of Einstein, following that of Benedict de Spinoza (1634–1677), is pantheistic.

Spinoza's form of pantheism is rather different from those surveyed thus far; it is a form of modal pantheism. Spinoza teaches that each individual thing is a mode or modification of God. God (or Nature, which is the same thing) exists in modes, in different forms of being, or in different points of view. You could say that a woman exists as a modification of God, as a wave is a modification of the sea. A woman could look like a separate individual and "might even be named Esther," quips Wallace Matson, but she is still a modification of God.[2]

1. "The Year of Dr. Einstein," *Time* (February 19, 1979), pp. 75–76.
2. Wallace Matson, *A History of Philosophy* (New York: Van Nostrand Reinhold, 1968), p. 316.

Historical Background

In 1492, Columbus sailed the ocean blue. He was sent on his way by Ferdinand and Isabella of Spain. In that year, the Catholic monarchs also sent packing all Jews in their realm who refused to embrace Christianity. Many Jews left Spain at great financial loss and personal risk, among them the forebears of a rabbinical student and lens grinder, Baruch Spinoza. Spinoza, who as an adult changed his name to the Latin Benedict ("Blessed"), was a rationalistic philosopher known for his creation of modal pantheism.

The history of philosophy boasts few heroes, perhaps because philosophers do not tend toward hero worship. But there are several exceptions. One is Socrates, whose convictions led him to submit to the death penalty when he easily could have escaped with the help of influential friends. Another is Spinoza, whom Bertrand Russell calls "the noblest and most lovable of the great philosophers."[3] The source of this admiration for the Jewish pantheist derives from his single-minded pursuit of freedom of opinion at great personal cost.

As a young man, Spinoza began to question the pontifications of the rabbis. His doubts so distressed members of the Jewish community that they offered him a considerable yearly stipend to keep his questions to himself. He declined the offer. Later, in 1656, after someone attempted to murder him, the Jews finally excommunicated him from their community and left him to his own resources:

> With the judgment of the angels and the sentence of the saints, we anathematize, execrate, curse and cast out Baruch Spinoza . . . in the presence of the sacred books with the six hundred and thirteen precepts written therein, pronouncing against him the malediction wherewith Elisha cursed the children, and all the maledictions written in the Book of the Law.[4]

When the curses did not faze him, Spinoza began to support himself by the manual trade he had learned, lens grinding. He often lived with families, grinding just enough lenses in his chambers to meet his expenses and spending the rest of his time reading and writing philosophy. His fame spread, and he received numerous and notable guests, including some wealthy businessmen who insisted on conferring on him a regular stipend. Heidelberg University offered him a post as professor of philosophy, but he declined, for he feared losing his freedom to think independently: "I do not know within what lim-

---

3. Bertrand Russell, *A History of Western Philosophy* (New York: Simon and Schuster, 1945), p. 569.
4. Willis, *Benedict de Spinoza* (London: 1870), pp. 35–36.

its that freedom of philosophizing ought to be confined in order to avoid the appearance of wishing to disturb the publicly established Religion."[5]

Herein lies Spinoza's claim to the status of hero. He preferred his simple life of grinding lenses with its complete freedom of thought to a life of duplicity in either the synagogue or the university. Spinoza spelled out his disturbing views on God most fully in a book entitled *Ethics*, and it is on this work that his lasting reputation chiefly stands. He finished *Ethics* in 1665, but waited until 1675 before trying to have it published. Opposition predictably developed, although it came principally from Reformed ministers and Cartesian philosophers, not Jewish rabbis. So Spinoza decided against publication. *Ethics* finally appeared after Spinoza died of tuberculosis.

Spinoza's rationalism stands in the tradition of the Frenchman René Descartes (1596–1650), although it is also in some ways a reaction to Cartesian philosophy. Descartes is known as the father of modern philosophy for his pivotal role in shaping several centuries of philosophy. In contrast to the medieval period, when philosophers focused primarily on the nature of being, the modern period followed Descartes in shifting attention to the question of knowing. His interest lay in finding an epistemology that would lead to an absolutely certain apprehension of truth. Beginning with certain clear and distinct ideas as axioms, Descartes deductively inferred what he thought were indubitable conclusions.

Spinoza depends on Descartes for his method, for some terminology, and for defining some important questions. But his answers to those questions differ from Descartes's in important ways. The most foundational of these differences is, of course, Spinoza's modal pantheistic metaphysic. This world view may have been inspired by the strong emphasis on divine oneness in certain Jewish sources, including Maimonides, but it surely did not come from Descartes. Descartes emphasized dualism, not monism, and he was a theist, not a pantheist. God and the world are distinct; mind and body are separate in the human person. But Spinoza accepted neither of these basic metaphysical premises.[6]

God as Nature

Spinoza's modal pantheism is built on his concept of absolute substance. 'Substance' is a common philosophical notion used since the time of the ancient Greeks. For Spinoza *substance* means "that

5. Benedict de Spinoza, letter 48, in *The Correspondence of Spinoza*, trans. and ed. A. Wolf (New York: Russell and Russell, 1966), p. 267.

6. Frederick Copleston, *A History of Philosophy*, vol. 4: *Modern Philosophy: Descartes to Leibnitz* (Garden City, N.Y.: Doubleday, Image Books, 1963), pp. 213–15.

which is in itself and is conceived through itself . . . which does not need the conception of another thing from which it must be formed."[7] Spinoza believes that substance is self-caused or self-existing. 'Self-existence' is an attribute of a thing that is explained simply by itself; we have no need to look for something else in order to explain its existence. Substance cannot be caused by or acted upon by anything else. Because it is completely independent, it depends entirely and only on itself. Though everything else depends on substance, substance depends on nothing.[8]

This concept of self-existence implies infinity. Spinoza interprets Aristotle's notion of substance literally and rigorously to mean that no substance could ever be acted upon. Only a reality that can be acted upon would be finite and limited. It follows with logical necessity, given these two premises, that no substance would be finite and limited. Thus substance must be infinite.[9]

The infinity of substance as Spinoza defines it leads to his pantheism. Substance is identified with God or, what is the same thing, with Nature. "God or Nature" is his way of expressing this identity.[10] Suppose, for example, that there were two infinite, all-powerful Gods. If they both had substance and being, they would both possess the ability to affect all other beings. At the same time, they would both be completely free of others' power. The supposition assumes, therefore, two beings who both can act upon each other and are immune to being affected by each other. This is clearly absurd. There can be only one God; a substance other than God is impossible and inconceivable.[11] Spinoza believed that his Jewish ancestors realized this basic oneness of God, although only "as if through a cloud."[12]

Because substance is infinite, it is indivisible. If substance were divided, that is, if God were distinct from Nature, it would not be infinite. This is impossible, for substance is indivisible.[13] Whatever exists in nature, therefore, also exists as part of God.[14] Spinoza does not deny that individual things or people exist or that everyday events occur. He denies only that they occur independently of God. God or Nature is the indwelling cause of all.[15] As the experience of

7. Benedict de Spinoza, *Ethics*, ed. James Gutmann, based on the White–Stirling edition, The Hafner Library of Classics (New York: Hafner, 1963), pt. 1, def. 3.
8. Ibid., pt. 1, defs. 1, 3.
9. Ibid., pt. 1, prop. 8.
10. Gordon H. Clark, *Thales to Dewey* (Grand Rapids: Baker, 1957), p. 334.
11. Spinoza, *Ethics*, pt. 1, prop. 14; cf. pt. 1, prop. 10, scholium; pt. 2, prop. 4.
12. Ibid., pt. 2, prop. 7, scholium.
13. Ibid., pt. 1, prop. 13, cor.
14. Ibid., pt. 1, prop. 15.
15. Ibid., pt. 1, prop. 16, cor. 1; prop. 18.

color depends on the presence of light, so the existence of everything depends on God.

Another important technical concept in Spinoza's system is 'attribute.' An attribute is whatever the mind perceives as constituting the essential character of substance. God, being infinite, says Spinoza, necessarily possesses an infinite number of attributes that describe his character necessarily.[16] These attributes are contained in the very idea of God. For example, the sum of the angles of any triangle necessarily equals 180°. The mind conceives this fact to be entailed in the very concept of triangles. In the same way, God's attributes flow from the nature of his being with the same necessity as does the sum of those angles.[17]

But this is not to say that our minds can grasp the infinity of God or Nature. There are many attributes, but we can perceive only two, namely, thought and extension. From what we know of God, in other words, he is a thinking thing and an extended thing. Saying that God thinks does not surprise any orthodox believer, but saying that he is extended does. The attribute of extension implies that God fills space as a material being. In other words, God has a body![18]

In contrast to Spinoza, Descartes believed thought and extension are found in different substances; they are not just different attributes of one substance. Descartes believed that mind is thinking, non-extended substance while body is extended, non-thinking substance. Obviously, Spinoza borrows his categories and concepts from Descartes. But since he posits that substance is necessarily infinite and united, Spinoza must ascribe thought and extension to the same substance rather than to different substances.[19] In this way, Spinoza uses the categories from Descartes's dualism and theism to build his own monism and pantheism.

Given Spinoza's premise that only one substance exists, he naturally infers that individual humans cannot be different substances. He does not deny that we exist,[20] but assigns us to a lower status, what he calls modes. He defines 'modes' as finite "modifications" of substance, that is, substance conceived or thought about from a finite point of view.[21] Thus, a human being consists in the modification of God.[22] Our bodies are God conceived through the attribute of extension; our minds are God conceived through the attribute of thought. Both our bodies and minds, in other words, are God in different

16. Ibid., pt. 1, def. 6.
17. Ibid., pt. 1, prop. 17, scholium.
18. Ibid., pt. 1, prop. 14, cor. 2; pt. 2, prop. 2.
19. Matson, *History*, p. 316.
20. Spinoza, *Ethics*, pt. 2, prop. 10, scholium.
21. Ibid., pt. 1, def. 5.
22. Ibid., pt. 2, prop. 10, cor.; cf. pt. 1, prop. 25, cor.

forms. In fact, "seeing . . . that our mind subjectively contains in itself and partakes of the nature of God, . . . we may rightly assert the nature of the human mind . . . to be a primary cause of Divine revelation."[23]

An important theme in Spinoza's modal pantheism is his emphasis on the correlation of ideas and things. *"The order and connection of ideas is the same as the order and connection of things,"* he writes.[24] To be sure, substance is divided into thinking attributes and modes, on the one hand, and extended attributes and modes, on the other. But the difference between these is really one of perspective; mind and body are really one thing considered from two different points of view.[25] Here we find Spinoza's solution to Descartes's perplexing mind/body problem: What is the relationship between thinking/non-extended things (minds) and extended/non-thinking things (bodies)? Because his dualism posited such a sharp division between mind and body, Descartes could not easily show how they are related. Spinoza's answer? There is no problem. Mind and body are one thing viewed from different perspectives. This is called the "double-aspect" theory.

In Spinoza's system, on the metaphysical scale between the infinite attributes and the finite modes lie mediate, infinite modes. These form a halfway house between absolute substance and the individual objects of the material universe. The mediate, infinite mode of extension is the totality of physical reality, the material universe as a unity. Spinoza calls it "the face of the whole Universe." The mediate, infinite mode of thought is "absolutely infinite understanding."[26] Spinoza built in this way a complete hierarchy of realities. Each level of reality exists in and expresses the level above it. Only absolute substance exists, and all the levels of reality flow from it: two infinite attributes (thought and extension), the mediate, infinite modes, and all the finite modes like Esther, James, and the coffee table.

The finite modes cannot be distinguished as different substances or different existing beings, since only one substance exists. Instead, factors like motion and rest differentiate the modes. All bodies are determined to be either at rest or in motion by other bodies that are in turn determined by other bodies and so on and so on and so on. The "whole face of the universe," that is, Nature, is a system of particles and bodies all of which are caused to be exactly what they are by the huge interlocking network of particles in motion.[27] This implies a closed system of causes with no agency from beyond. The only causal

---

23. Spinoza, *Tractatus theologico-politicus* in *The Chief Works of Benedict de Spinoza*, trans. R. H. M. Elwes (London: George Bell, 1883), vol. 1, p. 14.
24. Spinoza, *Ethics*, pt. 2, prop. 7.
25. Ibid., pt. 2, prop. 21, scholium.
26. Spinoza, letter 64, *Correspondence*, p. 308.
27. Ibid., pt. 2, prop. 13, lemmas 1, 3.

explanation lies within the system of moving particles, which just happens to be all there is.

This idea has led some to think of Spinoza as a precursor of the modern, scientific world view. Modern physicists conceive of reality most basically as energy. Albert Einstein, who claimed to believe in the God of Spinoza, taught us that energy is equivalent to matter. The material universe is patterns of energy acting according to regular laws. In Spinoza's thinking, you could say, God is the Energy that acts upon matter; matter is what the Energy acts upon. Yet in a sense $E=mc^2$—the Energy and the matter are one.[28]

Whatever may be said of this analogy, one parallel between Spinoza and Einstein's scientific world view is explicit: what happens in Nature happens by necessity. Though some of Einstein's adversaries among physicists, for example, opt for genuine randomness at the subatomic level, Spinoza's system implies a complete mechanism. No finite mode has freedom; each is determined to be what it is by the laws of Nature. Spinoza defines 'law' as "that by which an individual, or all things, . . . act in one and the same fixed and definite manner, which manner depends either on natural necessity or human decree."[29] From the ultimate perspective, natural necessity rules all. God exists necessarily, not by free decision, and he acts as he exists. Therefore, "in Nature there is nothing contingent, but all things are determined from the necessity of the divine nature to exist and act in a certain manner."[30]

We could illustrate by thinking of a card game. The hand you will be dealt at the beginning of the game, assuming the dealer is honest, is predetermined by the order of the cards in the stack. Once the deck is cut, nothing could change the hand you will get for it is "in the cards." In just this way, the events of history are in the cards.

Among Spinoza's friends were two businessmen, the DeWitt brothers. In 1672, a mob loyal to the House of Orange lynched these friends at the Hague where Spinoza was living. Uncharacteristically, the philosopher wanted to rush out to denounce the crowd publicly for its criminal behavior. But friends locked Spinoza in his room, probably saving his life. According to his philosophy, however, Spinoza's understandable emotional reaction was inappropriate. Everything happens as it does because it is determined to happen. Nothing could have changed the DeWitts' lynching. Regrettably, it was already in the cards.

Spinoza does try to affirm the freedom of God in a sense. This sounds contradictory, for his system requires that "God's will cannot

28. Matson, *History*, p. 318; Copleston, *History*, vol. 4, p. 224.
29. Spinoza, *Tractatus*, p. 57.
30. Spinoza, *Ethics*, pt. 1, prop. 29.

be other than it is. . . . Things therefore cannot be differently consti-
tuted."[31] But Spinoza calls a thing "free" if it "exists from the necessity of its own nature alone and is determined to action by itself
alone."[32] By this definition, God is free. But, of course, this really
means only that God is self-sufficient, independent, unaffected by
others. It does not mean that God is a personal, loving God who could
choose one alternative instead of another. For this reason, Harry
Austryn Wolfson calls Spinoza's God "an eternal paralytic."[33] In
Spinoza's view, the world is a network of natural causes and events for
which no transcendent God is necessary. Such is the shape both of certain modern scientific viewpoints and of Spinoza's modal pantheism.

A Geometric Method for Knowledge

Spinoza follows Descartes in seeking knowledge through the use of
the geometric method. Thus, in *Ethics* he uses words like *axiom* and
corollary to express his philosophy, including his ideas on human
emotions. He tells us in part 3 that for some

> it will doubtless seem a marvelous thing for me to endeavor to treat by
> a geometrical method the vices and follies of men. . . . [But Nature's]
> laws and rules . . . are everywhere and always the same, so that there
> must also be one and the same method of understanding the nature of
> all things whatsoever. . . . I shall therefore . . . consider human
> actions and appetites just as if I were considering lines, planes, or bod-
> ies.[34]

There is some debate as to the exact significance of the geometric
method. Spinoza himself apparently thought that it produced certain
knowledge. He wrote to a friend, "I do not presume that I have found
the best Philosophy, but I know that I think the true one. If you ask
me how I know this, I shall answer, in the same way that you know
that the three angles of a triangle are equal to two right angles."[35]
Today, however, most philosophers agree his writings do not have
quite the logical rigor that geometry itself achieves. "Spinoza's
rhetoric is magnificent," writes Matson, "but it is not geometry."[36]

Spinoza believed that the geometric method could lift us above
lower, more inadequate forms of knowledge to higher forms. He

31. Ibid., pt. 1, prop. 33, scholium 2.
32. Ibid., pt. 1, def. 7.
33. Harry Austryn Wolfson, *The Philosophy of Spinoza: Unfolding the Latent
Processes of His Reasoning* (Cambridge: Harvard University Press, 1934, 1983).
34. Spinoza, *Ethics*, pt. 3, preface.
35. Spinoza, letter 76, *Correspondence*, p. 352.
36. Matson, *History*, p. 324; cf. Russell, *History*, p. 580.

delineates in *Ethics* three levels of knowledge: opinion or imagination, reason, and intuitive science.[37]

Knowledge of the first level includes ideas derived from the senses. These ideas may be true as far as they go, but in fact they give only "confused" and "inadequate" knowledge. We may come to know other bodies in that they affect ours. But if we think in purely physical terms, we will be thinking inadequately. Confusion and inadequacy derive from the fact that sense knowledge is external and comes to us by "chance coincidence."[38]

Our general or universal concepts often come from imagination. We conceptualize 'humanity' in our minds by abstracting the element of 'humanness' from the individual human persons we perceive. We then conceive the concept by mentally joining this element of 'humanness' into a composite idea. But this process begins with sense perception and thus belongs to the lowest level of knowledge. This is not to say that there are no adequate general ideas. But concepts like 'being' and 'thing' partake in the confusion of imagination. "It is in this way that those notions have arisen which are called *universal,* such as, *man, horse, dog,* etc." Confusion reigns because none of us is capable of perceiving all humans. So each of us conceives of humanity in terms of whatever particularly impresses him. Thus, we end up with various definitions of humanity: "an animal of erect stature, . . . an animal capable of laughter, a biped without feathers, a rational animal, and so on—each person forming universal images of things according to the temperament of his own body."[39]

Clearly, Spinoza thinks of imagination as the lowest form of knowledge, but we must not infer that this means it is entirely false, even if it is vague and confused. He does tell us that we know everyday matters via imagination. That we shall die, that oil burns, that water does not, that dogs bark—in fact, nearly all our knowledge of everyday things comes through imagination.[40] This knowledge, as far as it goes, is not false in isolation. Indeed a positive idea, even though rooted in imagination, cannot be false.[41]

Yet whenever error arises it can be traced to knowledge from imagination, because only imagination is confused and inadequate.[42] The inadequacy arises from the lack of complete knowledge. There is no positive ignorance. A positive idea that is partly true is true as far as it goes. Its falsity lies in that it leaves out other important aspects

---

37. Spinoza, *Ethics,* pt. 2, prop. 40, scholium 2.
38. Ibid., pt. 2, prop. 26, cor.; pt. 2, prop. 29, scholium.
39. Ibid., pt. 2. prop. 40, scholium 1.
40. Benedict de Spinoza, *On the Improvement of the Understanding,* ed. James Gutmann, The Hafner Library of Classics (New York: Hafner, 1963), p. 8.
41. Spinoza, *Ethics,* pt. 2, prop. 33.
42. Ibid., pt. 2, prop. 41.

of the larger truth. In this sense, Spinoza can say that an idea is true but inadequate. "Falsehood, therefore, consists in the privation of knowledge which is involved by inadequate knowledge of things or by inadequate and confused ideas."[43]

Spinoza obviously has a place for errors in thinking. Imagining another body (which is the same as sensing it), for example, can never yield adequate knowledge. When it comes to explaining Nature via the senses, there are as many imaginations as there are heads. Each person has his unique views, and none of these is any more objectively certain than matters of personal taste.[44]

Spinoza argues that the source of errors must be external to the mind. He castigated Francis Bacon, for example, for teaching that both the senses and the mind could cause error.[45] The senses may cause error, but the mind never does. For example, suppose someone adds a column of figures and comes to an incorrect answer. What could cause such an error? Spinoza argues that the problem lies in our mathematician's senses. The numbers in the mind are added correctly, of course, since the mind does not err. ("As far as the mind is concerned there is no error.") The only explanation is perceptual error: the numbers on the page could not be the same as the numbers in the mind. People assume the mind errs only because they do not have direct access to the numbers in the mathematician's mind, and they assume them to be the same as those on the page.[46]

Another example clarifies Spinoza's views on the senses and the mind. He mentions that the sun appears to the senses to be only 200 feet away. Now we know, he says, that the sun is at a distance from us of 600 times the diameter of the earth. So the belief based on the senses is in error, and we can know that it is in error.[47] (There are several problems here. One is that 600 earth diameters would equal about five million miles. This figure is about eighty-eight million miles short. Were we five million miles from the sun, we would be burned to a crisp. More important, however, how could we discover, except by another imagination, that the sun is 600 diameters of the earth away?)

Spinoza, however, infers that our imagination would not be completely false, since the positive part of a larger error is still true. When we come to a correct awareness of the distance, our bodies still tell us that the sun *appears* to be 200 feet away. It is still true that this is the way it looks, even though we may know this is not the way it is.[48] So

43. Ibid., pt. 2, prop. 35.
44. Ibid., pt. 2, prop. 26, cor.; pt. 1, appendix.
45. Spinoza, letter 2, *Correspondence*, pp. 76–77.
46. Spinoza, *Ethics*, pt. 2, prop. 47, scholium.
47. Ibid., pt. 2, prop. 35, scholium; pt. 4, prop. 1, scholium.
48. Ibid., pt. 2, prop. 35, scholium.

long as we consider this idea as a statement of what the body experiences, we are not in error. The problem would come in passing to the objective statement that Nature exists as we sense that it does. Significantly, even when we know the true distance of ninety-three million miles, this does not change the fact that the sun *looks* to be 200 feet away.

In contrast to imagination, the lowest level of knowledge, stand the second and third levels. The second, reason, is necessarily true because it is adequate. To qualify as adequate, an idea must display the intrinsic marks or inherent properties of a true idea.[49] The second level of knowledge takes us beyond concrete, individual objects to a system of abstract statements that reveal the essential properties that all objects in a class share. Spinoza tells us that these common elements cannot be conceived except adequately.[50]

To conceive these common qualities as adequate ideas and clear propositions in a logically related system is to reach the second level of knowledge. This should not be confused with the universal or abstract concepts that are produced at level one by inference from the senses. These are influenced by personal prejudices and impressions. Therefore the universal concept that I might have would differ from yours. Confusion results.[51] At level two, we are talking about the common elements that we all agree are known to be part of the very essence of some thing. These truly common features are known rationally, that is, adequately, clearly, and distinctly.[52]

In moving from the first to the second level of knowledge we go from doubt and uncertainty to certainty. Spinoza believed that following the proper method would lead to this assurance. Doubts come from careless disregard for proper method. Good method will produce good results. "If a man proceeded with our investigations in due order . . . , he will [sic] never have any ideas save such as are very certain, or, in other words, clear and distinct."[53] He has little use for skeptics who must be either arguing from "bad faith" or suffering from "complete mental blindness." He writes with some sarcasm that skeptics are "afraid of confessing that they exist, so long as they know nothing; in fact, they ought to remain dumb, for fear of haply supposing something which should smack of truth."[54]

The intellectual awareness that God exists cannot be attained through the first level, but depends on the higher forms of thought. Spinoza tells us repeatedly that proper method is imperative in the

49. Ibid., pt. 2, def. 4.
50. Ibid., pt. 2, prop. 38.
51. Ibid., pt. 2, prop. 40, scholium 1.
52. Ibid., pt. 2, prop. 38, cor.
53. Spinoza, *Improvement*, p. 28.
54. Ibid., pp. 15, 16.

search for truth.[55] The proper order does not take us from our senses to God, but rather from God first to our senses second.[56] This implies that Spinoza will use an ontological argument for God. The ontological argument, associated first with Saint Anselm of Canterbury (1033–1109), is built not on the senses but on the very idea of an absolutely perfect being. Spinoza's premise lies in the first statement in *Ethics:* "by cause of itself I understand that whose essence involves existence, or that whose nature cannot be conceived unless existing."[57] Since God fits this definition and is self-caused, it follows that his nonexistence is inconceivable. As soon as we think of a being like God, we are rationally forced to think of him as existing. Spinoza writes in a note, "since [God's] essence shuts out all imperfection and involves absolute perfection, for this very reason all cause of doubt concerning his existence is taken away, and the highest certainty concerning it is given—a truth which I trust will be evident to anyone who bestows only moderate attention."[58]

As his aside shows, Spinoza is sure both that adequate ideas are true and that we can know them to be true. Those who know, he is saying, know they know.[59] But what is the standard of knowledge? In Spinoza's words, "Who can know that he is certain of anything unless he is first of all certain of that thing?"[60] Spinoza answers that truth serves as its own criterion; it contains its own intrinsic standard. Light reveals both light and darkness; truth illuminates both truth and falsity. A true idea agrees with its object, the thing of which it is an idea. If we have an adequate idea, its very adequacy assures us that we know it adequately. From self-evident axioms we can deduce a system of propositions that cannot be doubted. In Spinoza's opinion, here lies the benefit of his geometric method.[61]

Spinoza uses another way of expressing the relation of true and false ideas. True ideas, he says, have more being. They have "more reality" and are "more excellent." Truth relates to falsity as being to nonbeing.[62] If we remember that all positive ideas are true and that falsity is a gap in or lack of positive truth, this analogy may make sense. But if it does not, Spinoza pulls rank: do not forget, he reminds us, that our minds are part of God's infinite mind. So our clear and distinct ideas are no less true than God's. Of course, this power play may still leave me stranded, for my mind is part of God's only "in so

---

55. Ibid., p. 13.
56. Spinoza, *Ethics*, pt. 2, prop. 10, cor., scholium.
57. Ibid., pt. 1, def. 1.
58. Ibid., pt. 1, prop. 11, scholium.
59. Ibid., pt. 2, props. 34, 43.
60. Ibid., pt. 2, prop. 43, scholium.
61. Spinoza, *Improvement*, p. 23.
62. Spinoza, *Ethics*, pt. 2, prop. 43, scholium.

far as it truly perceives things."[63] In order to know if my mind is part of God's, I have to know if it is perceiving things truly. In order to know if I am perceiving things truly, I have to know if my mind is part of God's. A classic Catch-22. Nevertheless, Spinoza gives assurances quite similar to those of the mystical pantheists—if you really know, then you know you know.

The second level of knowledge leads to the third, intuition, and is its necessary prelude. The third level does not move qualitatively above the second as the second does above the first. It leads to a perfect knowledge of God. In fact, Spinoza claims that he has as clear an idea of God as he does of a triangle![64] Even though intuition is "more potent" than reason, it is organically related to reason and builds upon it. Intuitive science may be the highest level of thought to which we should aspire, but it depends on reason, without which it cannot be attained.[65]

The exact relationship between these two levels is open to discussion. In one interpretation, Spinoza is telling us that reason gives a logical deduction of the essential elements and structure of reality. This is the prelude for seeing God or Nature as a total system, for grasping a synoptic vision of reality as a whole. Parts are now seen in their necessary relation to the Whole instead of as isolated bits. Coherent knowledge of the individual parts in this Whole is, of course, knowledge of God.[66] This level of knowing, since it is the highest possible, has religious overtones. This leads us to consider Spinoza's beliefs about the religious dimensions of a rational person's knowledge.

The Religious Dimension of Knowledge

Knowledge at the third level possesses religious importance. Spinoza calls this intuition "the intellectual love of God." It gives the philosopher peace of mind and a sense of delight and joy.[67] This love partakes of divine attributes, for it is eternal and infinite. In fact, since we are modes of God, our love for him is actually part of the infinite, intellectual love that God has for himself.[68]

This "intellectual love of God" has important practical implications. Understanding Nature better means understanding God better, for Nature expresses God. When we come to see that law operates in Nature so that all events are determined to happen as they do, we

63. Ibid., pt. 2, prop. 43, scholium.
64. Ibid., pt. 2, prop. 36.
65. Ibid., pt. 5, prop. 36, scholium; props. 25, 28.
66. Copleston, *History*, vol. 4, p. 242; Spinoza, *Ethics*, pt. 5, prop. 24.
67. Spinoza, *Ethics*, pt. 5, prop. 27; prop. 32, cor.
68. Ibid., pt. 5, prop. 36, cor.

increase our knowledge of God.[69] Recognizing determinism, or, to say it anthropomorphically, realizing that everything happens according to "God's will," we may experience blessedness through resignation. We learn to accept fortune, good or bad, since life's joys and sorrows are inevitable. We come to see that virtue is its own reward, and we are satisfied just to be good without hope of reward. Since each one is what he is by God's decree, we appreciate the importance of despising no one and helping everyone.[70]

This life of which Spinoza speaks is the highest virtue. The knowledge of God that leads to blessedness is the highest human good. The potential for this knowledge of God is built right into the very structure of the human mind.[71] Spinoza even uses the language of obligation, or 'oughtness,' to speak of this knowledge: "This love of God above everything else ought to occupy the mind."[72] Of course, moral exhortation of this kind is difficult to square with a belief in necessity. Exhortation implies we ought to alter our choices about the future; determinism says these choices cannot be altered. For this reason, Russell thinks Spinoza means only to describe our behavior, not to tell us how to change it.[73] We shall see in light of further evidence whether this interpretation is adequate. In any case, the basic point of Spinoza's doctrine is clear: it is in the life of reasoned resignation to God's will that humans find blessedness.

Although blessedness is possible through reason and intuitive science, we should not infer that God created us for this purpose. Spinoza attacks the notion of purpose, Aristotle's final causality, in a celebrated section of *Ethics*.[74] Consider a rock that rolls off a roof and kills a man. Unenlightened people immediately infer that the rock fell in order to kill him. If someone notes that the wind blew the rock off the roof, the popular mind will still jump to its conclusion: the wind blowing just enough to push the rock off the roof just as the man passed by indicates an ultimate purpose. The speculating never ends, complains Spinoza, for people "will not cease from asking the causes of causes until at last you fly to the will of God—the refuge for ignorance."[75]

Although Spinoza sometimes explains his own work by talking about his purpose in writing, his philosophy leaves no room for genuinely purposive action. He explains that the illusion of purpose arises from our normal inclination to seek fulfillment of our desires.

69. Spinoza, *Tractatus*, pp. 59, 86–87.
70. Spinoza, *Ethics*, pt. 2, prop. 49, scholium.
71. Ibid., pt. 4, prop. 28; prop. 36, scholium.
72. Ibid., pt. 5, prop. 16.
73. Russell, *History*, p. 576.
74. Spinoza, *Ethics*, pt. 1, appendix.
75. Ibid.

We come to believe (incorrectly) that our own actions are purposeful, directed toward the end of self-satisfaction. We then observe useful things in Nature (eyes, for example, are useful for seeing) and conclude that Nature was created by someone for our use. Thus, we invent gods and create ways to worship and placate our own inventions. Thinking that our God must have created Nature for our good, we come to believe that Nature does nothing in vain, that every event has a purpose.

But this approach only mires us in absurdity. The harmful things in Nature are inexplicable. Given the prevalence of natural disasters, if God created Nature for our good, he did a rather poor job. This line of thinking, Spinoza affirms, leads us to think "that Nature, the gods, and man are alike mad."[76]

Too long everything has been attributed to the capricious will of a mysterious God. This view has bound us in darkness. We have tried to believe that good rewards the virtuous and evil punishes the sinful. But experience tells us that the righteous sometimes suffer and the wicked sometimes prosper. Because experience belies our sense of justice, some appeal to the mystery in God's will. Only God knows, say some, why good people do not seem to get their true rewards.

Spinoza has only contempt for those who hold this view. Such people are "triflers who, when they cannot explain a thing, run back to the will of God; this is, truly, a ridiculous way of expressing ignorance." The solution to the insanity is, of course, a true knowledge based on the geometric method. Spinoza advises that we abandon belief in a God whose inexplicable and mysterious will is used to solve explanatory problems. We should recognize instead that mathematics holds the key to Nature. Geometry does not deal with final causes and purposes. It emphasizes instead the eternal "essences and properties" of reality. Only knowledge of this kind leads to real blessedness.[77]

Abandoning the purposeful will of God in favor of the deterministic law of Nature means eliminating miracles. Miracles are supernatural events brought about by the will of God to achieve some special purpose. But Spinoza rejects miracles not only because they are purposeful but for other reasons as well. His belief in the completeness of the law-like system of Nature means that every event has a scientific explanation. Because they go contrary to Nature, miracles are ruled out. Actually, any event claimed as a miracle can be explained in principle by scientific understanding. But even if the explanation is not forthcoming, we should not immediately jump to the fantastic conclusion that we have just experienced a miracle. In fact, since by

76. Ibid., pt. 1, appendix.
77. Spinoza, *Tractatus*, p. 86.

natural law we actually mean God's decree, to think that God by his decree could contradict natural law is to suggest that God could act against his own decree, and this is "an evident absurdity."[78]

The Bible itself teaches that nature cannot be contradicted because of the immutable nature of its laws. Spinoza quotes Ecclesiastes 3:14, among other texts, to show that nature is fixed: "I know that whatsoever God doeth, it shall be for ever; nothing can be put to it, nor anything taken from it."[79] Silly, naive people do not understand that even the Bible contradicts their religion: "Anything which excites their astonishment they believe to be a portent signifying the anger of the gods or of the Supreme Being, and, mistaking superstition for religion, account it impious not to avert the evil with prayer and sacrifice. Signs and wonders of this sort they conjure up perpetually, till one might think Nature as mad as themselves, they interpret her so fantastically."[80]

Spinoza's argument leaves one wondering why the Bible is reliable when speaking of the orderliness of Nature but suddenly unreliable when speaking of miracles. He seems to judge it unreliable whenever it contradicts his antisupernatural bias. Nevertheless, he plows ahead, suggesting that miracles call into question Nature's absolutely immutable character. Since we are led to knowledge of God by awareness of this immutability, doubts about Nature lead to doubt about God. Thus, miracles, were they real, would actually lead us to doubt and atheism![81]

The absolute knowledge of Nature gives us the sense of peace we need for living here and now. This is the essence of religion and 'salvation' in Spinoza's thinking. Blessedness consists of a "constant and eternal love toward God," but this love can also be called "repose of mind."[82] This love is called eternal, but this does not necessarily mean that we survive death as individuals. Actually, it is difficult to say exactly what Spinoza means by *eternal*. He does indicate that we know we are eternal.[83] But he seems to imply that life here has the quality of eternity. Following his definition of *eternity*,[84] we may say that calling me eternal would mean that my existence follows necessarily from God's nature. Religion, therefore, is important for this life even without individual immortality. Its primary significance is motivating piety and overcoming the fear of death. We accomplish these not by promises of immortality by and by, but by knowledge of

78. Ibid., pp. 83–85, 97.
79. Ibid., p. 96.
80. Ibid., pp. 3–4.
81. Ibid., pp. 85–87.
82. Spinoza, *Ethics*, pt. 5, prop. 36, scholium.
83. Ibid., pt. 5, prop. 23; prop. 23, scholium.
84. Ibid., pt. 1, def. 8.

the second and third levels. Pragmatically speaking, in this life alone we find the importance of religious experience.[85]

Here we may also find the significance of the Bible. Scripture teaches piety and obedience only. It is not concerned with philosophical truth. The Bible teaches only what is consistent with the results of philosophy. But revelation and reason are not handmaidens. They are distinct, operating on entirely different grounds to perform the same function.[86] Scripture motivates piety among the common masses as philosophy does among the wise. For this reason the Bible is accommodated to the masses. This leads to its use of rhetorical and symbolic language as well as to errors. Spinoza writes, "Scripture does not explain things by their secondary causes, but only narrates them in the order and the style which has most power to move men, and especially uneducated men, to devotion; and therefore it speaks inaccurately of God and of events, seeing that its object is not to convince the reason, but to attract and lay hold of the imagination."[87]

Spinoza has defined "love of God" in intellectual terms. He rejects the idea that God has a will in the usual sense of that word. Indeed, Spinoza actually equates "God's will" with the order of Nature. He eliminates any thought that God should be seeking some purpose in this world. He refuses to consider that God might act miraculously or that the Bible speaks literally when it records miraculous events. This all implies that our experience of God, our love for God, is an intellectual satisfaction, but not a love between persons. He defines "religion" as what we desire to do in light of our idea of God. This desire, if it is noble and good by the standards of reason, is "piety."[88] But nothing here suggests a communion with a personal God who calls me by name and counts the hairs of my head.

Although *Ethics* says much about loving God, we should not understand Spinoza's words to mean personal love. God is not affected by any emotion like joy or sorrow. We cannot hate God, and we should not expect God to love us in return for our love of him.[89] In a letter he clarifies his view: "Speaking philosophically we cannot say that God demands something from someone, or that something wearies or pleases Him, for all these are human attributes, which have no place in God."[90] Spinoza purges all anthropomorphic description from God, for God is Nature; he is not a person with whom I may experience a love relationship. Spinoza's God is blind, deaf, and dumb, and he is ultimately impersonal.

85. Ibid., pt. 5, props. 36, 41, 38, scholium.
86. Spinoza, *Tractatus*, pp. 9–10, 190.
87. Ibid., pp. 190, 90–95.
88. Spinoza, *Ethics*, pt. 4, prop. 37, scholium 1.
89. Ibid., pt. 5, props. 17. 18, 19.
90. Spinoza, letter 23, in *Correspondence*, p. 191.

The Role of Ethics

Spinoza entitled his most important work *Ethics.* Undoubtedly this is significant. He believed that his philosophy had its payoff in everyday life. No matter how speculative, philosophy must also be practical. His achievement in producing an ethic based on reason is admired by some as the most valuable contribution of his philosophy.[91]

Initially, Spinoza makes it clear that Nature has no evil. No evil can be ascribed to the law of Nature for "she is always the same and everywhere one." Everything, even negative emotions, follows from the laws of Nature with the same necessity. These negative emotions must be understood by delineating causal explanations just as any other event would be understood.[92] Of course, this may seem to imply that God is responsible for evil. Spinoza's response to this gets at the heart of his ethics: "in so far as we understand the causes of sorrow it ceases to be a passion . . . , that is to say . . . , it ceases to be sorrow; and, therefore, in so far as we understand God to be the cause of sorrow do we rejoice."[93]

Descartes and Leibniz thought this the best possible world because an all-good God would never freely choose anything but the best. Spinoza held to determinism. Thus, this is the best possible world because everything happens necessarily. It is the best possible world because it is the only possible world. Evil arises not because there is anything wrong with the world but because we make judgments about it based on our passions. Spinoza reminds us, "the perfection of things is to be judged by their nature and power alone; nor are they more or less perfect because they delight or offend the human senses, or because they are beneficial or prejudicial to human nature."[94] Nature herself is good; our passions give rise to evil.

This leads us to wonder whether there exists any intrinsic standard for good and evil. Spinoza answers unabashedly in the negative. Good and evil, he says, are judged extrinsically; they are not inherent qualities.[95] Good and evil are defined entirely in terms of their pragmatic consequences. *Good* refers to things that bring joy and satisfy desires. *Evil* refers to things that bring pain and thwart desires. What is useful is good; what is not is evil.[96]

In societal settings, of course, ordinances that guide everyday behavior would be necessary. Yet these are only pragmatic rules. In a

91. Russell, *History*, p. 570.
92. Spinoza, *Ethics*, pt. 3, preface.
93. Ibid., pt. 5, prop. 18, scholium.
94. Ibid., pt. 1, appendix.
95. Ibid., pt. 4, preface; prop. 37, scholium 2.
96. Ibid., pt. 3, prop. 39, scholiums; cf. pt. 4, defs. 1, 2.

society, a common agreement among persons determines the meaning of *good* and *evil*. But in Nature, without any social consensus, these designations have no inherent meaning.[97]

Ultimately, the standard of good that commands universal consent is based on self-interest. Every being naturally seeks self-preservation. This is part of the essence of anything.[98] Since Nature gives us the right to do what is necessarily implied in our natures, we have the right to act egoistically to promote self-preservation. Reason, in fact, dictates this form of egoism.[99] In society, self-interest operates corporately when we all join in a common pact of mutually beneficial egoism. In this way we see that "all should together seek the common good of all."[100]

Given his enlightened corporate egoism, Spinoza's response to Christian virtues is mixed. Since men do not live by reason, repentance and humility sometimes can produce more good than harm. If we sin against the laws of society, these emotions are necessary. But Spinoza really believes that humility and repentance indicate failure to follow the dictates of reason.[101] Yet at the same time he affirms the importance of forming communities to meet the obligation of caring for the poor and of recognizing that we ought to repay evil with good. If these sound like Christian admonitions, do not forget that Spinoza promotes them as the dictates of reasoned self-interest.[102]

The heart of Spinoza's ethic, however, lies in his naturalistic account of human emotions. He defines emotions, or passions, in physical terms: they are "modifications of the body by which the power of acting of the body itself is increased, diminished, helped, or hindered, together with the ideas of these modifications."[103] He begins with the premise of *conatus*, the passion for self-preservation. When we consciously reach a greater state of perfection or reach a greater power of existence, we experience pleasure; when we become conscious of a movement to a lower state, we experience pain. When we become conscious of *conatus*, pleasure, and pain, they may be called desire, joy, and sorrow.

Spinoza's account details forty-eight emotions, all of which are defined in terms of desire, joy, and sorrow, the basic passions. For example, love is joy in conjunction with some external cause while hatred is sorrow connected with an external cause. These external causes could be anything at all; no object relates necessarily to a cer-

97. Ibid., pt. 4, prop. 37, scholium 2.
98. Ibid., pt. 3, prop. 6, 7.
99. Ibid., pt. 4, prop. 37, scholium 2; prop. 18, scholium; prop. 24.
100. Ibid., pt. 4, prop. 18, scholium; cf. pt. 4, prop. 35, cor. 2.
101. Ibid., pt. 4, prop. 54, scholium; props. 53, 54.
102. Ibid., pt. 4, appendix 17; prop. 46.
103. Ibid., pt. 3, def. 3.

tain emotion. In fact, different persons have different reactions to the same objects. And one of Spinoza's favorite virtues, cheerfulness, is the emotion of joy when it is equally related to both mind and body. He similarly defines each of the other forty-eight emotions.[104]

Spinoza analyzes the human predicament in light of this understanding of emotions. Our basic problem is bondage, inability to control or govern our emotions. If we are in a state of bondage, we are out of touch with Nature. Spinoza understands the root cause of this imbalance in intellectual terms. The passions place us in bondage in direct proportion to the number of inadequate ideas in the mind. One of the most important of these is the belief that humans are free. The illusion of freedom comes because of our ignorance of the real causes of behavior. The point of ethics is to correct this intellectual inadequacy and in this way to live with a proper emotional disposition.[105]

We might suppose that this solution to ignorance and its moral consequences demands that humans be free. But Spinoza's analysis of human behavior eliminates freedom; all action occurs by the necessity of natural law. He states explicitly, "It follows that a man is necessarily always subject to passions, and that he follows and obeys the common order of Nature, accommodating himself to it as far as the nature of things requires."[106] "I do not place Freedom in free decision," he states firmly to one detractor, "but in free necessity."[107]

Given this view, we should expect Spinoza to defend himself on this question: If actions are determined, how can we account for moral praise and blame? Can a wicked man be blamed for his vice, or a good woman be commended for her virtue? If determinism reigns, it seems, wickedness should not be blamed. Now, if Spinoza did not mean to defend determinism, answering this question would surely give him opportunity to say so. But his responses continually presuppose the necessity of human action. At one place he answers that though evil actions are excusable, those who commit them are nevertheless rightly punished.

> A horse is excusable for being a horse and not a man. . . . He who goes mad from the bite of a dog is, indeed, to be excused, and yet is rightly suffocated, and, lastly, he who is unable to control his desires, and to restrain them through fear of the laws, although he must be excused for his weakness, is nevertheless unable to enjoy peace of mind, and the knowledge and love of God, but necessarily perishes.[108]

We doubt that this answers the question.

104. Ibid., pt. 3, prop. 11, scholium; prop. 13, scholium.
105. Ibid., pt. 4, preface; prop. 32; pt. 3, prop. 1, cor.; prop. 2, scholium.
106. Ibid., pt. 4, prop. 4, cor.; pt. 2, prop. 48.
107. Spinoza, letter 58, in Correspondence, p. 295.
108. Spinoza, letter 78, in Correspondence, p. 358.

In contrast, Spinoza also acknowledges that human behavior is supposed to be governed by human will. Consider this paradoxical passage: "The law that men must yield, or be compelled to yield, somewhat of their natural right, and that they bind themselves to live in a certain way, depends on human decree. Now, though I freely [sic] admit that all things are predetermined by universal natural laws to exist and operate in a given, fixed, and definite manner, I still assert that the laws I have just mentioned depend on human decree."[109] The answer to this apparent contradiction (Spinoza *freely* admits determinism) lies as usual in Spinoza's careful definitions. He does not mean by *freedom* what others mean. Human freedom is at work when "we are the adequate cause, that is to say . . . , when from our nature anything follows, either within us or without us, which by that nature alone can be clearly and distinctly understood." Will, he explains, is the equivalent of the mind. Will is a "faculty," an ability by which the mind acknowledges truth or falsity, not a "desire" by which it chooses one object and rejects another.[110] Freedom, therefore, may be ascribed to a person whose actions are adequately caused by his own mind as governed by reason.

Hope for freedom from the passions comes from knowledge. Knowing the causes of pain neutralizes the suffering. To understand emotions means to control the emotions. Emotions are limited in power while the mind is limited only by lack of knowledge. Thus, the mind of one who knows can dominate the emotions through its superior power.[111] Moral progress depends completely on intellectual advance. Salvation comes by proper knowledge, a claim that threatens to diminish the number of the virtuous to a tiny number of elite thinkers.

The motivation for right action is reason. Since every action determined through reason is good, the righteous person nurtures reason. Motivating right living through fear of evil is destructive. Rather, virtue ought to be encouraged by desire for good based on reason. Such desire is never excessive, but always moderate. Spinoza illustrated this by a parable. The sick man who eats nutritious food that he hates is not to be preferred to the healthy man who, for fear of death, enjoys what he eats and thus enjoys life more than if he feared death.[112] To sum up, Spinoza writes, "It is therefore most profitable to us in life to make perfect the intellect or reason as far as possible, and in this one thing consists the highest happiness or blessedness of man; for blessedness is nothing but the peace of mind which springs

109. Spinoza, *Tractatus*, p. 57.
110. Spinoza, *Ethics*, pt. 3, def. 2; pt. 2, prop. 49, cor.; prop. 48, scholium.
111. Ibid., pt. 5, prop. 18, scholium; props. 6, 3; prop. 20, scholium.
112. Ibid., pt. 4, appendix 3; prop. 61; prop. 62, scholium.

from the intuitive knowledge of God, and to perfect the intellect is nothing but to understand God."[113]

Many wonder whether Spinoza really can have it both ways. If it is really true that every event is determined, then how could anyone seek the reasoned path of virtue? If there is no purpose, no final causality, how could anyone plan ahead to reach virtue? Would not reason be as determined by causes as emotions? Spinoza partially solves the problem by redefinition. *Freedom* essentially means inner coercion as opposed to external coercion. But inner determination is still determinism. Determinism of behavior reigns, and freedom in its usual sense is eliminated.

Once again the question comes: How could anyone strive to be virtuous? Frederick Copleston believes this leads to a contradiction in Spinoza's ethic.[114] Russell writes that Spinoza's ethic merely describes human behavior without actually prescribing how it ought to be different. Either way, Russell concludes, "His attempt was magnificent, and rouses admiration even in those who do not think it successful."[115]

Conclusion

Some commentators have debated whether Spinoza is a pantheist. Because his "God or Nature" identifies the two disjunctives, some believe it is as accurate to describe Spinoza's views as naturalism. Naturalism is the world view in which nature alone is real. In one sense, Spinoza would fit this model.

But naturalism and pantheism are not that far apart. In fact, pantheism may be thought of as a religious form of naturalism. For this reason, New Age pantheists are finding soul mates among those scientists, especially physicists, who think, as did Einstein, in pantheistic terms. Some of these scientists treat nature with semireligious awe. One example is Carl Sagan, who states, "Our ancestors worshiped the Sun, and they were far from foolish. And yet the Sun is an ordinary, even a mediocre star. If we must worship a power greater than ourselves, does it not make sense to revere the Sun and stars?"[116] The God of Spinoza, it appears, is not dead.

113. Ibid., pt. 4, appendix 4.
114. Copleston, *History*, vol. 4, p. 257.
115. Russell, *History*, p. 571.
116. Carl Sagan, *Cosmos* (New York: Random House, 1980), p. 243.

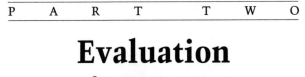

Evaluation of New Age Pantheism

Common New Age Themes

The idea that 'all is one' is foundational for the New Age.
—Douglas Groothuis

By now it is obvious that pantheism is not a monolithic world view. It appears in many forms and displays many features. Though many think of pantheism as an Oriental philosophy, in fact it can be found in both East and West. Though many think the New Age movement is new, in fact this religion's philosophical roots, both in the East and in the West, stretch back to the centuries before Christ. The New Age is not new.

But the sheer variety of pantheism's various forms can be confusing. An overview of common themes will help tie together its many forms into a generic pantheism. We cannot suppose, of course, that every general descriptive comment in this summary applies to every pantheist, let alone to every New Ager. Yet the pantheistic commitment to the unity of reality inevitably entails certain corollaries. If we can recognize the values and limits of generalizations, we can describe profitably the patterns of thought that these commitments and their implications repeatedly weave. To aid us in this task, we will discuss pantheism's common themes in metaphysics, epistemology, religious experience, and ethics.

The Pantheistic World View

Since the philosophies included in this study were chosen because of their common metaphysic, it is no surprise that the pantheists' views of reality have several common threads. Seven of these can be identified.

1. Oneness of reality. All pantheists agree that reality is one. This, of course, distinguishes them as pantheists. Though many modify this oneness in one way or another, in the final analysis, each pantheist believes that God (by whatever name he or it is called) is all that exists. Perhaps the best example is Plotinus, who actually uses the word *One* to designate this unified ultimate reality. In this respect pantheism shares with naturalism the distinction of believing in only one form of reality. Naturalism, which says that Nature alone is real, affirms only one kind of reality, namely, the natural world described by scientific laws. Although many pantheists deny the reality of matter, with naturalists they affirm the oneness of all things.

A corollary to this central point is of great importance. Since God is the All, it follows that whatever is real will be found within his being. Therefore, and quite significantly, opposites like good and evil coalesce in God. Or, as pantheists more commonly put it, God is beyond good and evil. Additionally, it is asserted that God is beyond personality/impersonality, being/becoming, and finitude/infinitude. What it means to say God is "beyond" these concepts is an issue we shall raise again. For now, it is enough to recognize that affirming God as the All involves pantheists in saying that God swallows up every pair of conceptual opposites.

2. The independence of God. Pantheists generally assert that the highest reality is in no way dependent. Everything else depends on God; God depends on nothing. Typical of this point of view is Sarvepali Radhakrishnan's claim that even if the world should pass away, God would remain unaffected. Further, God is in no way limited by the world. The world and its creatures cannot force God's hand in any way. In general terms, pantheism sides with theism in emphasizing that God is impervious to outside influence. Both of these views reject various positions (such as Alfred North Whitehead's process philosophy) that affirm a finite God who is dependent on creation. In Christian theism, although God loves persons and chooses to answer their prayers, God's creatures cannot dictate their will to God or force God to be other than he is. God can listen to his creatures and willingly act on their behalf, but he is clearly not dependent on the world he has created.

An important result of this stress on God's independence surfaces in pantheists' descriptions of God. Precisely because God is so magnificent, pantheists wish to avoid ascribing any characteristics to him. To define is to "finitize," to make finite, to delimit. Even if we compliment God by ascribing to him what many take to be positive qualities like personhood or goodness, our concepts limit him. We have used our thinking and our logic to force God to be this way and not that way. But God cannot be so limited. He explodes all our puny concepts. Thus, pantheists typically avoid such descriptions altogether, preferring rather to leave him or it nameless. This method of emphasizing God's greatness and independence will become especially relevant in later discussion.

3. God as impersonal. Although theists may agree with pantheists on God's independence, the two positions differ significantly on the personhood of God. Is God personal or impersonal? Theists, of course, conceive God in personal terms. God is ultimately and maximally personal; humans are personal only in a derivative, finite, and truncated manner. Thus, God is far more than humanly personal; he is not merely personal as we experience personhood. Pantheists, however, generally argue that personhood is simply another of those delimiting concepts that reduce God to the level of our thought.

Additionally, personhood entails twoness, for to be personal is to be in relation to another person. (You cannot live personally by yourself, which is why solitary confinement is such a debilitating punishment.) Since pantheism militates against any form of duality, God must rise above personality into the impersonal. Many pantheists will use personal metaphors like *Father* to speak of God, and some will even allow for the worship of a personal God among unlearned people. But in the final analysis, the concept of personhood does not appropriately describe God.

4. Necessary creation. While pantheists and theists both speak of creation, they mean quite different things by that concept. When theists speak of creation, they mean that a personal God chose to bring other beings, his creatures, into existence. But pantheists view creation as a necessary event that occurs because it is God's very nature to do it. Creation is not freely chosen; it occurs by necessity. Indeed, if only persons can choose freely and God is not personal, then God could not freely choose to create. Remember Spinoza's statement that God "exists from the necessity of its own nature alone and is determined to action by itself alone."[1] This Spinoza calls freedom, but he cannot mean the sort of freedom in which an intelligent being chooses among several options. God acts "freely" only in that creation is not caused by something other than God. In reality, creation is necessary.

1. Benedict de Spinoza, *Ethics*, ed. James Gutmann, based on the White-Sterling edition, The Hafner Library of Classics (New York: Hafner, 1963), pt. 1, def. 7.

5. Creation out of God. In contrast to theists, who believe in creation out of nothing (*ex nihilo*), pantheists hold that creation is out of God (*ex Deo*). The universe (nature) is of the same substance as God. In fact, it is God. Whether it is spoken of as an emanation, a manifestation, or a dimension of God, the real world is not simply like God; it is God.

6. The divinity of humans. Pantheists naturally argue that every aspect of finite existence is an expression or extension of the divine. As part of this finite reality, humans are manifestations of God. This idea finds its classic statement in the Hindu doctrine, *tat tvam asi* ("that art thou"). Commenting on this theme, Shankara notes that union with God is not something to be sought. It only needs to be realized since it is already true—it is "self-established."[2] Each person contains the spark of the divine.

7. The world as a lower level of reality. Though critics sometimes contend that pantheism claims the world does not exist, this does not apply to all pantheists. Some explicitly reject this conclusion. In some cases they state rather emphatically that the world is real. Generally, pantheists try to ascribe to the world at least a rudimentary form of reality. For example, Radhakrishnan says that we must not infer the non-existence of the many from the higher existence of the One. At the same time, pantheists do affirm that the kind of reality they are talking about in reference to this world is at a lower level of being than the ultimate.

If the world has some sort of reality and it depends upon God, how does this differ from theism? Theists also assert that this world is dependent and yet real. The difference is that theists hold the world to be really different from God while pantheists do not. Though theists believe that creation is dependent, and in that sense a lower form of reality, they also affirm that the world is distinct from its creator. (The other possible position is held by deists, who, in contrast to both theists and pantheists, declare that the world is both distinct from and independent of its creator.) Pantheists believe that the world is neither independent of nor distinct from God.

8. Levels of reality as perceptual ignorance. Though pantheists often protest that this world is not completely denied, they also commonly affirm that it is real only from a certain point of view. Spinoza tells us that the solution to Descartes's perplexing mind-body problem is that mind and body are the same reality viewed under different attributes. Idealistic Buddhists will say that the objects of this world are simply states of consciousness. Initially, Hindus like Shankara will not accept this interpretation. The world is real from a certain,

2. Shankara, *The Vedanta Sutras of Badarayana with the Commentary by Sankara*, trans. George Thibaut, 2 parts (New York: Dover, 1962), 2.1.14; 1.1.

lower point of view. One should not say the world is like the horns on a toad, entirely non-existent. Yet at the same time, Shankara tells us, the lower point of view is the perspective of ignorance.

We may summarize Shankara's claims in this way: (1) reality is one beyond the multiplicity of everyday life, (2) yet empirical reality is not nothing, (3) empirical reality is real from a certain point of view, and yet (4) that point of view is ignorance compared to the greater truth of the union achieved through mystical insight. Despite protests, the effect of this set of beliefs appears to be that the world we live in each day is not, as such, real.

We turn now to relate these historic pantheistic themes to the claims made in the current manifestations of pantheism in the New Age movement. In what ways do New Agers promote these metaphysical ideas? Teaching about the unity and independence of God is omnipresent in New Age circles. The impersonal nature of the ultimate is emphasized by the Force of *Star Wars*. The little guru, Yoda, teaches us that the Force is within each of us, just as *The Karate Kid* informs us that *ki* is within. The divinity of each person is reinforced repeatedly. For example, Jack Underhill of *Life Times* magazine says, "You are God. Honest. I know your driver's license says differently, but what does the DMV know?"[3]

Since each of us is God, our innate human potential can solve world problems and holistic health can yield a higher degree of wellness than ever before. Because of the connection with the divine, New Agers promote human potential for stress reduction, increased productivity, and personal transformation at weekend seminars and in corporate executive suites. The various elements of a "New Medicine" that taps inner energy sources are taught in several leading nursing and medical schools. The claim is that these can achieve a level of healing unavailable through traditional medical care.[4] Both soul (through the human potential movement) and body (through the holistic health movement) can achieve impressive new heights of wellness through the recognition of the organic nature of reality. Clearly, the pantheistic world view lies behind many New Age claims.

The Knowledge of Mystical Consciousness

Most pantheisms depend on mystical experience as the primary mode of consciousness. Mystic insight provides access to the divine in a way qualitatively different from sensuous experience. Seven common themes can be identified in this mystical mode of knowing.

3. Quoted in Russell Chandler, *Understanding the New Age* (Waco: Word, 1988), p. 29.

4. See Douglas Groothuis, *Unmasking the New Age* (Downers Grove: InterVarsity, 1986), pp. 57–91.

1. The abandonment of the senses. Pantheism tends to turn away from knowledge that depends on the observations of the senses. Instead, pantheists often use a mystical epistemology. But even when they use a more rational way, pantheists warn that naive dependence on the senses can be misleading. Typical of mystical pantheists' claims would be Shankara's statement that since ignorance is due to dependence on the senses, Brahman is empirically unknowable. Those who write in modern times, Radhakrishnan particularly, do incorporate the validity of science, which obviously depends on sensuous observation. At the same time, they believe that knowledge is inadequate if it is based only on the senses. Even though he believes that perception has a legitimate role, Radhakrishnan places it at a lower level than intuition.

2. Two levels of knowledge. In most pantheists the minimizing of sensuous knowledge leads to some sort of two-truth theory. This view affirms the correctness (at least initially) of two different modes of knowing, even though those two modes may ultimately lead to vastly different conclusions about the nature of reality. Very commonly, pantheists will acknowledge a rudimentary adequacy of everyday knowledge and language. But intuitive knowledge must transcend this level. Generally the intuitive is described metaphorically as higher knowledge; one rises above sensuous and logical knowledge to the heights of truth.

The higher levels of knowledge perform several functions. In general, all the pantheists believe that the higher knowledge corrects the distortions of the lower. More specifically, Shankara uses the two-levels-of-truth idea to resolve apparent problems in the Hindu scriptures: difficulties arise when we suppose that contradictory statements in scripture operate at the same level, but in fact they do not. Radhakrishnan uses the two-truth theory to support his pluralism: all religious doctrines, despite greater or lesser adequacy, point to the same God.

3. Knowledge by direct apprehension. Pantheists in general depend on a direct, first-hand grasp of reality. The lower levels of knowledge, which depend on the senses, give at best a knowledge based on logical steps. Since this knowledge must use logic to move from a sense experience to knowledge of the object of experience, it will always be indirect. But this lower knowledge gives way to a higher knowledge based on an immediate, direct, and intuitive experience. Even the rationalist Spinoza considers intuition the highest knowledge. Intuition depends on reason, but is "more potent" for it gives a knowledge that is clear, distinct, and perfect.[5] A claim more typical of

5. Spinoza, *Ethics*, pt. 5, prop. 36, scholium; props. 25, 28.

mystical pantheists is one by Plotinus, that we may achieve a kind of knowing where knower and known are one. Here one knows the One by becoming the One.

4. The self-certifying nature of mystical intuition. Since some experiences mislead us, many philosophers are interested in whether we have warrant for accepting certain experiences as genuine. For example, we might check our own experiences against those of others to minimize the chance that we might be misled by an unknown illusion. But mystics do not accept any factors external to their experiences that could certify the genuineness of their intuitions. They believe the mystical intuition carries its own stamp of authenticity. To someone who has experienced the mystical union, external verification procedures are no more necessary than fins on a cat. As D. T. Suzuki says, a mystic who has experienced the highest knowledge can say with assurance, "I am the Ultimate Reality itself" and "I am absolute knower."[6]

5. The inadequacy of logic. Pantheistic epistemologies of various types typically give logic a preliminary validity at best. Logic always involves a division between A and not-A. But the unifying thrust of pantheism seeks to overcome this distinction at the ultimate level. Shankara surprises us by his admission that logic plays a vital role in knowledge. In fact, he argues that to insist on an absolute distinction between self and Brahman opposes true logic. At the same time, Brahman is clearly beyond logical distinctions. Plotinus says the same of the One. And Suzuki, in his desire to achieve shock effect, provides the most extreme example of this tendency when he says that Zen can "serenely go its own way without at all heeding . . . criticism" about logical contradictions.[7]

6. The inadequacy of language. Pantheists generally agree that the self-certifying knowledge of direct union cannot be expressed in words. Language necessarily depends on the either/or of logic. Without A/non-A, language would not communicate content. If A = non-A, if *black* equals *white* and *cat* equals *dog*, what would *The cat is black* communicate? To accept the essential correctness of linguistic description is to acknowledge that the law of noncontradiction relates to reality. This they believe suggests that reality is made up of more than one thing, of A and non-A. This conclusion the pantheist cannot accept. So language is universally thought by mystical pantheists to be a distortion. Speaking of the holistic knowledge of the One,

6. D. T. Suzuki, "Zen: A Reply to Dr. Hu Shih," in D. T. Suzuki, *Studies in Zen* (New York: Delta, 1955), p. 147.

7. D. T. Suzuki, *Mysticism: Christian and Buddhist* (New York: Harper and Brothers, 1957), p. 49.

Plotinus reminds us, "we are forced to apply to the Supreme terms which strictly are ruled out."[8]

7. The ineffability of mystical objects and intuition. The inadequacy of language leads to an important corollary, ineffability. Ineffability means that since linguistic description must break things into logical opposites, things that cannot be so broken must be indescribable. As Radhakrishnan explains, "God is too great for words to explain. He is like light, making things luminous but himself invisible."[9] When mystics, whether Western or Eastern, do use language, they often limit themselves to negative language. That is, though they will not say what God is, they may try to say what he is not.

To what degree are these themes reflected in New Age affirmations? New Age advocates commonly denigrate logical, conceptual, and empirical ways of knowing. Instead, they practically deify mystical and intuitive knowledge. For example, Shirley MacLaine places the hero of a novel in an acupuncture session where the "doctor" says, "Now relax. . . . Let your mind go. Don't evaluate and don't let the left brain judge what you are thinking. Give your right brain more space. As a matter of fact, don't think."[10] Ironically, as this quote suggests, New Age proponents are fixated on the right brain/left brain research. The irony lies in the fact that the distination depends on the rational, left-brain methods of science. New Agers use the rational, left-brain distinction between left and right brains primarily to promote holistic, immediate, intuitive right-brain thought to the exclusion of dichotomistic left-brain thought.

Many New Agers also defend the self-certifying and ineffable character of the higher consciousness. The author of *The Aquarian Conspiracy*, Marilyn Ferguson, says that you reach genuine knowledge "only when you get yourself out of the way. You have to be willing to have experiences and not have words for them."[11] When we shut down the analytical left brain, reach beyond the logic-chopping words inherent in all conceptuality, and open ourselves to Mind-at-Large, then the Higher Consciousness breaks in. For those who hope to apprehend true knowledge, this is the New Age party line.

The Religious Dimensions of Pantheistic Mysticism

The pantheists' views of religious experience and of salvation follow closely their epistemology. The mystical experience that panthe-

8. Plotinus, *The Six Enneads*, trans. Stephen MacKenna and B. S. Page, 6 vols. (Chicago and London: Encyclopaedia Britannica, 1952), 6.9 [3, 10, 11]; 5.3 [13].

9. Sarvepali Radhakrishnan, *An Idealist View of Life* (London: Allen and Unwin, 1932), p. 97.

10. Shirley MacLaine, *Dancing in the Light* (Toronto: Bantam, 1985), p. 312.

11. Interview with Chandler, *Understanding*, p. 38.

ists depend on to show that God is the all is the same experience that provides liberation from our most basic human dilemmas. In general, we can specify six common ideas about religious experience and salvation that pantheists share.

1. Knowledge is salvation. In the classic question of faith and reason, several positions have been proposed. For most theists, faith (that is, our trust in and relation to God) and reason (that is, our cognitive knowledge about God) are different. Some have said that faith and reasoning about God are mutually exclusive. Søren Kierkegaard and Karl Barth have taken this position. But many theists believe that they are mutually supportive. Pantheists generally hold that the two are the same; there is no substantive difference between faith (salvation) and reason (experiential knowledge). Salvation *is* knowledge, though this knowledge is intuitive, not rational. To be enlightened through mystical intuition or higher consciousness about the true reality of our oneness with God is in itself to be saved from our false experience of pain in the world.

2. Ignorance as the source of evil. If knowledge is salvation, the cause of the problems from which we are saved is our own ignorance. We languish far from our heavenly home because we do not realize our true identity. Oriental writers tie their view of reincarnation to this problem of ignorance. If we fail to realize our oneness with God, we suffer through the debilitating series of lives full of pain and sorrow. Enlightenment enables us to begin walking the path toward God. Through this ascent we can overcome the evil caused by ignorance. Similarly, Spinoza tells us that viewing God as a mysterious person who controls things by an omnipotent will leaves unexplained all the absurd and evil things that happen to us. This false view of God leads to spiritual blindness.

3. Salvation through human effort. Pantheists affirm various techniques for arriving at true knowledge, the mystical experience of enlightenment that is salvation. Generally, however, achieving higher consciousness involves human effort and discipline. Although Spinoza is unique among the pantheists we have discussed in his use of geometry to achieve knowledge, favorites in the East are yoga and other forms of meditation. Suzuki's Zen Buddhism leaves nothing either to chance or to the will of a capricious personal God. Through the use of *koan* (those maddening mental puzzles that bring reason to a standstill) and *zazen* (sitting meditation) the Zen novice begins the journey toward enlightenment. The Vedanta Hindus usually permit the three avenues to salvation: meditation leading to intuitive consciousness, good works of service, and devotion to a personal God. But the latter two are given legitimate status only grudgingly; the real path to Brahman is mystical union. Here most emphatically can we

experience that indescribable sweetness by which we rise above this world of pain and find union with God.

4. The mystical ascent. Pantheists often describe the path to salvation as an ascent. We have "fallen," metaphorically speaking, and we need to rise again to our true oneness with God. Although this fall is sometimes given moral overtones, the pantheists' use of the metaphor is not identical to the Judeo-Christian idea of a fall into sin. Instead of holding to a moral fall, pantheists teach a fall into ignorance. Salvation reverses this fall, and for this reason the concept of an ascent into something higher (both a higher point of view epistemologically and a higher reality metaphysically) dominates pantheists' descriptions of salvation. In Plotinus the language of ascent is prominent, for he speaks most directly about the descent from God in his idea of emanation. Matter and this world are things that weigh us down. Through mystical devotion and ethical living we cast off this excess baggage like sailors throwing weight off their ship during a storm. Thus lightened, we move back up the ladder to Mind and finally to the One, our home.

This aspect of Plotinus finds parallels not only in the other pantheists who speak often of the higher and lower points of view, but also in many medieval Christian writers. We should note, however, that in the majority of cases, Christians speak of ascending to a personal union with God. The culminating stage of the Christian's climb is the two-in-one union of personal love, not the absolute oneness of impersonal identity.

5. The peace of salvation. As with any religious philosophy, pantheism claims to give a solution to life's problems. This solution includes a sense of peace, tranquility, and repose. Although it is sometimes heavily philosophical, the whole point of pantheism is not philosophical in the traditional sense in that pantheists do not seek rational truth for its own sake. Pantheism's goal is the religious sense of assurance, peace, and contact with God that religions seek.

Put another way, pantheists do not seek primarily to *explain* our experiences of the world and of evil; they seek instead to *resolve* our problems with evil. Consequently, each pantheist in this study ends his chain of thinking by promising a sense of peace and release from tension and worry. Even the rationalist Spinoza believed that knowledge brought the tranquility we need for living; he argued for a blessedness that he described as "constant and eternal love toward God."[12] Similarly, each pantheist, no matter how philosophically oriented, finds the purpose of his philosophy fulfilled in this religious goal.

12. Spinoza, *Ethics*, pt. 5, prop. 36, scholium.

6. Pluralism of beliefs. The pantheistic emphasis on experiential knowledge leads very naturally to religious pluralism, a perspective that has gained a firm foothold in this century. Because pantheists deem our experience to be so important, they imply that the concepts we use to describe God, ourselves, and the world are correspondingly less important. Historically, Western pantheists have not generally followed this logic; they affirmed instead that differences in religious beliefs are important. Certainly Spinoza, at least, thought that certain concepts about God (say, the idea of miracles) were both philosophically false and religiously dangerous. But Oriental pantheists do commonly hold that differing religious beliefs can all be "true." Suzuki's Buddhism does not really accept any doctrine. Actually, he affirms that no religious doctrines are ultimately true. This is within the spirit of the original Buddhist teaching.

Hinduism, however, most emphatically states that contradictory theoretical conceptions can be accepted as true. This all-embracing religious pluralism of Hinduism is at home in a modern world where the mood is characterized by the statement, "Your faith is good for you; mine is good for me." The willingness within Hindu faith to accept alternative conceptions means that Hinduism includes pantheism, polytheism, and even theism. In fact, scholars generally concede that Buddhism no longer survives in India, the land of its origin, because Hinduism's inclusive nature simply swallowed up Buddhism's distinctive teachings. Radhakrishnan, the modern Hindu, explicitly affirms this pluralism in his belief that various religions are all acceptable paths toward the religious goal of happiness and goodness. Even though Westerners historically have been more exclusive, this aspect of Hinduism is increasingly becoming part of the dominant religious perspective of our time.

How does the New Age movement today display these ideas? Salvation from the suffering of reincarnation and the pain caused by ignorance are common pantheistic themes. These find expression in the writings of typical New Age proponents. That ignorance causes pain and requires a change in consciousness is a primary theme of the many seminars that promote the new awareness necessary for enlightenment. Famous examples include the *est* training sessions of Werner Erhard (he now has a new group called Forum) and the Esalen Institute in California. The Esalen Institute has attracted a number of famous psychologists, including Carl Rogers, Rollo May, and Abraham Maslow. These seminars preach the same message: you are ignorant of your true divinity, so gain a new perception through (insert one of a number of techniques here) and experience a transformed personal consciousness.

This new consciousness must come through your own initiative, but it can be achieved in a number of ways. This fits the pluralistic, do-your-own-thing tendencies of the New Age movement. Following the lead of ancient Hindu thinking, New Agers believe that any religion can help you find truth. Follow the Buddha, Krishna, Jesus, one of many others. They all teach the same basic message. (In this view, the teachings and example of Jesus, not his unique deity or sacrificial death, or physical resurrection, are what New Age proponents consider important.) The New Age radio program "Dimensions" succinctly articulates these ideals in its introduction: "It is only through a change of consciousness that the world will be changed. This is our responsibility."[13]

The Problem of Good and Evil

Every world view and every religion must respond to good and evil. Humans in all cultures find themselves prompted to seek religiously and intellectually satisfying explanations for evil. Both moral evil and personal tragedy clamor to be explained. Like every other world view, pantheism must face this theoretical and practical problem.

1. Our responsibility for pain. Though pantheism generally blames ignorance for our experience of evil and at times says that evil is necessary, it also teaches that we are responsible for our sorrow and pain. In Hindu thinking, the law of karma accounts for our station in life. We are rewarded or punished in this life for our actions in previous lives. Though in our current situation we may think inequities abound, still, when we consider the virtues and vices of previous lives, we conclude that the apparent injustice in this life is not unfair at all. We are all simply reaping the consequences of our own actions. In other forms of pantheism, we are at least culpable for our ignorance and for our failure to find salvation through knowledge. Spinoza, for example, tells us that everything is necessary, yet it is our passions that give rise to sorrow and evil.

2. Ethics as a means to salvation. Pantheists agree that immoral living brings sorrow and pain while ethical living contributes to salvation. On this point the agreement is universal: though good and evil are not ultimately real in God, yet in this life ethical discipline is the means by which the ascent toward God begins. Among preconditions for the pursuit of Brahman, Shankara lists renunciation of desire and development of self-restraint.

Radhakrishnan opposes the biblical idea of transferring guilt to another person on the grounds that salvation must be achieved at great cost: 'Cheap grace' is not the way to redemption. Suzuki argues that although Zen values life just as it is, this does not imply antino-

---

13. Quoted in Groothuis, *Unmasking*, p. 25.

mianism. Ascetic retirement is necessary for moral development. The Zennist can simply do what needs to be done without a second thought. Zen admires the "secret virtue," the "deed without merit," but it does not abandon ethics.[14] Plotinus teaches that the soul must be liberated from vice before it can begin the ascent to the One. And Spinoza argues that reason demands the enlightened self-interest by which we control our passions and live with a proper emotional disposition. In this way, we can live without the sorrows the passions cause. Every pantheist identifies ethical effort as the boot camp of salvation.

3. The illusory nature of good and evil. Yet, paradoxically, pantheists generally believe that the distinction between good and evil is not real. In God the division between good and evil must be transcended since all distinctions collapse in the oneness of God. In the Hindu religion, Nirguna Brahman, God without qualities, is beyond all categories of good and evil. Hindus believe that such attributes would limit Brahman. Similarly, Plotinus's One is beyond any duality like good and evil.

4. The lack of moral altruism. If good and evil have no meaning in God, is there any point in doing what is good and avoiding what is evil? Of course, the benefit of personal discipline contributes to the ascent by drawing our attention away from the outer, sensuous world and onto the inner life of the spirit. But would serving another person be a good act in and of itself? It appears that the pantheistic world view could not allow for such service. Why serve a person who does not exist separately from ourselves?

Various pantheists respond differently on this point. Traditional Hinduism has no place for service as an intrinsically good act. The doctrine of karma cuts the nerve of social compassion. Presumably every suffering person suffers justly. But the Mahayana Buddhist ideal of a *bodhisattva* makes service to others possible. (The *bodhisattva* is a saint who delays his own "salvation" or entrance into Buddhahood to help others achieve their Buddhahood.) This expression of Buddhist compassion gives place to moral effort, not just as a personal discipline but as service to others.

Like the Hindus, Western pantheists do not have room for ethical altruism for its own sake. Plotinus's discussion of virtue generally revolves around the need for moral purification as the first step of the return to the One. Though Spinoza's major work was *Ethics*, he does not defend altruism. He does argue for a kind of social ethics in that each person acts from enlightened self-interest to benefit society, but his major emphasis is on cultivating the virtues that benefit the indi-

14. D. T. Suzuki, *An Introduction to Zen Buddhism* (New York: Grove, 1964), pp. 130–31.

vidual by preventing needless pain. Spinoza tells us to develop and admire chiefly the personal habit of cheerfulness. With the exception of the Buddhist concept of *bodhisattva*, therefore, pantheists generally do not prescribe ethical behavior on the ground of service to others.

5. The illusory nature of pain and sorrow. As good and evil are moral categories that have no ultimate reality, the same can be said for the experience of pain and sorrow. Though sorrow has reality from the lower point of view, in the ultimate perspective, our sorrow is illusion. We suffer because we *believe* we are in pain, not because we really are. Shankara says sins that, through the law of karma, lead to suffering are part of the ignorance of this world: "The pain of the individual soul also is not real, but imaginary only, caused by the error consisting in the non-discrimination of [the Self from] the body, senses, and other limiting adjuncts which are due to name and form, the effects of [ignorance]."[15] Similarly, Spinoza the rationalist argues that things are simply what they are. They are not inherently good or evil. We may treat events as good or evil because they bring pleasure or cause pain. However, we must understand that each event is necessarily caused to be what it is. If we possess this knowledge, then every event "ceases to be sorrow."[16]

Can we find parallels between the usual pantheistic claims in this area and the themes prominent in the New Age? As in the other areas, the New Age bristles with the ideas that the typical pattern of pantheistic thinking leads its advocates to accept. The New Age view of evil follows the dual answer found in pantheism. On the one hand, suffering is caused by karma, the cosmic law of justice where virtue is rewarded and vice is punished. Thus, in one report, Shirley MacLaine told a rape victim that she very likely had been a rapist in her last life and was now working off her karma.[17] On the other hand, evil is not ultimately real. According to another report, MacLaine held a $300-per-person meditation session in New York. A woman revealed that she had suffered pain for years. But MacLaine took it in stride: "Sometimes people use pain to feel alive. . . . Pain is a perception, not a reality."[18]

The ethical demands of the New Age movement on its adherents are low. In this respect, the traditional religious pantheists who defend the need for rigorous self-discipline as the means to enlightenment have found their teachings modified by the desires of a narcissistic Western society. Yet the belief that no ultimate standards of good and evil can be imposed on all persons finds adherents among

15. Shankara, *Vedānta Sūtras*, 2.3.46.
16. Spinoza, *Ethics*, pt. 5, prop. 18, scholium.
17. Timothy Philibosian, quoted in Chandler, *Understanding*, p. 243.
18. "New Age Harmonies," *Time* (December 7, 1987), p. 63.

both traditional pantheists and New Age proponents. Since God is within, we do not need artificial moral dogmas. We simply need to be true to ourselves.

At the same time, ironically, some pantheists find that the divinity within serves as the basis for an agenda of ethical norms. Radhakrishnan bases his plea for interreligious toleration on the reality of God within all persons. Similarly, New Agers argue for the moral rightness of ecological concerns, nuclear disarmament, and world peace. In the swirling current that is the New Age movement, these varied pantheistic themes mix together in colorful, if confusing, ways.

Conclusion

The New Age movement, loose and diverse as it is, does not fit neat boxes. Yet the historic pantheistic themes we have discussed do, in general, form the intellectual content of New Age teaching. Into this philosophical context individual New Age proponents place the more bizarre trappings of their movement: "channeling" (consulting mediums), crystals (rocks with cosmic power), various occult practices, "Harmonic Convergences," and much more. Further, the ideas we have been developing are the backdrop for the multitude of self-help books, tapes, and seminars and the myriad business seminars geared toward stress reduction and productivity increases.

Additionally, this pantheistic philosophy grounds social and political movements designed to get New Age teaching into the mainstream of Western culture. These include political lobbyists, environmental groups, educational consultants, artistic productions both highbrow and low, psychological therapies, and more. The New Age movement is not centrally organized. But it incarnates in a bewildering number of ways the fundamental philosophy we have been discussing: God is all, you are God, so get in touch with the divine within.

We must warn again that we have identified themes in this chapter, not doctrines. Pantheism and its many New Age expressions have a variety of details. Not all pantheists agree with each other on every point. We do not wish to leave the impression that pantheism lacks variety. At the same time, this chapter has identified certain recurrent ideas, moves, and arguments that tend to repeat themselves in various pantheisms, including the New Age movement. These common themes make it possible to develop lines of criticism that apply to various forms of pantheism. To this critical task we now turn.

The Pantheistic World View

*Awaken to the god who sleeps at the root of the human
being.—Theodore Roszak*
*[The] knowledge of absolute unity represents either nature as an
illusion or God as an abstraction.—Robert Flint*

Previous chapters have been primarily descriptive in purpose. In
addition to introducing the thought of these influential philosophers,
however, we hope this discussion has driven home two other points:
first, the variety of pantheisms and, second, the unity of pantheism.
On the one hand, this world view, like any other, manifests itself in a
variety of concrete historical forms. This multiplicity should not be
compressed or overlooked. On the other hand, common threads also
can be detected, and this important fact must not be ignored either.
Though we should not seek a flat uniformity among pantheists, certain typical positions and moves make a unified discussion possible.
The thrust toward oneness typical of pantheistic commitments entails a pattern of beliefs that is repeated by various pantheists from
East and West.

A Word about Method

Having sketched this pantheistic web of beliefs in several of its
forms, we are ready to turn to the far more difficult task of evalua-

133

tion. This process is fraught with so many difficulties that exponents of criticized positions often believe their views have not been fully appreciated. This occurs even when the specifics of a single person's philosophy are subjected to criticism. But the problem is compounded in our situation, since we will respond to a generic pantheism when, as the various descriptive sections reveal, the world view takes on many subtly different forms. Indeed, that the currently prominent version of pantheism is described by the phrase *New Age movement* itself indicates this very multiplicity: the New Age movement is not a view or a school, it is a movement, a loosely related network of people and ideas that share a web of common characteristics. But New Agers display no monolithic structure of thinking.

How can we evaluate something this diverse? If we evaluate pantheism in general (as opposed to one particular form), the advantages are obvious. The greater applicability and broader relevance of the discussion will enhance the value of any critical remarks. But we face several dangers that could erode the significance of this evaluation. On the one hand, we must resist the temptation to compress the variety of pantheisms unduly in order to criticize the whole. On the other hand, we must avoid criticizing only the less sophisticated forms of pantheism, assuming that this testing process weakens also the strongest forms. A similar thing happens, for example, when critics hold Christianity responsible for the eccentric beliefs of its less thoughtful adherents. Some may find themselves tempted to take this low road when testing the New Age movement, for this conglomeration of ideas and practices attracts true believers who display bizarre beliefs. But such a procedure is surely unfair and virtually useless.

Our approach in these evaluative chapters must be to raise questions about the kinds of moves pantheists typically make. In no case can we assume that every comment applies to every pantheist or to every New Ager. Critical remarks will be made concerning the kinds of positions one typically finds pantheists taking. We depend therefore on individual readers to think creatively with the raw materials of our critique to shape thoughtful responses to the particular forms of pantheism or New Age thinking they encounter. Given this understanding, we believe the patterns in pantheistic styles of thinking are similar enough to justify raising certain evaluative questions about the world view in general. With this caveat, applicable to all evaluative sections, we can begin our discussion in earnest.

The Problem of Criteria

In addition to the sheer variety of pantheistic expressions, philosophers point out several other problems that confront us when seeking proper evaluations of world views.[1] First, Westerners commonly think that the critical process involves testing theories or hypotheses against facts. This, we presume, is the way of science. In testing a philosophy like pantheism, we treat the world view as a theory and see if it stands up to the facts. Like Sergeant Friday on the old television show "Dragnet" we say, "Just the facts, ma'am."

But philosophers have wondered where we get the facts with which to judge world views. As we shall argue in some greater detail in chapter 8, facts are not the pure, conceptually innocent little things most people think they are. Even in their purest state, they are contaminated by theory. To a degree, what counts as a fact is influenced by the point of view of the perceiver. As an example, imagine the "facts" the fans of opposing teams "see" when the umpire makes a critical decision in the final seconds of a close game. Since facts are not entirely neutral with respect to world views, a theist and a pantheist may not even agree as to what the facts are. Therefore, straightforward appeal to facts as such cannot be decisive in choosing between two macroscopic world views.

Second, assuming we could agree on the "facts," how are they to be related? The connections between data, as David Hume has helped the modern world see, do not arise from the data themselves. We do not readily find in those facts the secret codes that reveal how they fit together. We find some elasticity in how we may relate facts. Though they may not be open to an infinite number of relationships (since the flex in facts is not unlimited), certainly several mutually incompatible systems of relating experiences can be spelled out. So even if there were some agreement on what counts as fact, the choices about the decisive facts, those central data that stand out and perform a critical organizing function, can differ in two perspectives.

For example, suppose a theist, an atheist, and a pantheist agree that Christ said, "I and the Father are one." The Christian theist might think this points to Christ's unique deity. The atheist might think it proves Christ to be self-deluded. But the pantheist might think (as Alan Watts did[2]) that this proves Christ to be among the few truly enlightened persons who understand that all of us are one with God.

1. Though a person who takes a common-sense approach to life might be tempted to reject the problems we shall mention here briefly, these conclusions are not uncontroversial in much of contemporary philosophy. Since this book is not about the current philosophical debates on evaluative judgments, a detailed discussion is not possible here. For an introduction to some of these issues, see David L. Wolfe, *Epistemology: The Justification of Belief*, Contours of Christian Philosophy, ed. C. Stephen Evans (Downers Grove: InterVarsity, 1982), or Basil Mitchell, *The Justification of Religious Belief* (New York: Seabury, Crossroad, 1973).

2. See Alan Watts, *Cloud Hidden, Whereabouts Unknown: A Mountain Journal* (New York: Random House, Pantheon Books, 1973), p. 129.

Examples, including biblical examples, of different interpretations of similar facts could be multiplied.[3]

Third, as Basil Mitchell points out, world views are notorious for their ability to incorporate new information into their own systems of thought and to resolve the questions raised by new criticisms.[4] This assimilating function leads some contemporary philosophers toward a relativist conclusion. They assume that the criteria we use for evaluating world views are to be defended entirely on the grounds of individual systems. Rules for deciding the relative merits of competing philosophies, it is argued, can be defended only within the context of world views. Given this claim, if we are to make meaningful and respectful evaluations, the question of standards or criteria for judgment must be addressed.

When we make judgments, we apply standards. If Thomas says that a gymnast's routine should be scored a "10," he indicates his awareness of a standard of gymnastic perfection that the individual has attained. If there are no commonly accepted standards, or if Thomas has little or no knowledge of any standards, his comment that the routine warrants a "10" has little cognitive significance. Maybe Thomas loves the gymnast passionately, and so his statement might rightly be dismissed as the emotional overflow of a fan's partisan feelings. Similarly, when we evaluate world views, describing them as true or false, consistent or inconsistent, coherent or incoherent, meaningful or unintelligible, we should use some criteria in making the judgment. The key question is, Where do we get these all-important criteria?

As we have already intimated, philosophers have suggested two essentially distinct avenues by which to warrant or justify the standards we use. One of these operates on the premise that every criterion for criticizing or defending world views grows out of a particular system of thought. On this view, for example, theism has certain principles and pantheism has others. When theistic criteria are used, theism is confirmed and pantheism disconfirmed. When pantheistic ones are used, the opposite occurs. So the world view we confirm in the end depends on which set of principles we chose in the beginning, and that in turn depends on which world view we accept. The arguments become circular, and the choice of criteria is arbitrary. Consequently, no decisive inter-world-view criticism is possible, and many perspectives theoretically could be acknowledged as true by

3. See the various interpretations given to explain the results of Jesus' healing ministry as recorded in Matthew 12:22–28 or the three different explanations given the sound of God's voice in John 12:28–29.

4. Mitchell, *Justification*, pp. 62–63.

their own principles even though they contradict other reasonable points of view.

The other avenue posits at least some criteria as world-view-independent principles of evaluation. Naturally, many criteria do depend on world views, and this is certainly acceptable. For example, "Is it biblical?" may be used legitimately as a test question within Christianity. But this second approach claims that at least some criteria are independent of world view, and if this is so, the possibility of grading world views by considering genuine and honest evaluations lies open to us. Participants in inter-world-view dialog need not inevitably speak past advocates of other perspectives. We should be able to posit the rationality of certain principles of thought upon which we might all agree at least to some degree.

Now, many in the inter-world-view dialog may not want to accept any common criteria. Despite this, some participants in the dialog, while overtly rejecting certain rational principles, reveal by their actions or words a necessary dependence on or implicit assumption of these rational criteria. Examples of this phenomenon will come up as our discussion proceeds. One reason we feel justified in using such criteria and in assuming their inter-world-view relevance is precisely this: even while rejecting such criteria, pantheists implicitly affirm them in their actions. Thus, something like the criteria we seek do seem to be at work even in those whose overt philosophy does not permit them. These standards of rationality, we believe, do warrant inter-world-view evaluation.

Thus, without arguing the question in great detail at this point, we assume that the criteria for evaluating world views are neither completely arbitrary nor entirely dependent on one's world view. Instead, the criteria we seek are embedded in the very task upon which we have embarked, namely, of finding a comprehensive interpretation of our lives that makes sense of our experience of the world. Another task would require different criteria. If our job were to find the best technique for selling women's clothing, for example, we would use other criteria—standards that themselves grow out of our marketing goals. Whether we should concentrate on making sense of the world (i.e., finding an adequate world view) or selling women's clothes is not the question. Assuming we wish to find a way of making sense of the world, what standards shall we follow in doing it? On this issue, we believe, some general agreement can be found.[5]

What criteria shall we use? Different philosophers have their own suggestions. One individual posits four that are typical of the kinds of principles philosophers in general have identified. *Consistency* means the lack of logical contradiction. This test, operating negatively, elimi-

5. Wolfe, *Epistemology*, pp. 46–51.

nates perspectives that are self-contradictory. *Coherence* entails the presence of genuine unity and relatedness among the claims in the world view. We can easily find examples of statements that are consistent but not coherent. Because they are entirely unrelated, "I drive a Chevy" and "The Pope is Catholic" are consistent but not coherent.

While the first two criteria are essentially conceptual, the next two are more empirical. The first two operate *within* a world view as we ask about the relationships among its claims; the second two operate *between* a world view's claims and our experience of the world about us. *Comprehensiveness* points to the world view's ability to accommodate large ranges of experience. In a graphic way, a psychologist says world views should "gobble up" experience. *Congruity* is the "fit" of the theory to the facts. Is there a sense of appropriateness or elegance in the match between theory and experience? Are the "facts" stretched and squeezed to fit the theory, or do they fit like a hand in a glove?[6]

Is positing such rational criteria justifiable? Many philosophers think so. For example, Mitchell, who discusses this question in some detail, concludes that when two macroscopic interpretive schemes disagree in their interpretations of the facts, mature individuals can make judgments about the relative adequacy of the two systems. Though detailed rules cannot always be specified ahead of time, general, system-independent criteria can be the basis for careful rational choices. Mitchell suggests "consistency, coherence, simplicity, elegance, explanatory power, [and] fertility" as candidates for these criteria.[7]

In addition to these basic logical criteria, we will also use the tests of unaffirmability and actual undeniability.[8] The former is a negative test related to, but broader than, the principle of consistency. The latter is a positive test that justifies acknowledging the fundamental evaluative criteria. We assume as basic principles that what is unaffirmable must be false and what is actually undeniable is true.

The test of unaffirmability may be explained in this way. Something that is affirmable can be stated meaningfully. Statements may be sayable or utterable, without being meaningfully affirmable, as anyone who has read *Alice in Wonderland* knows. Statements that

6. Ibid., pp. 50–55.

7. Mitchell, *Justification*, p. 95; Frederick Ferré, *Language, Logic, and God* (New York: Harper and Row, 1961), pp. 162–65, suggests consistency, coherence, applicability (roughly Wolfe's congruity), and adequacy (roughly Wolfe's comprehensiveness). Alvin Plantinga argues that such criteria must be determined inductively, from the ground up, rather than in an a priori or deductive manner: "Is Belief in God Properly Basic?" *Nous* 15 (March 1981): 41–52.

8. Norman L. Geisler, *Christian Apologetics* (Grand Rapids: Baker, 1976), pp. 141–45.

self-defeat are unaffirmable. The statement, "I cannot speak one word of English," self-destructs. This is not logically inconsistent as is talking about square circles; it is possible to express that statement meaningfully in Swahili. But uttered in English, the assertion is meaningless. If a statement is self-defeating, it may be uttered, but it cannot be meaningfully affirmed. So we would rightly judge it false. It is, to use a more technical phrase, self-referentially inconsistent. In our quest to evaluate pantheism, we shall find that the patterns of ideas that this world view commonly generates tend to be unaffirmable.

The principle of undeniability confirms the reality of our own existence and the necessity of the rational criteria we have been discussing. It is, in a sense, the flip side of the principle of unaffirmability. If a statement is undeniable, this means that it depends necessarily on some presupposition that it seeks to deny. This makes the statement necessarily false because it is unaffirmable. But it may also make that presupposition necessarily true because it is undeniable. If every attempt to deny some presupposition entangles one in self-defeat, we have strong warrant for accepting that presupposition.

Suppose, for example, that a man utters the logical statement, "Logic is always misleading." We would be within our rights to call that statement false. Since it presupposes the validity of logic, the statement is self-defeating and therefore is not meaningfully affirmable. But this illustration suggests that logic, the presupposition that the statement sought unsuccessfully to deny, is undeniable. More generally, because any attempt to deny the canons of basic rationality will assume those principles, we affirm them to be undeniable and therefore true. Pantheists can utter denials of the fundamental canons of thought, but they cannot do so meaningfully. We accept as a basic premise that something that is undeniable is true.

Our purpose in discussing these criteria is that they are beneficial in evaluating world views. World views are what we come up with when we seek to explain the sum total of things. Why would someone want to do this? Why would we seek "total explanations" instead of selling women's clothes? Frederick Ferré has argued persuasively that the human search for a comprehensive interpretation of things

> is generated by our very practical needs as conscious agents for oneness in conceptual orientation toward the environment with which we must cope. It is nurtured by the need for inclusiveness in the account of things by which we live. . . . It is reinforced by the practical needs of a finite intelligence for economy if order is to be intelligible. . . . And it is reflected in aesthetic preferences for elegance and harmony even in diversity.[9]

9. Frederick Ferré, *Basic Modern Philosophy of Religion* (New York: Charles Scribner's Sons, 1967), p. 392.

We believe everyone wants a coherent world view. Part of being human is having the itch for adequate explanation. Some people scratch this itch passionately—they spend their lives seeking true philosophy. Others are less motivated to seek proper explanations seriously, and they either grab the first hypothesis that happens along or staunchly accept tradition.

For example, both scientists and common folks seek causal explanations of our world. The difference is that scientists are more dedicated and rigorous in eliminating unworkable hypotheses. Therefore, we rightly judge them to be more likely correct when their results differ with "common-sense" conclusions. Most people admit that it is best to seek the "truest" world view, even if for personal reasons they cannot or will not do so. We presume that anyone who wishes to evaluate pantheism seriously will resonate with this attitude and find in the search for a unified, relevant, and true world view a worthy goal.

Ascribing Concepts to God

The groundwork we have laid in this chapter undergirds the rest of our evaluative journey. We are not concerned simply to ask whether pantheism is biblical or Christian. We wish to test its mettle against the sort of general criteria we have briefly enumerated: consistency, coherence, comprehensiveness, and congruity. We shall approach our critical task in this chapter by following key issues generated by familiar patterns of pantheistic metaphysics. In subsequent chapters, we will examine epistemology, religious experience, and ethics.

Our fundamental metaphysical evaluations grow from a basic fact: pantheists persistently resist predicating concepts of God. Although some pantheists do ascribe concepts to God in initial phases of a discussion, in the final analysis they tend to warn against taking such descriptions of God as literally true. When pressed, those pantheists who do describe God often reverse their field and assert that God cannot be captured by human concepts. While some pantheists believe that rational theories can have rudimentary applicability to God, they find it much more important to emphasize the inadequacy of conceptual descriptions than to affirm their appropriateness. If someone understands that concepts do not really describe the divine, pantheists may use them gingerly to point toward God. But if they sense that someone thinks he has said something literally true or even minimally adequate about God, they take great pains to set the record straight: the reality of God's being bursts every human rational concept.

The motivation for this skittishness about concepts is most honorable. Pantheists wish to preserve God from the limiting, finitizing effect of concepts. They wish to protect the absolute unity, supremacy, perfection, infinity, and independence of God. If God were small enough to be captured by human words, the divine absoluteness would be compromised. If concepts that depend on logical opposites were applied to God, the divine unity would be denied. Consequently, God cannot be described.

It is important to acknowledge fully the nobility of purpose evident in this maneuver. It is a tack with which traditional theists should have some sympathy, especially in a day when so many theologians are opting for finite views of God. We should commend pantheists for their desire to emphasize God's infinity, the inadequacy of our rational thinking, and the need for genuine humility even about our best thoughts of the divine.

As noble and well-intentioned as this program may be, however, it leads those who adopt it into several intractable difficulties. The desire to show that God is impervious to normal conceptualizing sometimes manifests itself in this claim: one who wishes to experience oneness with God must climb a ladder of concepts until he finally transcends all theoretical viewpoints. Buddhists like to say that our concepts are like rafts that carry us across the river. Once across the water, however, we abandon the rafts and continue the journey by walking. Similarly, in reaching for God, we use conceptual thinking in initial stages of our journey, but later abandon it as we move into higher forms of knowledge. The enlightened one no longer thinks about an object called God. He stands above all viewpoints and simply experiences God.

The claim to transcend all viewpoints and thus to get beyond all concepts seems extravagant. It is hard to see how we can avoid thinking of that new, higher perspective as a new viewpoint. Unfortunately for the pantheist, the viewpoint beyond all viewpoints is still a viewpoint. One does not get beyond all viewpoints. One rises to better, truer, more adequate viewpoints. If that were not so, what would be the point of the analogy of the ladder? In what sense does the enlightened one climb "higher"?

As Stuart C. Hackett points out, this metaphor does not quite get us past concepts. To visualize ourselves climbing a ladder to truth involves the assumption that higher rungs represent sets of concepts that are increasingly correct articulations of ultimate reality. If this were not so, all rungs would be equally adequate (or inadequate), and we could never move to higher rungs that are better or truer than the lowest. We cannot climb higher on the rungs of a ladder that is lying flat on the ground.

> If . . . there is a ladder of intellectual stages, the higher rungs of which more closely approximate the absolute truth precisely because they match corresponding stages of spiritual development, then it follows that not all viewpoints are equally distortions of the ultimate, and conversely that the Absolute Reality itself is in principle accessible to philosophical insight. If this last point were not essentially sound, then no viewpoint would be any more (or less) of an approximation to the Absolute than any other, since, as utterly devoid of all determinate qualities, that Absolute would be equally and infinitely remote from them all.[10]

The analogy of the ladder, it appears, implies that some conceptualities are truer than others, else there would be no point in the climbing. This makes it difficult to sustain the claim that we make some progress via concepts only to abandon them when we reach a perspective that is somehow beyond all conceptual viewpoints.

To avoid this problem, pantheists may assert straight out that no concepts apply to God in any way. They may admit that the rungs are on the same level and abandon the claim that progress up the ladder is possible. In this case, the point of the metaphor is lost. Alternatively, they may affirm that the progress up the ladder is moral, not conceptual. That is, they may admit that they are moving closer to God spiritually, but deny that the series of concepts in any way involves an improvement in degrees of descriptive adequacy. But this reverts to the admission that the rungs are on level ground conceptually. The analogy of climbing a ladder implies either that some concepts are truer than others (we climb up to truer ones) or that we make some other sort of progress. To avoid admitting that some concepts are truer than others, a pantheist must take the second option.

But this posture also carries unfortunate consequences even though it evades the dilemma posed by considering some viewpoints better (that is, some rungs higher) than others. While we do not wish to forget the noble purpose that stands behind this move, we should recognize that it carries with it an ominous implication: the word *God* becomes entirely vacuous; it becomes a word without any conceptual meaning. *God* becomes a symbol of nothing. Its referent is entirely amorphous, for no concept is allowed to shape it. Without a definition, we do not have a word that captures infinity, but one that captures nothing.

Pantheists are stuck. If they allow concepts, then according to their principles God's unity and infinity are compromised. But if they allow no concepts to describe God, the word *God* becomes void of

10. Stuart C. Hackett, *Oriental Philosophy: A Westerner's Guide to Eastern Thought* (Madison: University of Wisconsin Press, 1979), p. 111.

meaning; like an empty plastic bag it may have potential for content, but the potential is unfulfilled.

Though we cannot develop it fully, we believe that a theistic alternative is worth considering. In theism, God is given definition; God is declared to be good, for example. In other words, theists are willing to risk saying something meaningful about God. It is true that denying all concepts of God will guarantee that there could be no internal conflicts in what is said about God. But that victory is purchased at the price of saying nothing about God and leaving the word *God* with no shape at all.

Charles Hartshorne delights to accuse traditional theists of paying God a dubious compliment when they call God omnipotent. His point is that important negative side effects tag along when we compliment God in this way. These consequences, in Hartshorne's view, are unnecessary baggage: they entail that God cannot relate to the world as a person and that God becomes responsible for the existence of evil. While we do not concede Hartshorne's point about theism, the point we are making about pantheism is roughly the same: to go to the pantheists' extreme in defending God's infinity entails certain conceptual consequences. These consequences are rationally costly. The pantheist would be better off to modify his thirst for complimenting God and to avoid the negative baggage that it entails. Modifying in the direction of theism will at several points ease the conceptual tension pantheists must suffer because of their extravagant claims about God.

It is instructive that theists do carefully modify crude concepts of God in order to avoid conceptual tangles and to improve their performance against the tests of consistency and coherence. For example, though Hartshorne thinks theists ascribe omnipotence to God too hastily, in fact theists historically have been careful to affirm that omnipotence does not mean God has the power to do the logically or morally impossible act. God cannot create square circles because these geometric figures have logically conflicting attributes: they are four-cornered, no-cornered figures.

We must pause to ask whether ascribing a concept to God really limits him. Does it really make God less than infinite if we say, for example, that he is good and not evil? While in one sense this "definitizes" God (or "de-fines" him), in another sense this description actually becomes the necessary precondition for meaningfully affirming God's infinity. Only when God has been described as good does it help to add the qualifier *infinite*. If we know what *good* means and then say that God is maximally good, we can meaningfully (though nowhere near fully) grasp what is being affirmed. But if God is infinite without being good, what do we have? Infinity times zero is still zero. Or worse, if God is both good and evil, and infinitely so, we are in even deeper metaphysical water.

Theists are not afraid to predicate such concepts to God and, additionally, to say that they apply infinitely. But this ascription of concepts does not limit God's goodness at all. Ironically, predicating concepts to God does not limit him at all; it is the only way to guarantee that he is not limited in those attributes he does possess. As Saint Augustine says, "Neither do we lessen [God's] power when we say He cannot die or be deceived. This is the kind of inability which, if removed, would make God less powerful than He is. . . . It is precisely because He is omnipotent that for Him some things are impossible."[11]

It appears that pantheists need to learn this lesson and moderate their world view if it is to score well on the world view tests. If pantheists insist on paying God absolute but conflicting compliments, they will find their world view mired in a mass of logical tangles, and their philosophy will fail to achieve consistency and coherence.

The Concept of Being

We now turn to the examination of certain specific qualities or attributes that pantheists often refuse to predicate of God. One important philosophical concept is 'being.' To have being, to be, is to exist. Pantheism often seeks to avoid using the word *being* to refer both to God and to the world. Using *being* both of the infinite God and of the finite world or persons and objects in it drags God down and puts him in the same category with those finite objects. This is certainly unworthy of the Infinite, and so it is to be avoided at all costs.

The division between God and the world can go in two directions. Perhaps the obvious pattern would be to think that God possesses being while the world does not. Certain Hindu thinkers tend to conceive reality in these terms. God is the infinitely existing one, but in our finite individuality we are nonexistent in the ultimate point of view. Plotinus, however, thought in the opposite way. He ascribed being to the world, but then was forced to deny it of the One. Thus the One is beyond being; being must not be predicated of the One.

But the end result of these two moves is identical. If a concept applies to something or someone in this realm of existence, it cannot apply to God. And the opposite, too, is true; anything that is true of God cannot be true of things in this world. Ironically, the net effect of this is to place God entirely beyond this world, a very unpantheistic

11. Saint Augustine, *City of God* (Garden City, N. Y.: Doubleday, Image Books, 1958), 5.10.

thing to do. God and the world are so different that the same words, *having being* or *existing*, cannot describe both.

However, this move may be based on an unwarranted presupposition. It sometimes is assumed that words have singular meanings. No flex is permitted in definitions. For instance, given this assumption, if *existence* means "existing without limits" and if we say that we exist, then we are calling ourselves infinite. Since we are finite, this is obviously unacceptable. If the word *existence* applies to God, it cannot apply to us. If God exists, then we cannot. This reasoning virtually forces the pantheist to give the things of this world a nonreal status.

This illustration reveals the unwarranted premise. The assumption is the pantheist's understanding of the way the term *being* works. Some pantheists, it appears, assume that *being* must mean exactly the same thing everywhere and always, no matter how it is applied. Stated more technically, pantheists assume that *being* must apply to all objects univocally. Assuming that a word applies to all objects univocally involves presupposing that it has but one proper meaning. If we say words function univocally, we are saying that they must mean identically the same thing in all contexts. Instead of thinking of *being* as a word that properly could describe or denote existents of different kinds, those who assume a univocal predication of *being* insist that every existing thing must have the same sort of existence.

A similar difficulty is especially evident in the ancient Greek philosopher Parmenides. In his famous argument for monism (that is, for the absolute unity of being), he argued that things cannot differ in what they have in common, namely, their being. Their being, the fact of their existence, is precisely what all beings share. But neither can things differ in their nonbeing, for nonbeing is nothingness and to differ in nothing is not to differ at all. Since beings differ neither in being nor in nonbeing, they do not differ. Because he assumed that *being* had to be predicated of all existing things univocally, Parmenides concluded that two different beings could not exist. Only one being exists, and therefore monism is true.

This univocal view of our use of words has several problems. First, in assuming a univocal view of being and not allowing for any differences in kinds of existing things, Parmenides has allowed his assumptions to determine his monistic conclusion. By assuming a univocal view of being, therefore, Parmenides becomes entangled in question begging. By assuming that *being* must mean everywhere the same thing without qualification, he eliminates as nonbeing or nonexisting anything other than his one being. His unsupported premise (a univocal view of being) dictates his conclusion (monism).

Second, Parmenides' unsupported assumption (that *being* must always be used univocally) ignores an option that theists have long defended. One theistic alternative posits an *analogous* application of words like *being*. On this option, in the context of metaphysics, *being* means the quality of actually existing. However, the state of affairs denoted by *being* can be predicated analogously of different kinds of existing things. It can be predicated of independent, eternal beings as well as of dependent, temporal beings. Both God and human persons can be said to exist without thereby suggesting that we humans possess the qualities of deity or that we are deity. God, we may say, exists independently, while we exist dependently. Parmenides entirely ignores this option in his argument for monism.

Other pantheists may be less blatant in their assumptions about the specific category called 'being.' Oriental pantheists, for example, do not work with the categories common to Greek philosophers. Nevertheless, the tendency of pantheists to avoid the ascription of the same quality both to God and to individual human beings reveals that the analogical way of predicating qualities has not been considered as a viable option.

The analogical use of *being* can resolve the conceptual difficulties into which the univocal use drives us. If *being* is predicated of or ascribed to its object univocally, then either only God possesses being (as many pantheists say) or only the world does (as Plotinus says), but never both. In the former case, we are left wondering what metaphysical status to ascribe to the world. (This problem will be raised systematically later in our discussion.) In the latter case, we are left in doubt as to how to understand God. He is all that exists in one sense, yet in another sense that is important to the pantheist, he does not possess existence at all. Is this coherent? It appears that the dilemma could be resolved more adequately if the unwarranted assumption of a univocal view of being were dropped in favor of an analogical view.

This point does not prove analogy, to be sure. It only offers it as an optional way of thinking. Yet pantheists should consider whether this option might reduce the degree of conceptual tension involved in assuming univocity. The pantheist may in the long run wish to stand by something like this univocal concept of predication. But she should argue for the assumption and against the analogical concept rather than merely assuming her view. And she should only accept it with the conscious recognition of the conceptual penalties that come attached to it.

With respect to our broader theme, an analogical use of *being* has another advantage. If univocity is presumed, then ascribing the same concept to two beings either finitizes God or infinitizes the objects of the world. Neither of these alternatives is attractive either to the pantheist or to the theist. But if concepts can be applied analogically, then we can avoid the problem of saying that either God or the world has no being. Describing God as having 'being' need not limit his infinity because he need not exist in the way that objects in the world do. Why, without assuming univocity of *being*, would saying "God has being" or "God exists" be a metaphysical insult that reduces God to finitude? This is one instance of our general question about the advisability of assuming that any description of God involves finitizing God. Ironically, the unwillingness to predicate attributes of God limits God even when it is done in hopes of protecting the absolute independence of the divine.

The Deity and Personality of God

The word *pantheism*, because it contains the word *theos* (God), implies to those thinking theistically that the All is divine and personal. But pantheists do not want the attributes of deity and personality ascribed to the All, for they argue that any attribution of concepts limits God. To say that God is divine is to imply that God is not mundane; to say he is personal is to suggest that he is not impersonal. This divides the All into parts, the divine and the mundane, the personal and the impersonal. It limits God to a determinate character. It defines God and this amounts to finitizing him. If he is described by concepts, then he is "this, not that." Instead, say pantheists, he is "not this, not that" (*neti neti*).

This move is nobly motivated. Pantheists want to preserve the supremacy and absoluteness of God. And initially, it appears that saying God is "this, not that" does subject the Ultimate to limitation. But the pantheists' approach entails certain consequences, and these must be examined to see if the philosophical gain (the preservation of a sense of God's absoluteness) is worth the baggage it brings along. While it is a fine compliment to say God is not captured in merely human categories, the results are less attractive: saying that God is neither divine nor mundane, neither personal nor impersonal, makes God indistinguishable from an impersonal, naturalistic cosmos. This is why some theists have concluded that pantheism is metaphysically indistinguishable from atheism. H. P. Owen says, "If 'God' . . . is identical with the Universe . . . it is merely another name for the Universe. It is therefore bereft of any distinctive meaning; so pantheism is equivalent to atheism."[12]

Some pantheists, notably Zennists, can almost as appropriately be called atheists. They do not choose to use *God*. If pantheists do say

12. H. P. Owen, *Concepts of Deity* (New York: Herder and Herder, 1971), pp. 69, 70.

that All is God, they gain some religious appeal. The use of *God* conjures up images of a personal, divine being whom we can worship. But this is a false hope for anyone who conceives reality pantheistically. The pantheistic metaphysic cannot allow for such a being. *God* inevitably carries conceptual connotations. But within a pantheistic world view, because of the inapplicability of concepts, the meaning content involved in using *God* to describe the All must be minimal even if it has some emotional or rhetorical appeal. Even when the pantheist initially opts for religious symbols, therefore, these symbols are, in the final analysis, inappropriately used. They imply more than pantheism can deliver.

The point here is not that pantheism is different from theism and inadequate on that account alone. That clearly presupposes theism and amounts to circular reasoning. The point is to emphasize the implication of denying concepts of God. If God is really indescribable, it is entirely inappropriate for pantheists then to smuggle in a word like *God* and to use it for religious purposes. The word depends on theism for its meaning; placing it in a pantheistic context strips it of that meaning.

Zennists realize the implications of denying concepts of Reality, and they accept the consequences. Others, including many New Agers, do not. They want the wonder and mystery of the absolute One beyond all description as well as a God with determinate religious qualities. We claim only that the indescribable One and the describable God cannot both be ultimate. Either Reality is absolute and indescribable or God is personal, divine, and worthy of religious devotion. But pantheists cannot have it both ways.

In sum, the thrust for unity that animates pantheism leads its advocates to deny concepts of the ultimate Reality. But many people want a God with whom to relate. These two facts put certain pressures on the pantheists' world view. At least initially, many pantheists want to describe the All as God. But if the All is really one, then words like *personal* and *divine* are not appropriate. Thus, pantheism, especially in its New Age variety, entices us by offering divinity when it calls everything, including us, divine. But if it is consistent to its basic principles, it must ultimately dash our hopes by reducing everything, again including us, to the impersonal stuff of the cosmos.

Denying deity and personhood of the All has other important implications for pantheism. One of these touches its concept of creation. In most forms of pantheism, creation flows from the Ultimate by necessity. In contrast, theistic views conceive creation as deriving from God's free decision. If the Ultimate is not a personal God, free actions by the Ultimate are impossible. Impersonal things and forces do not act freely. If God is beyond personhood, then creation cannot be a free act.

Now there may be nothing inherently incoherent with viewing creation as necessary. But it is important to note our theme again: the pantheist tries to compliment God by denying any limiting and/or finitizing concepts to God. This in turn brings negative consequences that actually have the opposite effect. Instead of absolutizing God, pantheists unintentionally limit God. If God creates necessarily, then God *must* create. If creation is necessary, then God cannot not create. Ironically, therefore, in trying to protect the infinity of God by refusing to ascribe personhood to him, pantheism makes God subject to necessity. The unwillingness to define God does not liberate him from limits; instead it actually entraps him, making him (or it) a slave of his (or its) own nature. Again, the problem is not that this facet of pantheism differs from theism, but that conceptual moves taken to achieve the announced goal of liberating God from concepts have the opposite effect of enslaving God.

Denying deity and personhood of the All has another important consequence for pantheists. If denying concepts of God means viewing creation as necessary, then this must affect our understanding of human life. If creation is necessary, our lives do not result from a purposive act of a creator. No goal or end underlies human existence. We are not here for a reason (e.g., to serve God and to love our fellow human beings). We are just here. Our lives, it seems, would be devoid of ultimate meaning.

It might appear that this comment presupposes theism. In theism, the lives of individuals result from a God who has some end in view when he creates. Theists believe God creates for a purpose so that our lives are not meaningless bits of snowy static on the television screen of the cosmic process. However, we do not want to assume theistic claims of this sort in making our observations. We simply point out that to the degree a person experiences his life as possessing some nonarbitrary significance beyond itself, pantheism as a world view is incompatible with and cannot account for that experience. The implications of pantheism must be that my life just is—it "just is" in about the same way that a caterpillar's life "just is."

Zen Buddhism, of course, has explicitly affirmed this very thesis. Zennists believe that toil, pain, and trouble arise from our false impressions that our lives are supposed to mean something. Instead of seeking some significance to our lives to quench this thirst for existential meaning, we should instead recognize the thirst as a literally neurotic (i.e., out of touch with reality) desire for ego preservation. The Zennist wants us to explode this desire for ego preservation by experiencing *satori* (enlightenment), where the myth of the persisting substantial existence of my ego is exposed.

In other words, Zennists essentially agree with the atheistic existentialists like Jean-Paul Sartre, who said that ultimately our lives count for nothing: "It amounts to the same thing whether one gets drunk alone or is a leader of nations."[13] The claim of the Zennist, "What is, just is," presumably applies to the drunk, to the leader, to Miss America, and to the victims of the Holocaust. We argue simply that pantheism has no place for a life of significance and meaning. We are not here trying to prove that life does have such meaning (although we believe, based on a theistic world view, that this is the case). Rather, a pantheist or New Ager cannot claim that the Ultimate is beyond all concepts and then pretend that she can also consistently believe in a personal God who gives religious meaning to her life.

The point we have been pressing in this section has nothing to do with the notion that pantheism is wrong merely because it differs from theism. We mean to point out instead the inconsistency within the pantheist's world view if he claims both that the Ultimate is beyond concepts and that a personal God is available to us. Pantheism does not represent a viable option for those whose deepest sentiments convince them that God is a person to be loved, in whose life we share, and with whom we may communicate and commune. To whatever extent the practice of religion depends on these activities, pantheism cannot comprehensively incorporate the fundamental yearnings of the human soul for a God in whom to trust and with whom to share our lives. It is inconsistent for pantheism to assert that the Ultimate is entirely beyond concepts and then to speak as though his world view has a conceptual place for communion with a personal God.

In this vein, Hackett responds to Shankara's discussion of Nirguna and Saguna Brahman by finally rejecting the Hindu's attempt "to preserve the best of both worlds by conjoining a qualified Brahman, who is personal and creative, with an unqualified Brahman that, in the final analysis, is neither. In any such interpretive juggling, for me at least, the mask of personalism would simply have to go, with the shocking discovery that underneath that mask there had never been any real face at all."[14] What Hackett says about Shankara applies equally to New Agers who combine claims of the absolute indescribability of God with affirmations of personal communion with God.

Consistency and coherence operate as internal tests. They function negatively, eliminating world views that do not succeed in meeting their own standards. Our general claim has been that many forms of pantheism do suffer from conceptual tangles that prevent it from faring well against these tests. In many cases, the desire to preserve the

13. Jean-Paul Sartre, *Being and Nothingness: An Essay on Phenomenological Ontology*, trans. Hazel E. Barnes (New York: Philosophical Library, 1956), p. 627.

14. Hackett, *Oriental Philosophy*, p. 175.

unity and independence of God expresses itself as an overly active tendency to insist that God cannot be described by rational concepts and that God rises above all conceptual opposites. While this is rooted in noble motivation, its consequences are too costly. It leads to a concept of God that is vacuous and meaningless. It also leads to a God who in all his actions is subject to necessity.

Some pantheists have willingly accepted these implications. But most resist them, as evidenced by the tendency to speak of God in personal terms. Even if the great philosophical pantheists more successfully evade it, this inconsistency is especially common in New Age circles. In a word, precisely in the attempt to free God of all conceptual limitation, pantheism tends to make conceptual moves that, in the final analysis, limit God. Robert Flint said it well: "under pretence of exalting [God] above all categories of thought and existence [pantheism] reduces Him to the level of dead things, of necessary processes, of abstract ideas, or even to the still lower level of the unknowable and non-existent."[15]

Our Experience of the World

In addition to passing the conceptually oriented tests, pantheism's metaphysical system must pass the experience-oriented tests by incorporating the vast amount of human experience of the world. Apparently, everyday experience convinces most human persons of their own independent existence. Most persons also believe that the world and other persons exist as entities separate from themselves. Although philosophers debate the perennial question of how we know other minds exist, it is still obvious that most people believe they do. Our inclination, though we cannot elaborate it here, is to concur that we do know others exist. Any epistemology that entails that we cannot know the reality of other persons thereby reveals its own inadequacy. In any case, every world view must deal with our experience of others in some way if it is to meet minimal standards of comprehensiveness and congruity.

It is important to note that our experiences of other persons and of the world are classes of experience, not isolated or individual experiences. If John Jones believes that he was knighted by King Arthur at the mall yesterday, we should be able to fit that experience into our total world view. Most of us would likely interpret John's experience as a delusion. In general, we know that some people suffer from severe psychological problems and do experience delusions. In John's case, we judge his claims about the alleged knighting as illegitimate

15. Robert Flint, *Anti-Theistic Theories* (London: William Blackwood and Sons, 1899), p. 387.

based on the incoherence between the details of his claims and all the other things we experience. One way we identify dreams for what they are is by noting that the events in them do not make enough connections with other events in our lives. The total sweep of our experience becomes a standard against which questionable individual experiences are judged.

But the human experience of self, others, and the world is not an individual experience or an isolated delusion. It is not like the single experience of being knighted at the mall. It involves the whole complex web of experiences that remains recognizably consistent from day to day. Our experience of the world is the whole class of experiences had every day by everyone. It is imperative, therefore, that any reasonable world view incorporate this macroscopic web of experience into its framework of interpretation.

But it is precisely at this point that pantheism feels great tension, for it calls into question not individual experiences but the whole range of sensuous experience that we depend on each day. Our basic thesis here is that pantheism cannot adequately handle that vast wealth of human experience about the real existence of self, others, and the world. Pantheism must, by definition, say that our existence as separate egos is ultimately unreal. To acknowledge this range of experience, a pantheist would have to admit the reality of individual persons who experience the world through their senses. But to the extent a pantheist allows for the reality of individual existents, he moderates his view toward theism. To remain a pantheist, he cannot permit individual egos as such to be real.

The well-known Hindu notion of *maya* is one attempt to explain the experience of separate identity. It treats the whole class of experiences of ourselves and others much as most of us would treat John's belief about his experience with King Arthur. That is to say, *maya* essentially says our experience of the world is delusory. In all fairness, we must hasten to add that the word *maya* has many shades of meaning. Sarvepali Radhakrishnan says that *maya* cannot be explained; its inexplicability indicates a "gap in our knowledge."[16] Scholars have traced its uses without arriving at a consensus on a standard meaning.

Having acknowledged Radhakrishnan's objection, we must add that this sort of claim strikes us as an attempt to avoid an essential interpretive problem. It seems like an evasion of a dilemma so fundamentally insoluble as to suggest major structural flaws in the system. Shankara and Radhakrishnan claim that *maya* does not eliminate the individual in the world. They tell us emphatically that our experience

16. Sarvepali Radhakrishnan, *The Vedanta According to Samkara and Ramanuja* (London: Allen and Unwin, 1928), p. 135.

of separate existence is not, like the horns on a toad, absolutely nothing. *Maya* is not incompatible with existence that is real from the sensuous point of view. But then they turn around and tell us that this everyday point of view is mistaken, for it is like confusing a coiled rope and a snake.

This sort of explanation initially deflects the present criticism. Pantheists object forcefully to the claim that their world view reduces our experience as separate egos to illusion. But in supporting the objection, pantheists often resort to "interpretive juggling," to use Hackett's phrase, that takes with the left hand what is given with the right. We do not want to distort the intricacies of philosophical explanation concerning *maya* that accompany the resistance to the criticisms we have been raising. At the same time, we cannot avoid the impression that the intricacies have the effect not of illuminating the dark but of muddying the waters. Despite their protests, it appears that pantheists do not so much explain our existence as explain it away. The misshapen character of typical pantheistic explanations raises doubts as to the congruity, the smoothness of fit, between pantheism and the vast range of our experience of individual personhood.

Calling our explanation of self, others, and the world an illusion raises another problem: How did this pervasive mistake arise? How did it come about that virtually every human being experiences himself, the world, and their interaction wrongly? And note that this pervasive alleged illusion involves not a single experience or even set of experiences embedded in an essentially correct structure or mode of experience. This widespread error concerns the very structure of all possible sensuous experience itself.

This illustration suggests the sweeping nature of this claim. The claim is neither that Susan Thompson mistakes blue for violet in dim light, nor even that she is entirely colorblind in a colorful world enjoyed by many correctly sighted people. The pantheist's assertion is like claiming that color is perceived by all and integrated by all with maximal congruence into the total experience of life, but still essentially irrelevant to reality. We have a system of experience so complete and congruent that many see color "correctly" while others are identifiably colorblind according to accepted standards. Nevertheless, the whole mode of experience that includes color is essentially and fundamentally misleading.

This is an extravagant claim. It burdens the claimant with two tasks: the one who makes it not only must show the different sort of truth that serves as the standard by which the whole color mode of experience is judged misleading, but also must give some explanation as to why most of us miss all truth all the time and why all of us miss all the truth most of the time. With regard to the first, there must be very powerful reasons to justify overturning not just isolated experiences but the whole web of our empirical experience. Pantheism claims that mystical experience provides this warrant. We will examine this assertion in chapter 8. The second question is our focus here. Why are we so often wrong?

Several moves are open to the pantheist who senses this problem. One might argue that our minds give rise to the illusion. Zen Buddhists who want to deny the persisting ego take this avenue. They argue that our suffering arises from a craving for all sorts of impermanent objects. One of the most seductive of these objects is the enduring ego. The ego is a sort of castle into which one retreats in hopes of protecting and making permanent one's own existence. Ultimately, through centuries of convention, thinking of ourselves as isolated egos petrifies and becomes the "normal" way of experiencing our existence.

As attractive as this explanation sounds, one wonders how the process begins. On the one hand, the minds that supposedly initiate this process of calcification are themselves part of the illusion. As Hackett points out, "there is, for such an outlook, no way to explain how such an illusory realm could arise, either as an objective order apprehended by finite, conscious minds, or as a series of successive transformations within those minds. Individual minds are, by hypothesis, themselves aspects of the illusion and can therefore provide no basis for explaining it."[17] If the mind is part of and as such a result of the illusion, it cannot predate the illusion and thus it cannot serve as an explanation for it.

On the other hand, if our thoughts are not illusory thoughts of an illusory mind, presumably they are God's thoughts. If, as we experience mystical enlightenment, our knowing becomes God's knowing, then we become God thinking. But this, too, creates difficulties. C. S. Lewis raised objections to the notion that our thinking is really God thinking precisely because we are sometimes wrong. In his usual incisive way, he comments,

> The traditional doctrine that I am a creature to whom God has given reason but who is distinct from God seems to me much more philosophical than the theory that what appears to be my thinking is only God's thinking through me. On the latter view it is very difficult to explain what happens when I think correctly but reach a false conclusion because I have been misinformed about facts. Why God—who presumably knows the real facts—should be at the pains to think one of His perfectly rational thoughts through a mind in which it is bound to produce error, I do not understand. Nor indeed do I understand why, if

17. Hackett, *Oriental Philosophy*, p. 113.

all "my" valid thinking is really God's, He should either Himself mistake it for mine or cause me to mistake it for mine. It seems much more likely that human thought is not God's but God-kindled.[18]

If our individual minds exist as such (that is, as individual minds) but pantheism is true, they must be God thinking. In this case, we are at a loss for an explanation of our many errors in thought. If our minds don't exist as such, how can they adequately explain the origin of the ego illusion?

Perhaps the better approach might be to admit that this question is unanswerable. With candor, Radhakrishnan quotes another author: "How do we manage to deceive ourselves into seeing a transformation and a plurality, where in reality Brahman alone is? On this question our authors give no information." Radhakrishnan then comments, "They give us no information, simply because 'no information' is possible."[19] This is an appeal to mystery in the worst sense of that term. It is a classic case of using mystery as a stopgap for an irresolvable problem created by the very structure of a thought system. Such ad hoc appeals to mystery are clues that a world view has serious structural flaws.

To some, the appeal to mystery may be attractive. After all, the move does depend on a half-truth. Every world view, no doubt, comes upon issues that resist rational understanding. It is pointless to deny mystery entirely. None of us is remotely close to omniscience. But appeals to mystery that smell more like evasions of rational responsibility are less tolerable. This, of course, is not a judgment with which everyone would concur, but it seems worth noting that the pantheists' appeal to mystery on this point is especially damaging. If pantheists cannot say any more than "It's a mystery" when justifying their exclusion of a whole range of experiences from consideration, we can only respond that this appears to be an ad hoc maneuver. If a world view is better that smoothly incorporates and fruitfully illuminates large areas of our experience, pantheism is not, on this point, better. Pantheism does not explain the vast reaches of our experience. It explains them away.

Pantheism's Self-Defeating Character

Pantheism's analysis of our individual experience of the world brings up a final point: pantheism is unaffirmable and self-defeating. The principle of self-defeat comes into play whenever a statement does something that it affirms cannot be done. Though it can be

18. C. S. Lewis, *Miracles* (New York: Macmillan, 1947), p. 29.
19. Radhakrishnan, *Vedanta*, p. 144.

uttered or said, such a statement cannot be affirmed meaningfully because of its self-destructive character. The statement is philosophically suspect, for it tries to do something that it says cannot be done. If the sentence were meaningful, it would destroy itself. Therefore, it is unaffirmable.

A well-known example of this problem is found in our own century. Philosophers known as logical positivists developed what they called the Verification Principle. This axiom of positivist thinking stated that only two kinds of statements could count as meaningful: definitions and facts, with facts defined as statements that are empirically verifiable. On this criterion, logical positivism considered statements about theological, ethical, or esthetic realities meaningless because they were neither definitional nor factually verifiable. But here is the catch: the Verification Principle is self-defeating for it is neither a definition nor a fact. If the Verification Principle were somehow correct, it would be meaningless on its own criterion. The historic collapse of the positivists' agenda shows the power of this principle of self-defeat.

This principle makes it difficult to affirm pantheism meaningfully. A pantheist usually claims that he was once blind, lost in ignorance due to the dominance of the logical, empirical view of things. But now he has regained his sight, the ability to see the truth that only God exists and that the finite perspective of sensuous observation is essentially misleading. He is saying, in effect, "I came to realize that I don't exist. I came to see that I was always God." This raises an appropriate question: Who is talking? What does *I* refer to in these sentences?

Several possibilities confront us. Perhaps *I* in this statement refers to a finite individual. The pantheist is speaking from a limited perspective as an individual person. But in this case, his statement is self-defeating. He is saying, "I am telling you that I don't exist." What sense can we make of that? If someone exists to tell us this, the statement must be false. If the statement is true, there could be no speaker to utter it. If *I* means a finite individual, then the pantheist's affirmation declares that he does not exist as such, and in this way he pulls that rug out from under his statement.

To evade this glaring problem, he could claim that *I* in this statement is God. He is speaking from the ultimate point of view. But although this alternative solves the problem of self-defeat, it raises two more pressing questions. First, why is he trying to express this to me? Presumably, I do not exist either. But he is treating me as a real entity by recognizing my presence and responding to my questions. Second, how is it that the infinite mind of God was once deceived and has now come to see the truth? This implies both that God's understanding was once wrong and that it changes through time. If *I* denotes the ultimate being God, then the pantheists' statement implies that God is a limited being, not infinite, as pantheists claim.

The rational pressure these problems create puts stress on pantheism's view of the reality of the finite individual's perspective. For example, Shankara says that the lower perspective of the sensuous realm is true. In that perspective, my individual existence is real and God is personal. But from the higher perspective, my individual existence is not real, and God is beyond personhood. Both viewpoints, he says, are true. Yet from the higher perspective, the lower point of view confuses a coiled rope with a snake. In other words, we assume, the lower perspective is not really true. Yet here is the pantheist, writing as a finite individual to convince us in our finite perspectives that finite egos are part of that coiled-rope point of view.

So which is it? Do pantheists speak from the finite, individual perspective of empirical egos or not? If they do, it appears that the statements they utter concerning the unreality of their own finite existence self-destruct. If they do not and if they claim instead to speak from God's ultimate perspective, it seems that they are introducing into God hefty doses of fallibility and mutability. Shankara paints himself into a corner. Mutism, the refusal to say anything, would be better. But that, too, has problems, as we shall see in chapter 8. In a word, the noble desire to compliment God as the All negates the very reality of the one who compliments. God therefore cannot get complimented at all. This dilemma, it appears, is a powerful challenge to the coherence of the pantheistic philosophy.

Personal existence may have some reality in modified forms of pantheism. As our descriptive survey revealed, not all pantheists call the world absolute nothingness. They have various means for ascribing some sort of limited reality to individual persons. One would run roughshod over the pantheists' actual beliefs by considering only the extreme illusionist view of the world. But we can state the objection in another way to incorporate this fact: to the degree that the perspective of the experiencing/thinking person *as an individual* is claimed to be part of an illusion, pantheism is self-defeating. If the finite point of view is admitted, then the self-defeat is mitigated. However, to the degree that the pantheist admits the reality of the individual experiencing/thinking person he abandons his fundamental pantheistic premises and moderates in a theistic direction.

As a response, a pantheist might try to maintain his own existence just long enough to assert that he does not exist. But if he does this, we can only think that it is somehow ad hoc and unfair to exempt that one statement from the broader premises of his philosophy. This reminds us of the psychological determinists, who exempt their own rational choices that lead them to accept their deterministic theory from the general principles of that theory. The ad hoc nature of these self-licensed exceptions to the rule reveals basic conceptual flaws that, in our view, can be corrected only by major structural changes. In pantheism's case, this means the affirmation of the real existence of the person who affirms a world view. It means a modification in the direction of theism.

Conclusion

Our discussion of pantheistic metaphysics has revolved around the pantheists' persistent resistance to the predication of concepts to God. Pantheists have claimed that using concepts to describe God both divides what is unified and limits what is infinite. Concepts are always defined in terms of opposites. We know black because it is the opposite of white and good because it is the opposite of evil. So using concepts for description always divides unity and entails that what is so described is limited to only one of the two concepts. Therefore, if God is personal, then he is not impersonal, and there is something that he is not.

We have argued that this fundamental pantheistic urge arises from noble motives. But it also entails certain consequences that cannot be ignored. Some of these create problems internally in that they run up against the tests of consistency and coherence. If we cannot describe God at all, then the word *God* loses any intelligible meaning. If we cannot describe God as personal, then creation is necessary, and he *must* create.

Other consequences concern external problems in that they run into the criteria of comprehensiveness and congruence. If God alone exists, how do we explain the vast wealth of experience had by every person alive that apparently leads us to believe that selves, others, and the real world actually exist? And if God alone exists, how could we ever affirm his existence from our individual, presumably nonreal point of view? It is our judgment that these rational tensions make pantheistic metaphysics, despite its positive contributions and noble motivations, a poor choice if we are seeking the world view that best explains the total experience of our lives.

The Knowledge of Mystical Consciousness

*Intuitive perception comes through the right brain. . . . You . . .
will understand that you already know everything there is to
know.—Shirley MacLaine*
*[T]he occult nature of the ineffable alleged revelations of mystical
contemplation prevents their being safely included in the denotation of "truth."—F. R. Tennant*

Though the philosophical literature on the pantheistic world view
is not as extensive, technical discussions of mysticism abound.
Because there is a great deal of interest in the significance of mystical
experience, the epistemology typically used by New Age pantheists
has been subjected to a great deal of analysis and interpretation.
Though Spinoza the rationalist is something of an exception, each of
the other pantheists depends on mysticism in an important way. And
certainly the major manifestations of New Age thinking that com-
mand attention today find their epistemological basis in intuitive,
right-brain, mystical experience. We turn, therefore, to an analysis of
this form of epistemology.

Mystical and Sensuous Modes of Experience

Our evaluation of mystical epistemologies must begin with one
central fact. Most mysticisms revolve around a crucial idea: we can

159

have an experience of union that somehow lifts us above ordinary, everyday, logical, sensuous experience. This allegedly higher and truer experience we call mysticism.

Mystical pantheists either state explicitly or imply that knowledge based on this higher experience is superior to empirical knowledge. The higher intuition puts us in direct contact with the Ultimate instead of giving only second-hand knowledge. It avoids the problems of error and uncertainty that plague knowledge mediated by the senses or logic. For reasons like these, mystics prize the intuitive experience as genuinely revealing what is real and discount ordinary experience when it conflicts with the intuitive.

It is important to see why such an experience would be important to pantheism. People of widely divergent cultures and religions agree that sensuous experience presents the world as separate from and independent of the individual ego. Our senses reveal to our consciousness many persons and objects that appear ontologically distinct from us. Were we to accept the ordinary perspective as finally correct, we would be led to acknowledge the multiplicity of objects in a separate world. But pantheism, even when it gives some limited or secondary reality to the world of objects, ultimately must deny its independent existence. Therefore, if we were to accept the ordinary point of view as a genuine revealer of what exists, we would be led to conclude that pantheism is false.

For this reason, ordinary sensuous experience and the metaphysic of pantheism innately stand at odds with one another. To put it another way, an empiricist would never be a pantheist. Pantheists can be rationalists like Spinoza. The rational thrust for a unity of ideas does often lead to a depreciation or limitation of the multiplicity revealed in sensuous knowledge. Though there is no logical necessity here, some rationalists not surprisingly do tend toward a pantheistic metaphysic.

We cannot take time to offer a full response to rationalistic epistemology. That has been done in other places.[1] Perhaps it will be enough here to mention that most modern analysts find the rational hope for certainty in knowledge to be unfulfilled. Among other things, the fact that many rationalists, each claiming certainty, have so strikingly contradicted each other suggests strongly that the rational method cannot guarantee absolute knowledge. In any case, pantheists are most often mystics, and so we must concentrate our analysis here.

1. See Stuart C. Hackett, *The Resurrection of Theism* (Chicago: Moody, 1957); Norman L. Geisler, *Christian Apologetics* (Grand Rapids: Baker, 1976), pp. 29–46; for a fuller discussion of the issues raised in this chapter see David K. Clark, *The Relation of Tradition to Experience in Mysticism* (Ann Arbor: University Microfilms, 1982), pp. 35–212.

The mystics' even stronger thrust for unity leads them naturally to pantheism. Ordinary sensuous experience, whether interpreted in naive or in sophisticated form, will not accord with pantheism. Pantheists therefore are driven by an inner logic to posit a form of experience that avoids the apparent implications of sensuous experience, namely, that the world of external objects really exists as it appears to. Thus, they tend to ground their metaphysic on a mode of knowledge that is thought to be somehow superior to empirical knowing.

In order to make this procedure work, however, it is necessary to distinguish this superior knowledge from the ordinary. Pantheists must identify the unique characteristics of the higher knowledge if they are to appeal to it as a reason for rejecting the metaphysical implications that sensuous experience seems to thrust on people of widely differing beliefs. Here the common tenets we identified in chapter 6 perform their logical duty. The higher intuitive knowledge is nonsensuous, direct, supralogical, self-certifying, supralinguistic, and ineffable. It is critical to see that pantheistic epistemologies call on these unique qualities to defend two things: the uniqueness and the superiority of the higher, mystical form of knowing.

Any claim that mystical experience possesses these two qualities, uniqueness and superiority, raises two questions: (1) Can we show that there is a form of experience and knowledge that possesses these characteristics so as to be distinct from ordinary, sensuous experience and knowledge? Obviously, if the two levels of experience and knowledge are not distinguishable, then we should not accept the appeal to the allegedly higher level of knowledge in support of any world view. To reject sensuous knowledge in favor of a different, higher knowledge would be a serious mistake if there were no such different, higher knowledge.

Suppose that pantheists do show that there exists a mode of experience and knowledge distinct from the ordinary. This immediately raises the second question: (2) Were there a distinct form of experience and knowledge, would that experience provide good reason to abandon the sensuous experiences and empirical knowledge that lead us to believe in a real, independent world of objects? To look at it another way, suppose that the pantheists' experiences do possess unique characteristics, features that somehow show them to be different from those that cause most people to believe in a real, independent world. Would those unique characteristics give evidence that the pantheists' experiences are superior? Or would they prove only that those experiences are different?

We will discuss the second question first, granting for the moment that the two modes of experience and knowledge do have differing characteristics. When two forms of experience that lead to conflicting conclusions confront each other, the obvious question is, How do we know which to trust? Which mode of experience is genuine?

Suppose we have two fundamentally different forms of experience, Mode A and Mode B. If Mode A and the world view and epistemological rules it generates is taken as normative, then Mode B will fail the tests and be discounted. But equally, if Mode B and all its philosophical accouterments are taken as our standard, Mode A will be falsified. How will we know which experience to accept? If we accept Mode A because it passes Mode A's tests and reject Mode B because it fails Mode A's tests, we are obviously ensnared in circular reasoning. We know Mode A's tests to be valid because we already accept Mode A, but we cannot accept Mode A simply because it passes its own tests. The same problem surfaces if we turn the tables and take Mode B as normative.

This is exactly what happened with the logical positivists and their Verification Principle. The positivists rejected certain forms of knowledge that did not fit their rules. According to the Verification Principle, statements are meaningful only if they meet one of two qualifications: they are definitions (like "A husband is a married man") or they are based on sense experience. This principle entails that theological statements like "God is love" (along with ethical and esthetic statements) are meaningless. The Verification Principle turned out to be self-defeating because it is neither a definition nor empirically verifiable. It has therefore been consigned to the dustbin.[2]

For our purposes, this illustration emphasizes the inherent difficulty involved in simply positing one mode of experience and knowing at the expense of another. How did the positivists know that sense experiences and empirical knowledge, rather than some other mode of experience and knowing, are normative? What reasons could they give to support the sensuous over the intuitive, the suprasensuous, and the mystical? If they answer that sensuous experiences pass the Verification Principle, we will simply ask, How do you know the Verification Principle is an accurate measure of truth? If an empiricist answers that he knows the Verification Principle because his sense experiences corroborate it, he has argued in a circle. Of course, the positivists realized they could not say that. This is precisely why their movement ground to a halt.

So the fact remains: it is difficult to resolve the dilemma. If there are two fundamentally different forms of experience, it is difficult to justify accepting one entirely at the expense of the other. If there is an attempt at reasoning, circular reasoning often results. If there is no

2. Morris Weitz, "Introduction," in *Twentieth-Century Philosophy: The Analytic Tradition*, ed. Morris Weitz (New York: The Free Press, 1966), pp. 7–11.

attempt, the decision on which form of experience to take as normative is arbitrary.

Yet another difficulty with rejecting whole classes of experience is the sheer facticity of those other experiences. One could argue that a particular mystical experience (say, an alleged vision of Krishna) misled the Krishna devotee. But to assert that mystical experiences as a class must always mislead us is a very bold statement. Those who believe that only one kind of experience avoids error can assert baldly that another whole realm of experience breeds illusion; they cannot deny that people have the other kind of "illusory" experiences and that they have them frequently. The very persistence of the other experiences (whether "other" means for you the mystical or the empirical) must at least be acknowledged fairly.[3]

The arguments we just reviewed apply equally to the mystic who wants to discount sensuous experience because it pushes us to acknowledge the reality of the world of objects and persons. The unsupported assertion, "Sensuous experiences are illusion," can be uttered verbally. But whether it could ever be supported by reasons that any thinking person (let alone all thinking persons) might accept is quite another question. And if no reasons can be given, how are we to distinguish between claims like "I am one with God" and "I am Henry VIII"? Are not both of these statements unvarnished claims that, though utterable, are unsupportable?

On the other hand, to begin giving reasons for the authenticity of a mystical experience can be problematic. If a sensuous experience (say, sighting a rare bird) is in doubt, many reasons to accept the claimed experience at face value are possible. A corroborating photograph, a sighting by another person, or a tape of the bird's call could confirm the experience. But mystics claim their experiences certify themselves, so they generally resist offering external certification. They claim their experiences do not conform to rationality. To begin using logical procedures for confirmation seems inappropriate. Mystics often remain content with the sheer claim based directly and only on the firsthand experience. And that will not satisfy many who wish to live life based on rational reflection of its meaning and purpose.

In sum, it is arbitrary to discount one whole mode or type of experience simply because it differs from another whole class or kind of experience. This applies to the logical positivists when they summarily discount the theological, ethical, or mystical realms. But this could apply equally to the pantheists who reject sensuous experience on the basis of an allegedly "higher" mystical experience. And the mystical pantheist runs into an additional difficulty. How could any-

3. Asher Moore, "Mysticism and Philosophy," The Monist 59 (1976): 494.

one argue rationally for the allegedly "higher" experience when the pantheist describes this experience as beyond logic and language? If there were indeed two fundamentally different forms of experience, each pointing to different metaphysical conclusions, sorting out the genuine and the illusory would remain an intractably thorny process.

The Two-truth Theory

One alternative remains to handle this dilemma: the two-truth theory. This theory suggests that two independent realms of experience and thought both possess validity within their own spheres. According to the two-truth theory, the two realms of truth are fundamentally unrelated. These realms of truth are not two different positions within the same arena of experience and thought. Such would be the case with two competing scientific theories: For instance, the views that light is composed of waves and that it is made of particles oppose each other, but they are theories that operate within the same field of experience and thought, and neither is a complete model of the reality it represents. The advocates of these two theories can debate over the same sensuous evidence and appeal to the same kind of facts.

The two-truth theory implies a more fundamental distinction. The two realms of truth have no connection. In the two arenas of truth, what counts as a fact, what rules are used to deal with the facts, and the theories that are developed out of those facts are entirely unrelated. The ordinary way of viewing life from the sensuous perspective (and all the scientific ideas, theories, and debates that go along with it) comprises one whole network of truth. In addition, there exists the supraordinary mode of truth, complete with its forms of experience and thought. According to the two-truth theory, the two arenas of truth are unrelated, yet both are "true" within their own realms.

Many mystical pantheists, especially from the East, develop this theory in some form to explain the relation of everyday experiences to their supraordinary experiences. Shankara, for example, accepts the ascription of qualities or descriptive characteristics called *guna* to Brahman among those who want to worship a personal deity. This may be "true" from their perspective. Yet from his viewpoint, Shankara knows that Brahman actually cannot possess such qualities. Thus, from differing perspectives, from two "true" points of view, both Saguna Brahman (Qualified Brahman) and Nirguna Brahman (Unqualified Brahman) can be correct. There are "two truths" about Brahman.

But this answer does not really commend itself to us. Rationality impresses us with the need to see reality and truth in a unified way.

We all sense the need for a unity of truth so forcefully that the notion of two truths works only as a temporary, stopgap measure. In the final analysis, most mystics admit that one realm of truth is not really true after all. It is only true *from a certain perspective,* a perspective that is ultimately false. Despite their denigration of logic, even mystics come hard up against the unavoidable conclusion that truth must be unified—truth cannot contradict itself and still be true.

To show this historically with any breadth would be a tedious task. If we can follow just the example of Shankara, however, the point should be clear. Shankara acknowledges that Saguna Brahman and Nirguna Brahman are both in some sense acceptable concepts of the ultimate. Yet at one point he writes,

> The same highest Brahman constitutes . . . the real nature of the individual self, while its second nature, i.e. that aspect of it which depends on fictitious limiting conditions, is not its real nature. For as long as the individual self does not free itself from [ignorance] in the form of duality—which [ignorance] may be compared to the mistake of him who in the twilight mistakes a post for a man—and does not rise to the knowledge of the Self, whose nature is unchangeable, eternal Cognition—which expresses itself in the form 'I am Brahman'—so long it remains the individual soul.[4]

In other words, Brahman cannot, in the final analysis, be thought of as Saguna Brahman (Brahman in its "second nature" as defined by "fictitious limiting conditions," that is, by logical attributes). As long as people continue to think of Brahman in this way, they remain isolated in individual egos and will not reach release from the sorrow of reincarnation. Only when an individual frees "itself from [ignorance]," that is, from duality, can it rise "to the knowledge of the Self." Despite the two-truth concept and the initially generous view that you can conceive of Brahman either way you wish, in the final analysis there is only one correct view.

The result is the same where one form of truth and experience is finally taken as normative. Although initially the two-truth theory allows a greater openness to opposing points of view, that openness is temporary. The problems raised by the reduction of truth to one area of experience are not resolved by the two-truth theory. In the final analysis, when they are forced to get right down to the real issues, mystics admit that one mode of experience breeds illusion and the other truth. This brings us to consider again how we should decide which type of experience we should trust to reveal reality. At this

---

4. Shankara, *The Vedānta Sūtras of Bādārayaṇa with the Commentary by Sankara,* trans. George Thibaut, 2 parts (New York: Dover, 1962), 1.3.19.

point, the two-truth theory notwithstanding, the problem of circularity once again raises its head. The two-truth theory does not solve our problem; it only delays its appearance.

Immediacy of Experience

What we have said so far has granted the claim that there are two different modes of experience. Mystics generally want to make this claim, for it seems obvious that the everyday realm of experience will lead away from pantheistic conclusions. But what sorts of reasons might be given to support the claim that mystical experiences are really so fundamentally different? Surely no one would claim that every form of human experience should exhibit exactly similar characteristics. At the same time, it may be that all forms of human experience do display certain similarities even when the objects of experience are different. In fact, since every mystical pantheist is a human being (and this should imply great solidarity with other humans), it should not seem surprising that various forms of experience should display not only the differences rooted in various cultural backgrounds but also similarities grounded on common humanness.

Mystical pantheists could be content just to testify to the uniqueness of mystical experience without arguing for it. But they are not. They often point to immediacy of experience as evidence of the distinctive character of their experience. They claim that their experience involves a direct, unmediated awareness of the object of experience. As we have pointed out, many actually claim an ontological oneness with the object of experience.

In contrast, mystics say (or imply) that many distorting factors plague sensuous experience. Empirical knowing is necessarily mediated by the sensuous apparatus itself. In addition, our sensuous experiences of the world fit the either/or of logic and language. This tendency to bifurcate the knowing subject from the object of knowledge marks any empirical knowing as a distortion of the underlying ontological oneness. Further, sensuous knowledge is formed and shaped by the philosophical presuppositions, the interpretations, of those who seek it. Thus many factors create distortion in any empirical knowing. According to various mystical pantheists and philosophers of mysticism, however, the mystical oneness with the divine offers a route to knowledge that differs from empirical knowledge in its fundamental form. This alternate route by-passes the factors that lead to distortion in sensuous knowledge and therefore genuinely reflects reality.

Arguments like these raise important questions about the structure of mystical experience. If indeed it possesses an immediacy that by-passes the senses, logic, language, and philosophical background of the experiencer, then we must take that fact into consideration. If not, however, then mystical experience cannot be used to support a complete overturning of the metaphysical implications of empirical knowledge, including science. The question becomes, Will the mystical claim to immediacy withstand scrutiny?

To answer this question, it is important first to distinguish between purely experiential elements and interpretive elements in the total mystical experience. This is a complicated subject, and philosophers of mysticism have long debated this distinction. Almost everyone warns that these two cannot really be divided or separated in actual fact, even though they may be distinguished in language. A separation is a metaphysical or ontological division; a distinction is a conceptual or logical division. This distinction is important. For example, I can survive very easily a distinction between my head and my body, but if I separate them, I will not survive. While it is easy to distinguish conceptually between logic, language, and philosophical background (i.e., interpretation) on the one hand and a concrete mystical experience on the other, yet many fail to see that dividing is very difficult if not impossible.

A classic example is the seminal work, *Mysticism and Philosophy*, by W. T. Stace. A philosopher of mysticism, Stace writes, "It is probably impossible . . . to isolate 'pure' experience. Yet, although we may never be able to find sense experience completely free of any interpretation, it can hardly be doubted that a sensation is one thing and its conceptual interpretation is another thing. That is to say, they are distinguishable though not completely separable."[5] This is an admirable warning. We just made it ourselves. But the problem is that Stace does not heed his own warning. Soon after paying lip service to the impossibility of distinguishing experience and interpretation, he turns to discuss "the difficulty of deciding what part of a mystic's descriptive account of his experience ought to be taken as his interpretation." Later on he says, "it is perhaps only possible for a contemporary mind, philosophically trained . . . , to realize that all these interpretations are imported into the experience, to free it from its incrustations of traditional dogmas, and to present it to himself and to us as as near to pure uninterpreted experience as is possible."[6]

The importance of this debate must be highlighted. If a mystical

5. W. T. Stace, *Mysticism and Philosophy* (Philadelphia: Lippincott, 1960), pp. 31–32.

6. Ibid., pp. 74–75. Other examples of philosophers of mysticism who make sharp distinctions between experience and interpretation are Charles E. Scott, "Preconceptuality and Religious Experience," *Southern Journal of Philosophy* 7 (1969): 243, and F. C. Happold, *Mysticism: A Study and an Anthology*, rev. ed. (Baltimore: Penguin, 1970), p. 188.

pantheist's experience of God is able to by-pass the senses, logic, language, and philosophical background, it offers a road to knowledge of God uniquely unsullied by distorting interpretive factors. But if it does not by-pass these elements, then the mystical experience is not unique in its structure and deserves to be considered as but one of several possible routes for knowledge about God. In this case, we are obligated to build a world view that accounts for both modes of experience. We cannot assume that mysticism will provide unchallenged confirmation of the pantheistic world view to which it tends to point.

We must examine one by one the features of mystical experience that are said to show that it is unique. One of these features is immediacy. Mystics use the quality of immediacy to support their claim that their kind of experience is different from other forms of experience. But many philosophers have argued effectively that mystical experience is not uniquely immediate in nature. According to their critique, every mystical experience is mediated by the world view of the mystic, including the logical principles and language that are embedded in that view.

A significant number of recent works on the philosophy of mysticism have developed this thesis. The author of one of these writes,

> Experience is not a realm. It is not a space or range of events that transcends language, or that stands outside of the activities of the mind in thought and judgment. It is misleading to speak of experience as if it denoted a locus to which one could appeal in order to confirm or infirm [sic] particular propositions. There can be no access to any realm of experience that is not shaped by the forms and categories of the mind.[7]

The upshot of this view is of great importance and should be quite clear: if this view is correct, mystical experiences are mediated just as all other human experiences are. They are not uniquely unmediated; they do not deserve a special place in our learning about God.

How would we support this thesis? First, an analysis of religious experience suggests that philosophical interpretation actually affects mystical experience itself. Interpretations do not just report or record "pure" experience. Consider the claim by Zen masters that all conceptual analysis leads to error. Because of this claim, the whole system of Zen life is contrived to bring on the enlightenment, *satori*, in a

7. Wayne Proudfoot, "Religious Experience, Emotion and Belief," *Harvard Theological Review* 70 (1977): 343. See also Steven T. Katz, "Language, Epistemology, and Mysticism," in *Mysticism and Philosophical Analysis*, ed. Steven T. Katz (New York: Oxford University Press, 1978), p. 26; Bruce Garside, "Language and the Interpretation of Mysticism," *International Journal for the Philosophy of Religion* 3 (1972): 99; H. P. Owen, "Christian Mysticism: A Study in Walter Hilton's The Ladder of Perfection," *Religious Studies* 7 (1971): 36–37.

nonconceptual way. The *koan* and other tactics break down the conceptualizing of the mind and prepare the initiate to experience *satori* directly without the interference of rationality.

But it can be argued that the Zen masters would not bring about *satori* simply by giving nonsensical answers or beating their disciples with a stick. These may be necessary to *satori*, but they are not sufficient. If a question by a theological student in the United States were greeted by a Zen-like answer, it seems apparent that *satori* would not take place. Nor would a stock broker on Wall Street grasp enlightenment if she were simply beaten with a stick. Obviously, something more, some sort of conceptual context, is required if the unconventional techniques of the Zen masters are to bear fruit.

It seems that this "something more" derives from the Zen tradition and is grasped nonverbally by the disciple. The tradition provides an unspoken but still crucial interpretive context that "makes sense," in a Zen sort of way, of the "nonsensical" (to others) responses the initiate's questions receive. The disciple must "soak up" this tradition before *satori* becomes possible. Though the rules of Zen prohibit giving this interpretive context explicitly and verbally, it must be passed down in some implicit way if the unusual methods of the masters are to produce more than resentment or confusion. Thus, even in Zen, where the rigorous attempt is made to avoid logical and verbal interpretation, every experience is shaped by the philosophical background of the experiencer. There is no "pure" experience that by-passes the cognitive background of the mystic himself. The world view background shapes the experience. With no Zen background, you can have no Zen experience.

Second, mystics often claim that their own experiences are unique. A Christian mystic does not usually think of his own experiences as being the same as the Muslim mystic's experiences. Philosophers of mysticism may believe all mystical experiences are the same, but mystics themselves generally do not.

Now, if various experiences are mediated by world views, then the mystics' claims to uniqueness make sense. If, on the other hand, the mystics' raptures are direct, unmediated apprehensions of God, the philosophers of mysticism would be right, and we would have to tell the mystics respectfully that they are wrong about the uniqueness of their own experiences. A Christian mystic may think that his intuition of God is different from the Muslim's, but he is wrong. Only the interpretation he later ascribes to the experience is different. This seems, if not presumptuous, at best a curious thing for a philosopher to tell a mystic about something only the mystic has experienced.

Third, we should think about how concepts in general affect our experience of the world. We inevitably experience the world in the terms and categories our philosophy of life provides for us. Suppose, for example, that an atheistic psychologist observes an experience of religious conversion. Since the intellectual net formed by his categories allows only for psychological phenomena and not for spiritual or religious ones, he naturally will experience and explain the conversion in psychological terms. Other factors will slip through the psychologist's net. It is not that the psychologist will experience the spiritual dimension but reject it. Rather, it seems that the psychologist will simply not experience the phenomena as spiritual phenomena.

This explains the matter of selectivity in the reports mystics give of their experiences. Philosophers of mysticism recognize that different mystics report different features of experience as important. Some of these philosophers are tempted to posit that the experiences are all the same; the mystics simply remember the features that their own religious traditions consider important. But if the experiences are actually shaped by the mystics' philosophical interpretations, then this selectivity is more adequately explained. The mystics do not have to edit their reports either deliberately or inadvertently. They simply report what they actually experience, and the marks of philosophical background will shine through.

In sum, if mystical experience did have an immediacy that no other experience possesses, then it would deserve a special epistemological status. We would need to give priority to the results of mystical experience, trusting its results when conflicts arose between basic metaphysical claims that grow out of different forms of experiences. But our analysis reveals that on the issue of immediacy, mysticism is not uniquely unsullied by the philosophical background of the experiencer. There may be other factors that show the uniqueness of mystical experience. But in the matter of directness of knowledge, mystical experience is not demonstrably different in kind from other modes of experience.

Self-Authentication

Defenders of mysticism also use its self-certifying nature as evidence of the uniqueness of mystical experience. This often grows directly out of the claim of immediacy. If I experience God directly, it is claimed, I do not need external confirmation for the experience. If I infer God from nature or read about God in a book, naturally I will need some confirmation that what I infer or read is accurate. Because of the supposed immediacy of mystical experience, it is easy to conclude that such experience is uniquely self-authenticating.

Empiricists often criticize mystical experience by pointing out that testing procedures are necessary to knowledge and that mysticism cannot generate these procedures. For example,

No one would deny that there are moments when the world is experienced in a most unusual manner. But it is no more than misguided thinking to assert further that these unusual experiences entail an additional [metaphysical] claim. . . . It is incredibly naive for a mystic to think that the only reason he needs to offer for the putative claim of "seeing the world as it is", is that he has experienced it as such. This simply begs the question.[8]

Empirical critics suggest that mystics are really saying, "I know I encountered God because I have a genuine experience; I know it was genuine because I encountered God." While the question begging is rarely this blatant, a subtle circularity intrudes when loaded words like *awareness, encounter, enlightenment,* and *apprehension* are used.[9]

This empirical argument implies that the two modes of experience exhibit differing characteristics: the empirical has testing procedures, the mystical does not. On this point, the empiricists agree with mystics and philosophers of mysticism who believe that the issue of self-authentication versus external certification through testing procedures divides the two forms of experience. The difference, of course, is that empiricists think that having testing procedures is a virtue; mystics think it is a vice.

It seems best to argue, however, that both groups are wrong. The issue of self-authentication does not divide the two modes of experience as neatly as either empiricists or mystics believe. Empirical knowledge, like the mystical, depends on certain basic, self-authenticating experiences. In one sense, all knowledge, the empirical kind included, depends on such basic experiences. Empiricists argue that their favorite mode of knowledge is subject to checking procedures, while religious and mystical modes are not. They imply that the empirical sort of knowledge does not need these unconfirmed intuitions. This leads some to distinguish between "logical" certainty—"being right"—and "psychological" certainty—"feeling certain."[10] If checking procedures authenticate an experience (as in sense experience), we can know; if not, we may feel sure, but we cannot know.

But inferences based on the senses must also end at certain basic experiences. Conclusions based on arguments need premises. These

8. Joseph Gilbert, "Mystical Experience and Public Testability," *Sophia* 9, 3 (October 1970): 17–18. See also C. B. Martin, *Religious Belief* (Ithaca, N. Y.: Cornell University Press, 1959), p. 67; Antony Flew, *God and Philosophy* (New York: Dell, Delta, 1966), pp. 125–26.

9. Peter Donovan, *Interpreting Religious Experience* (New York: Seabury, Crossroad, 1979), pp. 61–62.

10. Flew, *God and Philosophy*, pp. 125–26; Donovan, *Interpreting Religious Experience*, p. 60.

premises, if they are argued for, need prior premises. But this process cannot go on forever. Sooner or later, as Ludwig Wittgenstein pointed out, "the giving of reasons must come to an end."[11] For this reason George Mavrodes writes, "If there is any knowledge at all then there must be some source of knowledge other than argumentation."[12] In this sense, empirical experiences also rest on a self-authenticating basis. Given the correctness of the realistic point of view, if our observational equipment is working properly and we have no reasons to doubt an experience, we are well within our rights to say, "I see the tree; the tree exists."

Empiricists claim that ordinary observations are always checkable. For example, C. B. Martin argues that the experience "I see an ashtray" warrants the claim "The ashtray exists" only because an ashtray *"Is the sort of thing that can be photographed, touched, and seen by others."* This is different from "I see God" because God is not tangible, and other tests cannot be specified to confirm God's existence. "I see God" is therefore more like "I seem to see an ashtray," which involves no claim about the existence of something in the world objectively.[13] It is only a claim about something I experience subjectively: "I seem to see water on the highway," when I might really see only heat waves. This claim about inner states of mind can be true and still be consistent with "I see a mirage; there is no water on the highway."

In defense of religion, Mavrodes responds that one fact has been overlooked. Even if a photo is taken to help authenticate "I see an ashtray," that still leaves an unauthenticated experience of the photograph. If we take a second photo to authenticate the first, we have only pushed the issue back a step. Obviously, we are off and running on an infinite regress. We will never get to a final photograph that will authenticate the whole series.[14]

In response to this rejoinder, Martin could point out that the first photo is confirmed not by a second photo but by the original experience of the ashtray. The experience and the photo authenticate each other. Thus we accept "I see an ashtray" as a genuine experience that authentically reveals the real because it relates to other experiences and beliefs. Experiences are authenticated not in isolation but by connection with the whole set of our experiences of the world.

11. Ludwig Wittgenstein, *The Blue and Brown Books* (New York: Harper and Row, Harper Torchbooks, 1960), p. 143.

12. George Mavrodes, *Belief in God: A Study in the Epistemology of Religion* (New York: Random House, 1970), p. 49.

13. Martin, *Religious Belief*, p. 88, emphasis original.

14. Mavrodes, *Belief in God*, pp. 75–76; William H. Capitan, *Philosophy of Religion: An Introduction*, Traditions in Philosophy (Indianapolis: Bobbs-Merrill, Pegasus, 1972), p. 138.

While so much is true, however, this response does not solve the basic problem. Our dilemma is not merely to authenticate individual experiences. Given the veridical or genuinely revealing nature of the whole web of experiences, authenticating an isolated experience is easy. The issue now becomes the authenticity of the whole mode of experience itself. We are not asking whether the judge properly applied the law in a particular case, but about the fundamental validity of the system of law itself.

Individual experiences are generally confirmed by connection to a broad system of experiences that fit the interpretive framework of the experiencer, that is, by a whole world view. If we treat experiences as isolated bits of data, no experience by itself demonstrates unequivocally the existence of the object it apparently reveals. In this sense, we have no procedures for proving that the sky is blue. We just see that it is blue. Taking a picture of the sky would not help to authenticate our initial experiences. We would still have to assume that the blue we see in both the sky and the photo really is blue. No amount of photography would by-pass this problem.

This discussion could entangle us in broader epistemological debates. But the point for our discussion is clear: the need for a broader background against which to judge experiences is felt both for empirical experiences and for religious experiences. Despite their initial claims, mystics act like empiricists when discussing their experiences. They, too, place their experiences within the context of a world view for interpretation and confirmation.

How, then, do we decide between an illusion and an authentic experience? Consider the well-known case of delusory experience. How would we distinguish seeing a mirage from seeing water? Each experience seems "real" to the one who has it at the time he has it. All other things being equal, we might say that both experiences justify our accepting the reality of what they apparently point to.

But all other things are not equal. We accept the sighting of water because it fits in with the rest of what we experience about the world. The mirage is rejected because it does not fit in. Facts, in other words, are not Lone Rangers; they are evaluated in contexts. The contexts are the world views of the experiencers. The whole realistic way of viewing the world includes water that lies on highways and is wet. We use this macroscopic view to identify genuine experiences. Thus, when we get close to the object of our sighting, we test to see if some wet stuff can still be found on the pavement. If it can, we conclude that this experience confirms the original sighting as a genuine experience of water.

The whole conceptual framework of the experiencer is used here to test questionable individual experiences. The world view itself is accepted because it passes the basic tests of rationality by explaining comprehensively and congruently the vast amount of the experience that seems to be in touch with reality. In empirical knowledge, therefore, a realistic world view usually helps us to judge questionable experiences and sift out illusions. Without developing a full-blown epistemology, the critical thing for our discussion is this: we must realize that this sort of testing operates in mysticism as well. Mystics use logical checking procedures, whether they admit it or not, to reach conclusions about different experiences. Those experiences that irresistibly elicit ideas that fit the mystics' world views are accepted. When some idea does not fit with the world view, however, the experience in which it is rooted is reinterpreted or rejected outright as delusory.

Checking an experience against a world view is a logical procedure. Given the mystics' skittishness about logic, we might wonder whether they do in fact use logical inferences to reach important conclusions about their experiences. Shankara, for example, says that logic has a preliminary validity. It can be used on the lower levels of truth where we assume the reality of this world with its various persons and things. But Brahman ultimately cannot be described with logical statements. Logic always divides into conceptual opposites. Applying these concepts to Brahman implies that Brahman is "this, not that." But Brahman is "not this, not that." Brahman has no determinate attribute that could exclude the opposite attribute. Brahman is beyond logical statements.

The obvious and simple problem here is that this line of thinking self-destructs. "Brahman is beyond logical statements" is itself a logical statement about Brahman (or else implies a statement about Brahman). Brahman is apparently not beyond this logical statement. In addition to this, Shankara has reached his conclusion that Brahman is beyond logic by following a logical train of thought. The flow of thought is something like:

(a) Logical description divides things into conceptual opposites.
(b) Nirguna Brahman is indivisible.
(c) Nirguna Brahman is not subject to logical description.

In other words, Shankara has arrived at a conclusion about Nirguna Brahman as the result of logical inference—perhaps implicit, not explicit—even though Brahman is supposedly entirely beyond logical inference and knowable only by direct apprehension. It is for this reason that we feel justified in positing basic rational criteria for evaluating world views.

A more graphic illustration of this point is provided by D. T.

Suzuki's Zen Buddhism, because Zen so adamantly refuses to allow logical thought. This persistence reveals itself in the nonsensical answers and mutism of the Zen masters. If a Zen novice asks a meaningful question about metaphysics, he receives no meaningful answer. He gets a slap, a laugh, or nonsense, or he is ignored altogether. The master deliberately uses a *koan* to trip up the novice's logical thinking. When the wheels of conceptual thought grind to a chaotic halt, then *satori*, or enlightenment, may occur.

But this Zen tradition reveals a logic of its own. Why does the master use nonsense or silence? Because logical answers will always distort, it is claimed. But how did the ancient sages of Zen come to realize that nonsense and mutism are necessary tools for passing the tradition to the next generation? Because, it seems, they understood, *as a result of logical inference,* the self-defeating implications of using verbal answers. The inference goes something like this:

(a) If I answer logically after denying logic, my view self-defeats.
(b) I do not want my view to self-defeat.
(c) I will answer illogically to preserve my view from self-defeat.

In other words, Zen sages have recognized the necessity of the nonsensical answers and the mutism by following logical trains of thought. The very irrationality of their answers suggests that they have followed rationality.

More specifically, how did Suzuki come to know that Zen can "serenely go its own way without at all heeding . . . criticism" about contradictions? It seems reasonable to think that his mind followed a path something like this:

(a) If Zen accepts logic, contradictions are a problem.
(b) If Zen does not accept logic, contradictions are not a problem.
(c) Zen does not accept logic.
(d) Zen can "serenely go its own way without at all heeding . . . criticism" about contradictions.[15]

Thus, while the Zen monks' nonsense and mutism are attempts to avoid logic, they are in fact the results of logical inference. No way exists to avoid this kind of basic rational process. Even the attempt to avoid rationality is made only because rationality leads us to conclude that the attempt can be made.

If the Zen masters really were completely illogical, there would be no difficulty in stating explicitly that language always distorts reality

15. D. T. Suzuki, *Mysticism: Christian and Buddhist* (New York: Harper, 1957), p. 49.

and then turning around to use language to describe reality. Of course, this would be a blatant inconsistency. Naturally, it would horrify other philosophers. But if logic really does not matter and inconsistencies really are acceptable, then expressing such contradictions should pose no problem. The masters believe mutism shows their conviction that rationality has been avoided. But resorting to mutism only shows that logic really does operate in the minds, if not in the words, of the Zen masters.

In sum, the discussion of self-authentication reveals no reasons to suggest that mystical experience is so radically different from other modes of experience as to warrant a special epistemological status. Mystical experiences are confirmed by logical procedures that compare those experiences with broader world views. Surely we can find distinguishing marks in those experiences we have come to call mystical. But these marks are not so fundamental as to imply radical differences between mystical and sensuous modes of experience. Indeed, even empirical knowledge possesses a certain immediacy, at least in the sense that inferences based on sensuous experiences must go back ultimately to experiences that are not the result of prior arguments. Furthermore, mystical knowledge depends to some extent on the inferences of those who have the experiences. It does not deserve to be accepted unquestioningly in the face of contrary evidence from other modes of experience.

Persistent empiricists and diehard mystics both want to believe that empirical knowledge uses testing procedures, while mystical knowledge does not. Empiricists employ this thesis to argue for the inadequacy of mysticism. Mystics use it to infer the superficiality of empiricism. But both, it seems, are wrong. Self-authentication and logical testing procedures do not neatly distinguish the two modes of experience. In this area of discussion, no concrete support can be found for the claim that mystical experience reveals reality in a uniquely undistorted, pristine, and true way.

Ineffability

Some philosophers of mysticism point to another feature of mystical experience to support mysticism's uniqueness. This feature is ineffability. Ineffability often has been cited as the real distinguishing mark of mysticism. Charles Hartshorne calls it the real problem of mysticism.[16] After criticizing William James because three of his four distinguishing marks of mysticism (noetic quality, transiency, and

16. Charles Hartshorne, "Mysticism and Rationalistic Metaphysics," *The Monist* 59 (1976): 467.

passivity) can be found in other experiences, Walter Kaufmann writes that "it must be ineffability that sets apart mystic experiences."[17]

Ineffability means that some experience or object of experience is indescribable. If language and logic fail, then ineffability results. Since mystics often assert that language and logic do indeed fail, the claim of ineffability naturally follows. This claim raises several questions. The most obvious concerns what the claim means. A second matter involves the implications for our larger problem of claiming ineffability. We want to know if mystical experience is unique and for this reason deserving of a special status in epistemology. We shall get at the second question by discussing the first.

Upon reading accounts of mysticism, we cannot help but be struck by one fact: mystics do not lack for words. How can they claim initially that the object of their experience is beyond words and then turn around and write about it page after page? This undeniable fact leads many to think that *ineffability* needs to be understood in a modified way, not in a strict or literalistic way. Some interpret the data by suggesting that some mystics just do not possess the skill to express themselves adequately. "Shakespeare finds words where lesser poets would not," claims Kaufmann.[18]

Others have suggested that certain languages simply lack the mechanisms necessary to express certain things. A classic article by semanticist Paul Henle illustrates this view. Henle argues that the idea of ineffability makes good sense because some languages do not have the categories to say certain things. He constructs a mathematical symbolism in which certain meaningful principles become either tautologies or contradictions because of the idiosyncrasies of the symbolic system. We know, of course, that these principles are meaningful, because we have broader symbolic systems in terms of which the principles are meaningfully affirmable. But within the narrower system, some things are unaffirmable. To one who knew only that system, it would seem that these principles were utterly ineffable.[19]

But mystics often assert that ineffability cannot be accounted for in these ways. The problem is not with particular mystics or particular languages. Language per se, language of any kind, fails to describe the mystic insight. One version suggests that the problem lies in the lack of shared experience. To take the commonly used example, you cannot explain the color steel blue to someone blind from birth. You might call it "cool and metallic," but this analogy is useful only to

17. Walter Kaufmann, *Critique of Religion and Philosophy* (Garden City, N. Y.: Doubleday, Anchor Books, 1961), p. 316.
18. Ibid., p. 323.
19. Paul Henle, "Mysticism and Semantics," *Philosophy and Phenomenological Research* 9 (1949): 416–22.

one who already knows the color and can understand the analogy in light of that experience. In the same way, for the nonmystic, the mystical experience always will remain a complete mystery because there are no similar experiences to which language can point.

Critics point out that this option is trivial. Ordinary experiences would be ineffable in this sense. A person who has recovered from a seemingly terminal illness will not be able to describe all the nuances of that experience to one who has never been in the hospital. In fact, the analogy of colorblindness makes its point as well as it does precisely because something like this form of ineffability is found in nonmystic experiences.

Another version that faults language of all kinds warns us that language cannot replace direct experience. This warning bears repeating, perhaps, but it is uncontroversial. The unfeeling soul who cannot understand why a man mourns so deeply for his late wife needs to hear this warning in no uncertain terms. Surely this warning, like the concept of shared experience, applies to both mystical and nonmystical modes of experience.

If somehow we modify the claim to ineffability as the options sampled here try to do, we find that mystical experience is not qualitatively different from ordinary experience. The sensuous experiences of life can be ineffable in senses like those we have already described. If ineffability is to be accepted as evidence that mystical experience is somehow different in kind from sensuous experience, it must be a strict concept of ineffability. Strict ineffability might suggest a complete lack of connection between mystical experience and any language whatever. Mystical experiences and objects are entirely undifferentiated; languages depend necessarily on differentiating logical opposites. Differentiated language seeks to capture undifferentiated reality, and distortion necessarily results.

Stace describes strict ineffability this way: "In that [mystical] experience there is subject and no object, and as the mystic is therein identical with God, so he is therein identical with all other mystics, and his mystic experience is identical with all other mystic experiences. . . . And hence there is, from within, no relation at all between one mystic experience and another, and therefore no likeness or unlikeness, and therefore no concept."[20]

This strict version of ineffability offers proponents of several positions some ammunition for their views. Some say that mystics use language as well as it can be used. Though this mystical language is laced with paradox, it is the only way mystics have to communicate transcendent reality. Thus, we should take it literally; it is as true as

20. W. T. Stace, *Time and Eternity: An Essay in the Philosophy of Religion* (Princeton: Princeton University Press, 1952), p. 84.

language can be. But paradox does not necessarily show the language to be false.[21]

Alternatively, others take the paradoxical language to be evidence that what the mystics think they are describing cannot really be. The contradictory language serves as the basis for a reductio ad absurdum argument. F. R. Tennant says, "Though there well may be more in the universe than normal experience can understand and comprehend, the occult nature of the ineffable alleged revelations of mystical contemplation prevents their being safely included in the denotation of 'truth'."[22]

A third group, comprised of mysticism's friends, asserts that the contradictions and paradoxes show that reality must be beyond language. Reality should not be talked about, it should be experienced firsthand. As Stace finally concludes, "[God] is unknowable to *the logical intellect*, but . . . he can be known in direct religious or mystical experience."[23]

The claims to strictly ineffable experience create some thorny problems. The first and most obvious is that such assertions appear to be self-defeating. How can anyone meaningfully affirm of God, "Nothing can be said of God"? The statement purports to do what it says cannot be done. It amounts to describing God as indescribable. If the statement is false, it is not true; if it is true, it self-defeats and so cannot be true. This logical difficulty forces us to wonder about the very intelligibility of the strict concept of ineffability.

Some may try to avoid the force of this dilemma by noting that "God is indescribable" is a statement about statements, not a statement about God. In saying that God is ineffable, the mystic is not making a statement about God to the effect that statements about God are impossible. He is making a statement about what kinds of statements achieve descriptive meaningfulness. Statements about trees and children do successfully describe their objects; statements about God do not. This tells us about language only.

This is a sophisticated move, but it may not succeed. Even if "God is indescribable" is not intended as a statement about God, it still implies describable knowledge about God. Whether this is intended or not, God is still being described as a being whom language fails to

21. Ronald W. Hepburn, "Nature and Assessment of Mysticism," in *The Encyclopedia of Philosophy*, ed. Paul Edwards, 8 vols. (New York: Macmillan, 1967), vol. 5, p. 430; Galen K. Pletcher, "Mysticism, Contradiction, and Ineffability," *American Philosophical Quarterly* 10 (1973): 207.

22. F. R. Tennant, *Philosophical Theology*, 2 vols. (Cambridge: Cambridge University Press, 1928), vol. 1, p. 317.

23. Stace, "Mysticism and Human Reason," Riecker Memorial Lecture, no. 1, *University of Arizona Bulletin* 26, 3 (May 1955): 20; see also *Mysticism and Philosophy*, p. 198.

describe. Even if "God is indescribable" only means "Language about God does not work," it also implies that "God is a being with respect to whom language does not work." This description of God is logically entailed in the statement about language. It seems impossible to make the statement about language's shortcomings without the implication about God tagging along. Thus, it does appear that a strict claim to the ineffability of language about God defeats itself.

Second, a claim to strict ineffability implies knowing all noncontradictory statements must be inappropriate as descriptions of the mystical object or experience. How could this be known? One would have to go through an infinite list of candidates for description and determine that each one fails. As Hartshorne rhetorically asks, "While having the experience, has the mystic run through his mind every possible nonparadoxical description and seen its inapplicability?"[24]

Third, the strict view runs up against the obvious fact that mystics do talk about their experiences and the objects of these experiences. They certainly must be assuming that someone will understand what they are saying. And this assumption is well grounded, for people do understand the mystics to a greater or lesser degree. This shows that the analogy of telling a blind person about "steel blue" misleads us. A better illustration would be explaining the color to someone with a glimmer of sight. Mystics speak to those with whom they have many experiences in common. Thus they skillfully weave descriptions by using analogies based on other forms of experience that mystics and nonmystics share. Mystics effectively describe their experiences, and nonmystics clearly understand those descriptions. After all, the mystic was at one time a nonmystic.

Fourth, philosophers of mysticism debate at length what is called the argument from unanimity. We have not discussed this argument in any detail, for mystics themselves show little interest in it. But their philosophical defenders like to point out that mystics from various cultures and religious traditions have certain experiential features in common. Though their theological explanations differ, mystics do have experiences that, by all accounts, display remarkable phenomenological similarity. Some philosophers take this as evidence that the mystics are on to something—mysticism breaks through the historical particulars of specific religions and puts the mystic directly in touch with the divine.

C. D. Broad presents a classic statement of the argument from unanimity:

> I am prepared to admit that although the experiences have differed considerably at different times and places, there are probably certain char-

24. Hartshorne, "Mysticism and Rationalistic Metaphysics," p. 468.

acteristics which are common to all of them, and which suffice to distinguish them from all other kinds of experience. In view of this, I think it more likely than not that in mystical experience men come into contact with some Reality or some aspect of Reality which they do not come into contact with in any other way.[25]

Were we interested in this argument for its own sake, we would elaborate a response to point out the circularity implicit in this claim. The mystics who serve as a sample for the study are selected because they exhibit a common set of characteristics. Then, after examining the experiences of those in the sample population, the argument concludes that the unanimity of characteristics in the sample gives evidence that mystics have experienced a special contact with God. Since the points of similarity among the mystics' reports were used initially to choose the sample, this argument clearly runs in a circle. One reviewer writes, "To be surprised at the [agreement among mystics] is like being surprised at the fact that all zebras have stripes."[26]

Broad's version of the argument is very chastened. Other examples tend to be far more extravagant. Yet it appears that even Broad suffers from the inherent circularity that plagues this argument. But the issue here concerns ineffability. The argument from unanimity, a favorite of mysticism's defenders, needs some data with which to work. The data that are compared and found to be unanimous are derived from the descriptions of the mystics. The argument from unanimity, in other words, depends on the mystics' descriptions for its data. It must therefore assume the general reliability of the mystics' language. This assumption clearly implies that strict ineffability is false. Any appeal to strict ineffability entails that the argument from unanimity has no data with which to work. Either strict ineffability is correct or the argument from unanimity has data to compare. But we cannot have it both ways.[27]

What seems significant here is that most defenders of mysticism place a good deal of evidential weight on the argument from unanimity. They must, therefore, implicitly admit that mystical experience cannot be strictly ineffable. Stace is honest enough to recognize this point: "If the mystical consciousness were absolutely ineffable, then we would not say so because we should be unconscious of such an experience; or in other words, we should never have had such an

25. C. D. Broad, *Religion, Philosophy and Psychical Research* (New York: Harcourt, Brace and Co., 1953), pp. 172–73.

26. W. E. Kennick, review of *Mysticism and Philosophy*, by W. T. Stace, in *The Philosophical Review* 71 (1962): 387.

27. Richard Gale, "Mysticism and Philosophy," *Journal of Philosophy* 57 (1960): 304; Katz, "Language, Epistemology, and Mysticism," p. 40.

experience."[28] If strict ineffability were correct, then any description, no matter how absurd, would be as appropriate as any other. An experience could be described with equal appropriateness as *"a Beatific vision . . . , seeing God . . . , feeling awe . . . , being tortured by an expert, eating a hamburger, or cursing one's fate."*[29]

The four criticisms of strict ineffability lead us inevitably to conclude that ineffability claims should be interpreted in some modified way. If this is so, the strict ineffability of mystical experiences cannot be used to mark off those experiences as radically distinct from sensuous experience and as therefore uniquely revealing reality. Mystical experiences may be ineffable in any of a dozen modified ways, but so are the sensuous experiences that point so forcefully to the reality of the everyday world. Without strict ineffability, the radical uniqueness of the mystical is undermined, and any special evidence mysticism supposedly provides for pantheism in light of the contrary evidence of other modes of experience cannot be accepted.

Of course, this assumes that mystics intend that we should take their language descriptively. Many theories in the literature suggest various functions for mystical language other than description. Without going into all these ideas, we note simply, for our purposes, that if mystical language is not descriptive, then it certainly cannot provide any epistemological basis for accepting metaphysical claims. Suppose the purpose of mystical language is to evoke mystical experiences in the audience. It then proves nothing. Parables have evocative power, but they cannot be accepted as evidence for the existence of ontological realities corresponding to the concepts they use. If the purpose of mystical language is not descriptive, then it implies nothing about the objective reality of objects allegedly pointed to by the categories it uses to accomplish its task.

This assumes, of course, that mystics do not intend their language to be taken as descriptions. But this assumption is highly questionable. Mystics usually assume that their words are descriptive, as do their critics and defenders. Thus, the concept of ineffability does not do the logical work that some have hoped for. It does not separate the mystical realm cleanly from other forms of experience. Mysticism cannot provide a unique area of evidence on the basis of which other modes of experience may be summarily ignored.

Conclusion

The course of this argument about epistemology has taken us through three areas sometimes used by mystics to show that their

28. Stace, *Mysticism and Philosophy*, pp. 290–91.
29. Keith E. Yandell, "Some Varieties of Ineffability," *International Journal for the Philosophy of Religion* 6 (1975): 177-78, emphasis original.

mystical raptures are distinct in kind from ordinary experiences. Mystical pantheists claim that their experiences of God are unsullied by logic and language. They assert further that this fact means that mysticism provides special evidence for the world view to which it tends to point. Because of the thrust for unity with God usually implied in mysticism, this world view, of course, is pantheism.

But despite the claims, our analysis reveals that mystical experience does not possess attributes that mark it as completely different from other forms of experience. It has no unique immediacy that bypasses the cognitive. It is not distinctly self-authenticating in a way that needs no external confirmation. It is not strictly ineffable. Mystical experiences do differ from ordinary experiences. But the differences are not so great as to warrant the claims of mystics who say they have a special pipeline to truth.

Any appeal to mystical experience in support of pantheism contains a basic irony. The mystical pantheist rejects empirical knowledge (which points away from pantheism) and acclaims mystical knowledge. He hopes thereby to avoid the logical bifurcations inherent in empirical knowledge and to achieve a supraconceptual knowledge of immediacy and unity. The final irony, however, is that this enterprise succeeds only when it posits the logical distinction between the logically conditioned empirical experience and the allegedly supralogical mystical experience. Thus, the appeal to mysticism, far from overcoming logic altogether, *actually requires a basic logical distinction* if it ever is to succeed. Once again, there seems to be no way to avoid rationality entirely.

In this vein, New Age mystics may claim that their world view is based on a higher, intuitive, right-brain arena of knowledge that does not participate in the distortions that mar "normal," logical, left-brain knowing. But upon closer analysis, these claims prove to be either self-defeating and contradictory or indefensible. Use of the right-/left-brain distinction as the ground for preferring unitive ways of knowing necessarily presupposes the logical distinction between left- and right-brain ways of knowing. The right-/left-brain distinction entails left-brain rationality and so cannot be used to denigrate conceptual thought. The claim that higher intuitive knowing is possible turns out to be a bald, unsupportable assertion. We must conclude, therefore, that the epistemological foundations usually offered for New Age pantheism are decidedly inadequate and do not support the metaphysical weight placed upon them.

The Religious Dimension of Mysticism

There is one mountain, but many paths to its summit.—Oriental proverb
Is it not a mark of maturity to be able to live peaceably with, and act properly toward, those with whom we might profoundly disagree?—Harold Netland

Pantheists find salvation through mystical knowledge. Because of this, their views of epistemology and of religious experience coalesce. Thus, the major criticisms raised against the mystical epistemology so common in pantheism bear directly on the New Age idea of religious experience. If it is not plausible to accept the claims for an immediate, ineffable, supersensuous experience of God radically cut off from rational knowledge, then the pantheistic concept of salvation is stripped of its privileged position. But one aspect of the pantheists' view of salvation still remains to be discussed. This topic deserves special attention because of its contemporary prominence not only among pantheistic and New Age writers, but among religious thinkers of other kinds as well. This idea is religious pluralism.

In a recent "Shoe" cartoon, Skyler is taking a philosophy quiz. There is only one question: What is the meaning of life? The would-be scholar looks blankly at his desk. Finally, in the last frame, Skyler thinks to himself, "This better be multiple choice." With Skyler many today believe there had better be several true world views from which to choose. In a day characterized by the "it's-great-for-you-but-it's-not-for-me" attitude, this religious pluralism deserves attention.

Basic Definitions

To begin, several definitions need to be addressed. We must first distinguish between phenomenological/factual and philosophical/normative uses of the word *pluralism*. We often say, "We live in a pluralistic society." But this ambiguous statement hides a subtle distinction. Do we mean, "Different people have conflicting viewpoints or opinions"? Or do we mean, "Conflicting opinions can be equally adequate or true"?

From a factual point of view, *pluralism* means that different people have different religious perspectives. *Pluralism* in this context refers to a sociological fact that is subject to confirmation or disconfirmation through social-science techniques. A cursory analysis of the history of religions or of the current religious scene confirms this phenomenological pluralism. We will reserve the phrases *religious variety* and *religious diversity* to denote the sociological fact of variety in religious beliefs and practices.

From a philosophical viewpoint, *pluralism* refers to a certain theory of the relations between the various religious traditions. In this sense, pluralism affirms that many religions, with their varied concepts and practices, can be appropriate modes of expressing our experience of God. In other words, different religions are able to lead to salvation (or whatever we call the religious goal). Though in practice, at different times and places, different religions may be more or less appropriate expressions of the experience of God, in theory, no one religion could ever claim an exclusive grasp of truth or a qualitatively higher contact with God. Because various religions are really different ways of conceptualizing and experiencing the same God, any religion can help its adherents to achieve contact with the divine. We will use the phrase *religious pluralism* to refer to the theory that many different traditions can help their adherents achieve the religious goal of contact with the divine.

Among those included in our study, Sarvepali Radhakrishnan most clearly defends religious pluralism. Consistent with the spirit of Hinduism, Radhakrishnan argues that religious doctrines are not absolutely true or false. They stand on a "graduated scale" of more true and less true. Even the crudest religious beliefs must be accepted because they bring good results for those who believe them. Every religion is valid, for "only through it have its followers become what they are. They have grown up with it and it has become a part of their being." Any religion is true so long as it leads its adherents to true spirituality.[1]

Religious pluralism like Radhakrishnan's stands in contrast to exclusivism, the more traditional view that only one religion is correct in its apprehension of God. Historically, most religions took this view of things in that each considered itself the sole guardian of truth. Exclusivism says that only one particular perspective teaches truth and leads to salvation.

A mediating position between exclusivism and pluralism has attracted some attention. This view, called inclusivism, affirms the truth of one religion, but suggests that adherents of other religions are covert followers of the one true faith. For example, a Buddhist inclusivist says Buddhism alone is the true religion. However, Christians and Muslims are or can be covert Buddhists. If inclusivism is true, only one religion is the "right" religion, yet all humans can potentially find salvation. Pluralists often argue that inclusivists have reinterpreted the substance of the exclusive claims of their traditions in essentially pluralistic ways. But the inclusivists have not revealed their abandonment of the tradition because emotional or ecclesiastical forces pressure them to retain orthodox theological language.

Most writers illustrate inclusivism by pointing to the "anonymous Christian" view of Catholic scholar Karl Rahner, even though others hold to inclusivism. Rahner claimed that Christianity is exclusively true, but he believed sincere believers of other faiths are "anonymous Christians."[2] Protestant theologian A. H. Strong held a more conservative version of Rahner's view. Strong believed that a few persons from non-Christian religions actually believe in the one true God, the God revealed in the Bible, even though they have never heard of Christ. Since these persons do not know anything about Jesus Christ, they cannot put their trust specifically in him. However, their faith in the God of the Bible and their rejection of the religion around them are "an implicit faith in Christ." This "implicit faith" theory posits that God gives salvation to these few individuals based on Christ's work of redemption because they trust in God to the limits of their knowledge.[3]

---

1. Sarvepali Radhakrishnan, *Eastern Religions and Western Thought*, 2d ed. (London: Oxford University Press, 1940, 1975), pp. 316–27; cf. *The Hindu View of Life* (London: Allen and Unwin, 1927), p. 32.

2. Karl Rahner, *Spirit in the World*, 2d ed., rev. J. B. Metz (London: Sheed and Ward, 1968). Other inclusivists are Archbishop William Temple, John Taylor, and Hans Küng.

3. A. H. Strong, *Systematic Theology* (Old Tappan, N. J.: Revell, 1907), pp. 842–43. See also Clark Pinnock, "The Finality of Jesus Christ in a World of Religions," in *Christian Faith and Practice in the Modern World: Theology from an Evangelical*

The Problem of Circularity

Our purpose here is not to examine these three positions, but to evaluate the common pantheistic view of pluralism. The most prominent philosophical advocate of religious pluralism is the British scholar John Hick.[4] Hick has been arguing for several decades that we need a Copernican revolution in religious thinking. No longer should we think exclusively; now we should think pluralistically. Different religions, he asserts, are "different human awarenesses of the Eternal One [that] represent different culturally conditioned perceptions of the same infinite divine reality."[5]

Borrowing from Kant, Hick claims that God himself, or the Real in itself, is different from the Real as we experience it. Thus the various Personae known in the history of religions—Allah, Yahweh, Krishna, Vishnu, and God the Father—reflect various experiences of the one Persona. In religions where the Real is not perceived personally, the Real is experienced as Brahman, Tao, Dharma, or *sunyata*. All of these reflect legitimate experiences of the same ultimate reality.[6]

In a discussion of the traditional Catholic teaching, "Outside the church, no salvation," Hick writes, "In the light of our accumulated knowledge of the other great world faiths, this conclusion has become unacceptable to all except a minority of dogmatic diehards."[7] What Hick implies here, though he no doubt knows better, is that the sheer facticity of religious variety shows religious pluralism to be correct. If not Hick, certainly the man on the street believes that the theory of religious pluralism follows from the phenomenon of religious variety. That different people have different viewpoints is the main evidence that all positions must be considered correct.

Hick says that religious pluralism interprets the facts of religious history: religious pluralism "is arrived at inductively as a way of making sense, from a religious point of view, of the facts described in the history of religion."[8] Pluralism, in other words, is a theory about religions. Its goal is to put the facts into a meaningful order. The view may be expressed with these two propositions:

Point of View, ed. Mark A. Noll and David F. Wells (Grand Rapids: Eerdmans, 1988), pp. 152–68.

4. The most prominent defender of pluralism from the field of religious studies is no doubt Wilfred Cantwell Smith, an expert on Islam and former professor at Harvard University. Another important pluralist is Paul Knitter.

5. John Hick, *God Has Many Names* (Philadelphia: Westminster, 1980), p. 52.

6. Ibid., pp. 52–53.

7. John Hick, "Pluralism and the Reality of the Transcendent," in *The Christian Century* (January 21, 1981), p. 48.

8. John Hick, "Religious Pluralism," *The Encyclopedia of Religion,* 25 vols., 1986 ed., vol. 12, p. 333.

(a) Different people have different religious views.
(b) Different religious points of view are potentially equally adequate.

The question of importance is this: Does (a) demonstrate (b)? The obvious answer is negative. Hick would probably admit that premise (a), a statement of religious variety, does not by itself prove conclusion (b), a statement of religious pluralism. But if this inference cannot be made, how could religious pluralism be defended?

One approach that supports pluralism depends on a skepticism about religious truth. Of course, if no religious perspective can be established by a rational process of some sort, then every religious viewpoint is on equal epistemological grounds. One could then turn to pluralism as an explanation of the epistemological impasse where no religion could provide rational grounds to support its point of view over another. To someone who believed that religious truth cannot be found through a cognitive process, pluralism could be an appealing option.

In fact, those who choose to combine this skepticism with pluralism sometimes believe that exclusivists argue in a circle. They posit that the exclusivist believes her view to be superior because it passes rational tests of some sort. But the exclusivist does not realize that the tests her world view passes are dependent on her own world view for their validity. In this way, exclusivists argue in a circle and fail to prove their point.

Several things should be said in response to this line of thought. For one, despite this criticism, exclusivism could still be affirmed by a fideist. Beginning with the skeptical premise that religious doctrines cannot be defended rationally, the fideist can choose simply to believe his religion to be the true one. While we do not endorse this move, clearly some thinking people today do. So we point out this option not to advocate it but simply to show that the facts of religious variety do not by themselves entail religious pluralism. Other explanations of the facts can be and are held by competent analysts.

Further, while some exclusivists probably do argue in a circle to support their view, it is not clear that they must do so. It is not enough to show that many people hold a position on defective grounds; it must be shown that the defective grounds are essential to the position. The pluralist who presses this point must show that circularity necessarily plagues the exclusive position, not that this or that exclusivist begs the question. This the pluralists have not done.

Finally, even if pluralists were to show that the exclusive position necessarily argues in a circle, this does not show pluralism to be superior until its adherents successfully avoid the same defect. The point

190

of our larger argument is this: pluralists run great danger of falling into a circle and thus of falling prey to the same difficulty they spot in some forms of the exclusivists' argument.

We are given a set of phenomena: the various religious opinions of different peoples, cultures, and traditions. In the West, these opinions traditionally have been interpreted by the exclusivist theory. This interpretation may not seem very open-minded initially, but it does give a coherent explanation of the facts. Now, the pluralists like Radhakrishnan and Hick want to interpret these facts pluralistically. But the fact of religious variety has been true for millennia. What new evidence forces a new interpretation? Without any qualitatively different evidence, the question becomes, How could we get these facts of religious variety that historically have been interpreted exclusively to support a pluralistic position? For pluralists, a modern religious skepticism, not new information or new unexplained facts, eliminates exclusivism as a possible candidate for the proper explanation of religious variety.

Consider this premise:

(c) No method exists for adjudicating conflicting religious viewpoints.

Premise (c) is, of course, entailed in the modern religious skepticism. By adding (c) to (a) and (b), pluralism becomes not just one possible interpretation of the facts, but the only correct interpretation.

(a) Different people have different religious views.
(c) No method exists for adjudicating conflicting religious viewpoints.
(b) Different religious points of view are (potentially) equally adequate.

Now this formulation of the argument effectively eliminates exclusivism. But it suffers from the obvious defect that it is viciously circular. For the skeptical premise (c) is in fact part of the pluralistic position. In order to preserve the argument from circularity, (c) has to be removed. But if (c) is removed, then exclusivism becomes at least as adequate an explanation for the facts of religious history as pluralism. So a defender of pluralism faces a dilemma: either he assumes (c) and argues in a circle, or he does not assume (c) and must at least admit that his interpretation is not the only possible option.

Of course, even the presumption of the skeptical premise does not lead necessarily to pluralism. As we have said, a theistic fideist can still believe pluralism is false and her theism exclusively true. Thus, the pluralist can argue in a circle and still not demonstrate pluralism to be true. For some fideists, even granting (c), the skeptical premise, does not decisively eliminate exclusivism.

Hick carefully says that pluralism is *"a way of making sense"* of the facts of religious history.[9] He implies that pluralism is only one of several plausible explanatory schemas to account for the phenomena of religious diversity. He seems to be admitting that he would not use (c) as a premise. But then the question is, How could pluralism be defended? The only area of evidence that could be appealed to in support of religious pluralism can be accounted for with equal philosophical adequacy in another way. Even if the all-important skeptical premise (c) is posited, pluralism is still not demonstrated. For reasons like these, Hick argues that "since all religions are aimed at the same goal[,] apparent conflicts in their truth–claims must be just that—apparent. This . . . is simply another unsubstantiated . . . assumption."[10] Maybe pluralists choose pluralism for psychological or sociological reasons, not for rational ones. The intellectual climate today is not conducive to exclusivist positions.

Exclusivism claims that one viewpoint is correct and that others that differ from it are incorrect. This account of the facts of religious history has some prima facie credibility. Historically, most religious people in most religious traditions have assumed exclusivism. And in everyday matters we generally assume that only one of two conflicting positions can be correct. Suppose that two individuals disagree on whether gun control reduces crime. Does the disagreement between the two prove they are both right? Normally we account for the sociological fact of differing opinions by affirming that one individual is right and the other wrong. This is an exclusive point of view. Naturally, something as complex as the choice between religious world views is even more difficult than the troublesome question about gun control and crime. But notice that our first inclination in interpreting a conflict of viewpoints is to say that one of the two debaters is in error.

The empiricist C. L. Stevenson has developed his famous distinction between disagreements in belief and disagreements in attitude. The first is a factual disagreement; the second is valuational. Disagreements in attitude mean having favorable or unfavorable feelings about something. Attitudes help determine questions like which beliefs are relevant in a particular disagreement. Stevenson assumes that while belief disagreements can be resolved by appeals to facts,

9. Ibid. (emphasis added).
10. Paul Griffiths and Delmas Lewis, "On Grading Religions, Seeking Truth, and Being Nice to People—A Reply to Professor Hick," *Religious Studies* 19 (1983): 79.

attitudinal disagreements cannot. Two debaters could agree on some facts and yet disagree as to which of those facts are the important ones. As an illustration of disagreement in attitude, Stevenson cites this example:

> Two men are planning to have dinner together. One is particularly anxious to eat at a certain restaurant, but the other doesn't like it. Temporarily, then, the men cannot "agree" on where to dine. Their argument may be trivial, and perhaps only half serious; but in any case it represents a disagreement *in attitude.* The men have divergent preferences, and each is trying to redirect the preference of the other.[11]

Whether we should accept Stevenson's distinction, the empiricism of which it is a part, and the whiff of positivism that accompanies it is a tangential question. But even if we do accept his analysis, the fact remains that in most cases, when a difference of opinion arises, we assume that we must first examine the facts to see if the problem does not lie there. Although we may conclude in the end that an irresolvable difference in attitude lies at the root of a disagreement, this is not the place to begin the investigation.

Normally, when a disagreement arises, we assume that someone has to be wrong: he either is missing information, has a conceptual schema that is inadequate, has limited experience, or is just plain bull-headed. Normally we believe that differences of opinion are resolvable and that irresolvable differences are due to epistemological shortcomings in someone's thinking. Consequently, we should not conclude too quickly that differences in interpretation prove all viewpoints correct, unless we have some very strong reasons for doing so.

The point we are contending for remains: even given Stevenson's distinction, most people in most situations assume that differences of opinion should not be interpreted pluralistically in most cases. Pluralism is not the interpretation that commends itself immediately. To affirm pluralism, one must give strong reasons for the view. The only reasons that seem relevant are the facts of religious variety. Yet it is difficult to know how these facts by themselves, without the importation of a hidden pluralistic premise (c), could demand a pluralistic interpretation. It seems that exclusivism is always equally adequate epistemologically as an interpretation of the facts of religious variety.

What has really changed in our culture is not simply the accumulation of new information about religious variety. Though our century has seen a great deal more knowledge of the history and literature of

11. C. L. Stevenson, *Facts and Values* (New Haven: Yale University Press, 1963), pp. 1–4.

religions come to light, this knowledge can be accounted for on exclusivist grounds. What is new is the consensus among scholars in some camps that we cannot achieve religious knowledge and that religious doctrines have a function other than describing actually existing religious realities.

In one common view, historical and scientific statements are fact oriented and therefore subject to confirmation and disconfirmation. But religious statements, it is claimed, are value oriented and therefore not open either to confirmation or to disconfirmation. The antecedents of this distinction between scientific and religious truth are very complex and numerous. It reflects the spirit of positivism with its failed Verification Principle. Positivists assumed that only definitional and empirical statements are meaningful. If that is true, then religious exclusivism cannot be defended. But tracing that story is not our purpose here. Our point is this: this latent positivistic mood and its skeptical mentality has contributed more to the acceptance in the West of the Hindu pluralistic mentality than any other single factor. Our culture has come to accept pluralism, but not because it is rationally necessary to do so.

The Parasitic Nature of Pluralism

This discussion raises yet another problem for the pluralist. The difficulty lies in the claim that pluralism is *the* correct view of religions. This, of course, is an exclusivist claim. Pluralists affirm exclusively their conviction that pluralism is true and deny exclusively that exclusivism is true. Thus pluralists become exclusivists at a different level; pluralism, we might say, is in this way parasitic on exclusivism. Pluralists attack exclusivism for failing to recognize the "deabsolutization of truth." In our day, they say, "absolute truth" is obsolete. But pluralists must "reabsolutize" truth at some level or they will have no platform from which to argue for the truth of pluralism. Without some "reabsolutizing" of truth, they will slide all the way to relativism. Pluralists are really closet exclusivists.

Hick certainly believes that exclusivism is false. His arguments for pluralism imply that. Of course, one could argue that Hick is simply suggesting pluralism as one of several possible views. Yet his statements strongly imply more than that. In one context, Hick raises the question of grading religions. He says that in different traditions, even in our own, we can see "different aspects [that] have to be regarded as higher or lower, better or worse, even divine and demonic."[12] He quotes as an illustration these words from the 1960 Chicago Congress on World Mission: "In the years since the war, more than one billion

12. John Hick, "On Grading Religions," *Religious Studies* 17 (1981): 451.

souls have passed into eternity and more than half of these went to the torment of hell fire without even hearing of Jesus Christ, who he was, or why he died on the cross of Calvary." Hick labels this claim "ridiculous."[13]

Apparently Hick is unwilling to accept this religious perspective as possibly true. His pluralism is not broad enough to include others' belief in hell. So now the question becomes, Has not Hick the pluralist become an exclusivist? It appears that Hick has indeed exclusively rejected a doctrine of hell. Of course, this may have been a statement made in one of his weaker moments. Perhaps to be true to his religious pluralism, he should allow that beliefs in hell are acceptable religious expressions and opt for exclusivism only at the philosophical level. In other words, a pluralist could achieve consistency by saying that religious pluralism is a philosophical view, not a religious one.

To grasp this point, distinguish between specific religious beliefs about God and a general theory about the nature of religious beliefs. For example, "God is a Trinity," "Allah is absolutely one," and "Brahman is beyond personhood" are specific religious beliefs about God. But "Religious doctrines are all true" and "Religious doctrines are all psychological projections" are general theories about religious beliefs. The statements in the first category express religious beliefs—beliefs about God. Those in the second category express metareligious beliefs—beliefs about beliefs. This kind of religious pluralism that claims all religions can be true is a metareligious interpretation about religious beliefs, so it is not itself part of any particular religious belief system. It is a higher-level philosophical view of religious beliefs.

Given this distinction, religious pluralists can resist our argument, at least initially. They can argue that they are committed to pluralism at the religious level and to exclusivism at the higher metareligious, or philosophical, level without contradicting themselves. Their commitment to *religious* pluralism need not involve a commitment to a higher-level *philosophical* pluralism.[14] Pluralists can achieve consistency by saying they are exclusivists only at the higher philosophical level. This response, as an initial move, seems justified.

But more remains to be said. The distinction between religious views and metareligious views means that pluralists need not contradict themselves by affirming both pluralism and exclusivism at the

13. Ibid., pp. 451–52; the quote is from *Facing the Unfinished Task*, ed. J. O. Percy (Grand Rapids: Eerdmans, 1961), p. 9. 14. Harold Netland, "Professor Hick on Religious Pluralism," *Religious Studies* 22 (1986): 254.

15. Radhakrishnan, *Eastern Religions and Western Thought*, pp. 316–27.

same level. Our point is different: sooner or later the pluralist must argue that religious views can be adjudicated. If pluralists want to defend religious viewpoints and exclude irreligious viewpoints, it must be possible to make rational judgments about the merits of religious truth claims vis-à-vis irreligious claims. But this stands in tension with the assumption of modern religious skepticism that lies behind contemporary pluralism. In order to infer religious pluralism from the fact of religious variety, pluralists assume premise (c), the claim that religious truth claims cannot be adjudicated. Now, to keep from sliding to relativism, pluralists reject (c).

Alternatively, if pluralists argue that irreligious explanations are as adequate as religious explanations, they move away from pluralism and into relativism. This means saying not just that different religious experiences and conceptions of God are adequate rationally but that any macroexplanation, religious or irreligious, is adequate. We are correct to hold any view of religion whatsoever, including Sigmund Freud's or Carl Sagan's. What is this but relativism? To evade irreligious interpretations, pluralists assume that religious truth claims can be adjudicated. If they do not, they cannot avoid the correctness of irreligious explanations. Accepting irreligious views as even partially correct is perilously close to relativism.

To avoid this relativism, in which every interpretation of religious experience (whether religious or irreligious) is acceptable, the pluralist must appeal to some criterion to show that religious explanations and conceptions are acceptable while irreligious ones are not. At this point, the pluralist necessarily will be parasitic on exclusivism. If we can find the level where the pluralist draws the line at which he stops allowing alternative explanations, we will find the point where he becomes an exclusivist. Of course, if the pluralist never crosses such a line, then his position reduces to relativism. Thus, pluralism is a position that can be held in the initial stages of a discussion, but sooner or later, at some level, it must reduce to either exclusivism or relativism.

The Appeal to the Pragmatic Test

Another avenue for understanding the significance of religious doctrines is to consider that they are means for achieving a religious goal. Perhaps the importance of religious beliefs is not that they describe reality in some way, whether mythical or literal, but that they are useful pragmatically for helping the believer to bring about a state of mind or to develop an aspect of character. An instrumentalist or pragmatic view of religious doctrine is coherent with religious pluralism because the pragmatic view interprets all religions as mechanisms for awaking a consciousness with God. The ancient Oriental proverb reflects this attitude: the different religions are like different paths up the same mountain.

Radhakrishnan makes just this move. He says we should accept any religion as true if it contributes to personal maturity and supports a life of the spirit. Even crude religions are to be granted legitimacy if they enable the believer to overcome egoism. Each religious doctrine is good if "it creates for those who use it a true path for spiritual life."[15]

Like Radhakrishnan, Hick uses the pragmatic test to grade religious doctrines. Hick concludes, "religious phenomena—patterns of behaviour, experiences, beliefs, myths, theologies, cultic acts, liturgies, scriptures, etc.—can in principle be assessed and graded; and the basic criterion is the extent to which they promote or hinder the great religious aim of salvation/liberation."[16] He defines this "great religious aim" as "the transformation of human existence from self-centeredness to Reality-centeredness."[17]

Notice that the pragmatic move does not avoid the question of truth. This is true in several ways. For one, the goal that is to be reached by the pragmatically justified doctrines cannot itself be defended pragmatically. If an instrumentalist says that religious ideas are true if they bring about selflessness, then this immediately raises the question, What makes selflessness good? Extrinsically justified dogmas, ideas we accept because they help us achieve some goal, cannot forever be justified by other extrinsically justified dogmas. Sooner or later the infinite regress must end at a goal that is intrinsically justified. At that point we are still within our rights to ask the pragmatist for epistemological justification.

When we raise the question of how we know that the goal the doctrines of various religions are reaching is correct, we are back to the question of truth. At this point, if one is pluralistic, several avenues of attack are open. One could argue that the religious goal of any particular religion whatever is acceptable, that only one goal of a particular religion is appropriate, or that a generally religious goal of salvation/liberation/enlightenment is to be sought. These three logical alternatives are the only options open to pluralists. We shall find it useful, therefore, to evaluate these three options in turn.

Suppose we say that just any religious goal is acceptable. This means that the Zen Buddhist doctrine is true because it leads to *satori* and Christian doctrine is true because it leads to forgiveness of sin. But these two goals are so different that it is hard to see that

16. Hick, "On Grading Religions," p. 466.
17. Hick, *God Has Many Names*, p. 9.
18. Hick, "Pluralism and the Reality of the Transcendent," p. 46.

there is any meaningful way in which they could both be said to be true. This move therefore reduces to a relativism: the doctrines of a religion are true if they help the believer achieve a goal that those doctrines say is acceptable. This approach validates every religion so that no external grading of religions is possible. Hick could not accept this option, for it is relativism.

But, suppose we say that only one goal is acceptable. The question then is, Which religion and which goal? The various religions conceive of the ideal spiritual state in quite different terms. Which one should be followed? This move reduces to exclusivism. It implies that only one view is correct and others are incorrect to the degree that they disagree with the correct view. No pluralist could accept this, for it is exclusivism.

But suppose the pluralist were to argue that something broad like salvation/liberation/enlightenment is the goal of religious doctrine. This avoids the problems of the other two choices. And Hick does speak in these terms. But again, this move raises problems. The main one is this: the concept of the religious goal is stated so broadly here as to be without specific content. What does *salvation/liberation/ enlightenment* mean? Shall we understand it to be freedom from moral transgression or from ignorance? Shall we understand it to be self-affirmation or self-denial? Does it mean the fulfillment of my deepest desires for relationship with God, as the Christian believes, or the extinction of all desires, as the Buddhist believes?

As soon as we try to decide what "the religious aim of salvation/liberation" means, we face a problem. Even talking about "salvation/liberation/enlightenment" as if there were such a thing presumes that pluralism is true. From an exclusive point of view, this phrase completely lacks coherent meaning. Therefore, to talk about it as though it were meaningful suggests that the pluralist has already assumed a pluralistic posture. This way of even raising the issue begs the question.

Fundamentally, an entirely pragmatic approach to the assessment of religious doctrine simply begs the question. Any use of the pragmatic test involves testing a doctrine by whether it reaches a religious goal. The test necessarily presupposes the validity of that goal. In the religious realm, the goal is itself a religious idea. Either that religious idea is itself justified by some other idea (that is, it is justified extrinsically) or it is not (that is, it is justified intrinsically). If it is justified extrinsically, then we are off on an infinite regress with no intrinsically justified reason in sight. If it is justified intrinsically, then the use of the pragmatic test begs the question, for it assumes the truth of the religious perspective that is supposedly being tested.

When Radhakrishnan states that religious doctrine is true if "it creates for those who use it a true path for spiritual life," the question-begging nature of the pragmatic move becomes evident. The truth of religious doctrine is being tested by a criterion that presupposes the truth of religious doctrine. Surely this begs the question unless there is some other criterion by which to judge whether the "path for spiritual life" is actually true. If another test could identify the "true path for spiritual life," then as a second phase of the argument this "true path" could be the standard by which all other doctrines are judged pragmatically. But to move right to this second phase by assuming the truth of the first phase without any basis is clearly inadequate. At the very best, only some, but not all, religious doctrines could be justified in a pragmatic way.

The same question begging can be seen in Hick's claim that "the basic criterion [for grading religions] is the extent to which they promote or hinder the great religious aim of salvation/liberation." As a standard for evaluating the truth of some religious doctrines, this claim clearly presupposes the truth of other religious doctrines. It assumes, for example, that there is a "great religious aim," that human beings ought to pursue this aim, that the aim is "Reality-centeredness," and that "Reality-centeredness" is better than "self-centeredness." These are religious ideas that need justification and cannot be justified pragmatically.

The pragmatic move leads to the dilemma mentioned above in a new guise. If we have no independently confirmed truth to judge the other truths, then pragmatism becomes question begging. If we use an independently confirmed truth to judge the other truths, then the pluralist is faced with an exclusively true religious doctrine. Once again, pluralists find their viewpoint dependent, sooner or later, on an exclusively true doctrine, even though the exclusivism appears at lower levels in the hierarchy of thought. If this exclusivism does not appear at some point, it may be argued, the pluralist is reduced to relativism. This conclusion pluralists do not generally like. Hick himself wishes to avoid relativism.[18] But a thoroughgoing pluralism is impossible; a complete pluralism is nothing other than relativism.

Pluralism and Tolerance

Among common reasons people reject Christian theism lurks the conviction that Christianity is too exclusive. For example, students polled by *HIS* magazine cited this as one of the top two reasons for rejecting Christianity.[19] One real problem for exclusivism may be the

19. Robert M. Kachur, "Why I'm Not a Christian," *HIS* (February 1986), pp. 7–10. By the way, the most commonly cited reason for rejecting Christianity was "Christians are hypocrites."

20. Griffiths and Lewis, "On Being Nice to People," p. 77.

perception that the rejection of pluralism entails intolerance. In our society today, with its freedoms of speech and religious exercise, intolerance is a cardinal sin. But as some of Hick's critics have pointed out, pluralists seem to assume that tolerance is possible only if one takes a nonjudgmental view of others' points of view.[20] Many assume that tolerance demands acknowledging the truth of others' views.

But this assumption is not correct. Tolerance in no way requires that we accept the truth of another person's beliefs. By definition *tolerance* implies a disagreement with the other doctrine. We never speak of tolerating a belief we ourselves accept. If we tolerate a doctrine, we are not approving but rejecting or disapproving that idea. Thus, as Harold Netland says, "Toleration has an element of condemnation built into its meaning."[21] If tolerance entails disagreement, then it is difficult for someone who accepts to some degree the truth of all the great world faiths to tolerate any of them. So it is a bit odd for pluralists to speak as if tolerance demanded pluralism. In a sense, tolerance demands exclusivism.

Solving this misconception requires that we distinguish between one's beliefs and one's stance. *Beliefs* refers to the doctrines, ideas, or opinions a person holds whether or not they are supported in an epistemologically acceptable way. *Stance* denotes the attitude, the posture, the degree of combativeness with which beliefs are held. Belief is an epistemological question; stance is largely a psychological issue. The degree of humility or arrogance, of openness or dogmatism, exhibited by a particular individual has to do entirely with stance. How and why people—whether snake-handling cultists or urbane, live-and-let-live pluralists—defend their views with the emotional zeal of a true believer is a question of stance and therefore a psychological issue entirely.

A particular set of beliefs has no logical connection with a particular stance. Pluralists assume that exclusivists have a corner on intolerance and that pluralism is necessary for tolerance. But nothing could be farther from the truth. Every combination is possible: tolerant pluralist and tolerant exclusivist; intolerant pluralist and intolerant exclusivist.

Essentially, pluralists assume that only their viewpoint is accepting of different perspectives. But paradoxically, pluralism does not really accept any religious tradition. The exclusivists say that all religious traditions are in error except one. The pluralists think they are doing better by saying that not just one religion is true, but all are. But pluralism forces us to abandon central claims of every religion,

---

21. Harold Netland, "Exclusivism, Tolerance and Truth," *Evangelical Review of Theology* (July 1988): 244.

22. Russell Chandler, *Understanding the New Age* (Waco: Word, 1988), pp. 210–14.

for these beliefs are simply irreconcilable. For example, New Agers like to present their views as "Christian." "A Course in Miracles" is a 1200-page compendium of New Age teachings (with a half-million copies sold) supposedly "channeled" by Jesus. It is the basis for hundreds of study groups around the country. The material uses Christian concepts like *God, Christ,* and *atonement.* But the meaning or content of these terms must be radically altered to achieve pluralistic unity of thought.[22]

Because they must generalize all religions in order to avoid interreligious contradictions, pluralists in effect tell the adherents of every religious tradition that they are in error at certain points. The proponents of a religious tradition who believe they have found the secret to contact with God are fundamentally wrong. There is no one secret; everyone has access to the divine. Two critics put the point this way: pluralism "does not even do the tradition with which it is concerned the favour of taking it seriously on its own terms."[23] By telling religious believers that unique central claims of their faiths must be given up to achieve interreligious tolerance, the pluralist assumes the very stance that Hick criticizes in exclusivists, a stance he calls "triumphalism and arrogance."[24]

This fact betrays the pluralists' deep-seated exclusivism. The pluralist must tell the adherents of every religious tradition that they are wrong not only about other religions, but even about their own. The pluralist knows more about the real content and implications of Religion A than does the devotée of Religion A. Pluralism can be as intolerant as exclusivism, because it is really parasitic on exclusivism at a different level. Since on the level of the conflict between pluralism and exclusivism and of the debate between the religious perspective and the irreligious, pluralists accept exclusivism, it is possible for the pluralist to be intolerant of exclusivists and the irreligious. Tolerance is a matter of one's stance, not one's beliefs.

What, then, is the appropriate stance for Christian theists? In general, if our analysis is correct, combining an exclusive understanding of theism with a tolerant posture is as logically feasible as being an intolerant pluralist. More specifically, these elements should be included in a stance that is becoming of Christian virtue:

1. Recognition of the need for humility. Christians, the saying goes, should be confident in the truth, but have doubts about themselves. Too many people do the opposite: they have doubts about the

23. Griffiths and Lewis, "On Being Nice to People," p. 78; cf. Netland, "Hick on Pluralism," p. 255.

24. Gavin D'Costa, *John Hick's Theology of Religions: A Critical Evaluation* (Lanham, Md.: University Press of America, 1987), p. 117.

truth, but are confident in themselves. Although we may believe we have the truth, we must admit that we do not grasp it completely or comprehensively. We should, therefore, be open to correction and instruction even by those who may not be Christians.

2. Recognition of the right of others to see it another way. Each person has the legal right (in most Western countries) and the moral right to believe as she sees fit. Christians who take the stance of tolerance should realize that others have the right to their views. Of course, we all have the right to try to persuade others. But in the end, others are responsible for their own views.

3. Recognition of the cultural factors that play important roles in the way we think. A person who takes the posture of tolerance will work to distinguish between things held for merely traditional and cultural reasons and ideas held for epistemologically adequate reasons. The posture of tolerance requires that we be open to those of other cultures who are in a position to identify our own cultural blind spots.

4. Recognition of the need for genuine dialog. We have the responsibility to listen to those who differ and to avoid even the appearance of a cultural imperialism. Again, genuine dialog does not mean accepting the truth of any claim another person makes. Nor does it mean suspending one's own beliefs as a precondition for discussion. But it does involve listening attentively and speaking honestly.

This posture of tolerance is not the exclusive possession of pluralists. Tolerance and pluralism are not logically connected. Some pluralists, of course, may adopt a tolerant posture, but that is incidental to their pluralism. In fact, if pluralism is correct, we can even wonder how the pluralist could conclude that tolerance is the only value that we ought to embrace. Maybe tolerance is a value we can defend exclusively because certain Christian doctrines like "God loves every person" are exclusively true. Be that as it may, the fundamental point is that the stance of tolerance is entirely consistent with an exclusive position that affirms the final truth of particular religious views.

In sum, as an interpretation of religious variety, religious pluralism has one very valuable asset: it allows us to take the stance of openness and tolerance toward those of differing perspectives. But this asset is balanced by several large liabilities. First, the pluralist cannot infer his pluralism from the facts of religious variety without presupposing a premise that is suggested by pluralism. This means that the pluralist runs the risk either of begging the question or of admitting that his view is not decidedly better than exclusivism as an interpretation of religious variety. Second, the pluralist must sooner or later become an exclusivist if he is to avoid a slide all the way to relativism. He may not be an exclusivist on the debate between

Christians and Buddhists, but he must be an exclusivist on the questions of pluralism versus exclusivism and of religion versus irreligion.

These liabilities are great. Of course, if accepting them is the only way to be tolerant, then they might be unavoidable. However, since we can assume the stance of tolerance in conjunction with exclusivism, we need not feel compelled to accept these liabilities. Pluralism's great advantage can be achieved in another way without having to shoulder its epistemological baggage.

Conclusion

New Age pantheists oppose exclusivism and promote pluralism. This is consistent with the myriad sources that flow into New Age thinking. The movement borrows from various Eastern religious philosophies, of course, but it also blends elements from ancient paganism, native American religions, occultism, Gnosticism, and Spiritualism. New Agers like to think that their religion is consistent with Christianity—at least with the best of Jesus' teachings.

But this pluralism, as we have seen, itself requires exclusivism. Indeed, one can hold an exclusive position, as many theists do, and still be tolerant. The posture of tolerance is certainly the morally appropriate attitude in this day when different religious perspectives have become known to all. Yet, though the stance of tolerance is to be commended, the position of pluralism should not be. Religious pluralism as a theory about religions follows neither from the moral obligation of openness toward others nor from the factual reality of variety in religious beliefs. This dimension of New Age views about religious experience cannot be defended and should not be espoused.

❖10❖

The Problem of Good and Evil

Buddhism does not share the Western view that there is a moral law, enjoined by God or by nature, which it is man's duty to obey.—Alan Watts
It was not easy to maintain . . . that good and evil, love and hate, life and death were One Reality.—Rabindranath Maharaj

Every world view must account for good and evil. The human encounter with the moral dimension of existence is so vivid it cannot be glossed over. Like the colicky baby that refuses to sleep, evil incessantly demands both philosophical explanations and practical solutions. The most privileged human beings, should they somehow avoid the suffering most of us sooner or later face, at the very least must face their own mortality. Evil presents every world view with both philosophical/theoretical and existential/practical problems.

The concepts 'good' and 'evil' refer also to morality. Every human culture commands some behaviors and prohibits others. Theorists debate whether all cultures require the *same* behavior patterns. But 'ought' and 'ought not' find a place in every culture. Though we cannot justify it here, we believe this fact derives from a fundamental sense of oughtness that is part of every person's human constitution.

The Problem of Evil

Our first task is to examine whether pantheism can fruitfully explain and solve the dilemmas created by the human experience of pain and suffering. This so-called problem of evil has annoyed theists in two ways for millennia. First, the problem of evil creates a philosophical puzzle: if God is all-powerful, he should be able to eliminate evil, and if he is all-loving, he should want to eliminate evil. But real evil exists. Therefore, either God is not all-powerful or not all-loving, or else God does not exist at all. Either way, traditional theism is false. Theism's antagonists press this philosophical problem, and their attack demands philosophical explanation. It is an intellectual question and needs an intellectual answer.

Second, the experience of suffering raises an entirely different kind of problem. Living with evil demands a practical solution. Philosophical arguments that seek to justify God's existence in light of an abstraction called human suffering say little to those who suffer concretely the loss of a loved one. This problem does not need merely cognitive explanation, it needs relational resolution. Caring, sharing a burden, encouragement, "being there" must accompany philosophical answers to resolve this existential dimension of the problem.[1]

We turn now to discuss whether pantheism responds adequately either philosophically or existentially to evil. We begin with the philosophical side of the problem: Can pantheism explain evil? Logically, we have available only a limited number of basic options to explain evil philosophically. They range from views that ascribe great importance to evil to those that treat evil as an illusion. First, we could posit that God is or contains evil. Though this is repugnant for all, it is a logically possible view. Second, dualism grants evil a separate metaphysical stature on a par with good or God. In this view, illustrated by ancient Gnosticism and Persian Zoroastrianism, the principles of good and evil coexist and combat each other eternally. But the dualistic nature of this view obviously contradicts pantheism. Third, some views posit that evil is an inherent part of the finitude of nature. Whether theistic, like some liberal Christians (Friedrich Schleiermacher, for example), or atheistic, like some evolutionists,

---

1. Theistic responses to the problem of evil often argue that God gives humans and other creatures freedom, which is necessary for real relationships of love with God. He has good reasons for allowing his creatures to misuse this freedom and to cause evil. For a classic statement of this position, see Alvin Plantinga's statement of "The Free Will Defense" in *God, Freedom, and Evil* (New York: Harper and Row, 1974). Less technical but equally competent treatments include C. S. Lewis, *The Problem of Pain* (New York: Macmillan, 1962); J. Tal Murphree, *A Loving God and a Suffering World* (Downers Grove: InterVarsity, 1981); Michael Peterson, *Evil and the Christian God* (Grand Rapids: Baker, 1982).

this option presupposes an actual world of nature and is therefore incompatible with pantheism.

Fourth, a theistic determinism, like some forms of Islam or extreme Calvinism, holds that God, who is sovereign over all, creates evil as well as good. Evil, therefore, is a direct result of God's causative action. However, this theistic view contradicts pantheism because it posits a world separate from God. Fifth, a free will view asserts that God creates free creatures whom he permits to choose evil. God so values freedom, it is argued, that he allows evil choices even when they go against his first and best will. This alternative, developed in various forms by many theists, also contradicts the unity of pantheism. Finally, evil may be an illusion or unreal in some way. Pantheism generally chooses this option.

Presumably, these alternatives are exhaustive. They have been listed starting with those that give great prominence to evil and moving toward those that give no place to evil. No other basic class of views has been advocated historically. Either

(a) evil is part of God's being;
(b) evil exists as an eternal reality separate from God;
(c) evil exists in nature as an unavoidable aspect of nature itself;
(d) evil is caused in nature by direct acts of God;
(e) evil is caused in nature by direct acts of God's creatures; or
(f) evil is unreal.

We have argued briefly that (b), (c), (d), and (e) assume the existence of a finite reality outside of God. Consequently, to the degree pantheists deny the existence of whatever is not God, each of these is logically incompatible with pantheism. This leaves pantheism two options: either (a) evil is in God or (f) evil is ultimately illusory. H. P. Owen sums up, "It is difficult enough to square this fact [of evil] with belief in an omnipotent and infinitely loving Creator. It is much more difficult to square it with the view that an evil world is an actual expression of God's perfect nature. There is in fact only one solution—to affirm that evil too is merely 'apparent.'"[2] We must examine these options more carefully.

To suggest that evil actually resides in God places any religious world view in an untenable position. If all that exists is in God and evil is actually part of all that exists, then evil has to be placed within the being of God. But surely this move compromises the very unity, perfection, transcendence, and infinity of God that the pantheist is so

2. H. P. Owen, *Concepts of Deity* (New York: Herder and Herder, 1971), p. 72.

much at pains to defend. The Hindu philosopher Ramanuja tries to conclude that the divine perfection suffers no external limitation by presupposing that evil is only an internal limit on God. This hardly seems adequate. As Stuart C. Hackett comments, "The attempt to solve these problems by making all these limits internal to God is rather like an American's dismissing . . . the national debt by the simple suggestion that after all we owe the money to ourselves—an observation which leaves that debt right where it was before."[3]

The remaining alternative is to relegate evil to non-existence. Pantheists generally find themselves pulled in this direction. Because of the alternatives logic allows, this option is the easiest path to follow for the pantheist who seeks coherence. Zen Buddhists hold to illusionism quite overtly. Others are less direct. Spinoza believed that our world is the best of all possible worlds simply because it is the only possible world. Thus so-called evil is a necessary part of the world as it is. What we call suffering could not have been other than it is; 'evil' could not have been avoided if only someone had chosen a different course of action. If we could understand the causes of sorrow, we would not experience it as sorrow. What is, just is. Suffering is caused by human ignorance of the true state of affairs.

To say evil is an illusion is an explanation in a sense. A world view is allowed to have certain explanatory principles by which it organizes the facts as it sees them. If one of pantheism's explanatory principles is "Experiences of alleged evil are misleading and illusory," it explains evil in a sense. But this explanation generates other difficulties. First, the principle of comprehensiveness comes into play. If I say that evil does not exist as such, I do not simply judge one experience to be an illusion. I eliminate in effect a whole class of experiences. We explored in chapter 7 the problems with rejecting whole classes or kinds of experience in toto (versus examining experiences individually), and we need not repeat them in detail. Stated briefly, world views run up against the test of comprehensiveness when they choose to dismiss whole regions of experience. Generally, a world view that incorporates and fruitfully illuminates larger areas of experience is better than one that obliterates whole ranges of experience.

Second, a judgment that a certain experience ought to be discounted generally calls for a warrant, a reason. Why does the United States Air Force judge that UFO sightings, for example, do not prove the existence of space aliens in our midst? *The National Inquirer* notwithstanding, the USAF has alternative explanations for these phenomena. Within their total USAF world view, these other explanations account more effectively for the sightings than does positing

---

3. Stuart C. Hackett, *Oriental Philosophy: A Westerner's Guide to Eastern Thought* (Madison: University of Wisconsin Press, 1979), p. 176.

real space aliens. Similarly, if pantheists could develop explanations as to how this whole range of experiences comes to be, their case for rejecting the experiences of evil as illusion could be considerably strengthened. Initially, both single experiences and whole classes of experiences that impress those who have them as revealing reality should not be discounted until we find significant reasons for discounting them.

One explanation given to account for these alleged illusory experiences is that they arise through errors in the mind. Pantheists generally argue that ignorance causes pain. We suffer because we do not have true knowledge of the nature of things. This explanation sounds reasonable initially. Who among us has not suffered because he was mistaken about something? Suppose I go to a job interview sweating and stewing because I think that the prospective employer is not likely to hire me. Only later do I find out that I was the first choice and the company had virtually decided to give me the job even before the interview. That knowledge might have saved me a lot of needless agony caused by ignorance.

Assuming individual minds exist, illusions with painful consequences do arise in our minds. Within a philosophical perspective of realism, as in our illustration, the explanation that ignorance causes suffering makes good sense. If our everyday lives are real, we can find many instances where our own ignorance causes our suffering. But it is implausible to say, *from a pantheistic point of view*, that evil is an illusion arising in the mind. In pantheism, neither we nor our minds exist as such. Our minds cannot be the source of the ignorance that causes suffering for they are themselves part of the illusion. To posit the human mind, which itself has no ultimate metaphysical status as finite mind, as the cause of the giant deception essentially explains a mystery by a mystery. Such a move does not really answer the question; it merely pushes the question back one step. How do we explain the new mystery?

An inquisitive young boy wants to know what holds up the world. Upon asking his mother, he is told, "The world stands on the back of a giant elephant." This satisfies him for a day or so, but the answer creates another problem: What does the elephant stand on? So the boy returns to his mother who tells him, "The elephant stands on the back of a giant tortoise." The boy feels satisfied for awhile, but again the answer poses another question. So he returns for yet another answer: "Mother, what holds up the giant tortoise?" Frustrated and realizing her dilemma, the mother retorts, "Son, there are tortoises all the way down."

This story illustrates the kind of answer we are talking about. Is the mother's answer really an answer? In one sense, yes, but in another sense, no. In that there is a limited response, the mother did answer the question. But the cure is as bad as the disease. The response raises another problem as difficult to solve as the original question. So the answer helps us gain no ground. It is a nonanswer. It leads to an infinite chain of questions and answers none of which will ever help us get closer to an answer of a different, more satisfying sort. Our contention is that this is exactly what happens when pantheists answer the all-important question, What gives rise to the great illusion? To say that the illusion is caused by another illusion immediately prompts us to ask, What caused that illusion? Since it appears that this is the first in an infinite series of answers, we wonder whether a different kind of solution will ever be found.

If we say that the mind creates misleading beliefs about our experiences of evil, a whole set of thorny questions appears. But if we do not take this general perspective, the alternative appears to be that we must allow for the reality of evil outside the mind. But since, presumably, only God exists, that real evil necessarily would have to reside in the being of God himself. This is a difficult dilemma: either evil is unreal or it is in God. Under pressure from the test of coherence, arguing that evil does not exist appears to be the more attractive horn of the dilemma. The concepts of pantheism fit together better if we disregard evil's reality. But given the force of comprehensiveness, admitting that evil does exist appears to be the better horn of the dilemma—even if it exists in God. At least this accounts for the universality of those experiences that persistently push us toward accepting evil's reality. Which horn of the dilemma would be better? In our judgment, neither one provides much conceptual comfort for the pantheist.

The conflict here is between the "truth" found in enlightenment and the "truth" found in everyday experience. Both of these cannot be true unless the flawed two-truth theory is refurbished. If the first is followed, evil is illusion. But that is difficult to square with experience. If the second truth is followed, evil is real. So presumably it must be in God since everything real is in God. This dilemma is vividly expressed by a guru who became a Christian:

> It seemed difficult to face everyday life after hours in trance. The conflict and contrast between these two worlds was irresolvable. The higher states of consciousness I experienced in meditation were supposedly approaching reality as it really was. Yet the everyday world of joys and sorrows, pain and pleasure, birth and death, fears and frustrations; of bitter conflicts with my Aunt Revati and unanswerable questions posed by my classmates at Queen's Royal College . . . was the world I had to deal with, and I dared not dismiss it as illusion. . . . My religion made

beautiful theory, but I was having serious difficulty applying it in every-day life.[4]

The Existential Problem of Evil

In addition to the conceptual aspect of the problem, evil also presents practical difficulties. This is the existential problem of handling actual, concrete instances of suffering, loss, and pain in life. In the logic of world views, the two sides of the question, the theoretical and the practical, are linked together. The practical generally finds its basis in the theoretical. Now, if pain and suffering are essentially not real, then solving the problem involves enlightening the sufferer. But does this solution really work? Does telling a person that his pain does not exist or that what he experiences is not painful solve the problem? Some critics have charged that this solution is existentially hollow. Like artificially sweetened drinks, it leaves a distinct after-taste.

Religions that say that evil is illusory do not, in our view, ring true. Christian Science, for example, because of its idealistic view of reality (that is, its view that reality is not matter, but mental, composed only of ideas), posits that no human sickness exists. This is all well and good in theory, but what do we do with a man who breaks a leg? Following a deductive thought process, the Christian Scientist is forced to the incongruous conclusion that the leg really is not broken. This view is coherent, perhaps, but suffers terribly at the hands of congruity. Stubborn facts must be forced unnaturally to fit the theory. The theory does not contradict itself exactly, but it has a rough time with the facts.

A world view should not only achieve consistency and coherence, it should also give a structure of practical meaning by which to live. If it were true that our practical experience of pain and suffering is only a nightmare, then obviously the proper solution is waking up. So the practical question, in large measure, hinges on the more theoretical. If pantheism's pattern of thought could provide some satisfying account of the illusory nature of evil, then the practical advice to retrain the mind to see through suffering would be well taken. In this case, we might be justified to accept the incongruity, the lack of smooth fit between theory and sensory experience. Without a reasonable account, on the other hand, the advice to retrain the mind to see that pain is not real becomes a cruel response to the most crying needs of human existence. By teaching without adequate basis that human pain is not real, pantheism could actually cut the nerve of human

---

4. Rabindranath R. Maharaj, with Dave Hunt, *Death of a Guru* (Nashville: Holman, 1977), pp. 104–5.

sympathy, encouragement, and healing. If suffering were real, this would be a very unfortunate, even inhumane, perspective.

In sum, if the world and its inhabitants are real, evil is real and must therefore be within God. In this case, it is hard to see how God's infinity and perfection can be sustained unsullied. Under this sort of conceptual pressure, pantheists usually revert to the view that the world of individual persons is not ultimately real.

Naturally, fairness dictates that we not criticize all pantheists for saying evil is an illusion if in fact they do not all say that. But since every conceptual commitment brings with it logical implications, we can state the argument as a dilemma. On the one hand, to the degree that evil is played down as an illusion to avoid placing it within the perfection of God, the world and its inhabitants become unreal. In this case pantheism will have difficulty providing either an adequate theoretical account of our experience of the world or a practical solution to universal human suffering. On the other hand, to the degree that individual existence is emphasized to recognize the persistent experiences of evil and thus to fulfill the tests of comprehensiveness and congruity more effectively, the all-inclusive nature of God, the central tenet of pantheism, is compromised. Either way, it appears, the problem of evil, both theoretically and practically, is an Achilles' heel for pantheism.

A Basis for Right and Wrong

The other aspect of good and evil relates to morality. The problem of evil emphasizes what happens to us: the suffering and pain we experience. The issue of morality emphasizes our responsibility to others: how ought we to act toward fellow humans? Pantheistic writers generally have much to say about ethics. At the same time, they deny any ultimate metaphysical basis in God for ethics. What are we to make of this paradox?

A long-standing tradition supports the claim that all humans are obliged to follow certain ethical norms. This position, sometimes called absolutism, is advocated by those who believe that some ethical norms cross cultural and individual boundaries and are therefore applicable to all persons. While the details of ethical beliefs may differ, certain common obligations are recognized in all societies. Although most people probably do not consistently follow these ethical principles in their lives, absolutists argue that this is irrelevant to the issue at hand: the question is not, *Do* people act morally? It is, *Ought* people to act morally? Absolutism affirms that all persons do have similar moral obligations.

Accepting an ethical version of pluralism or relativism, some today challenge the claim that ethical obligations and judgments possess universally binding character. Many, intelligentsia and commoners alike, believe that no universal ethical judgments are possible. They point out that people in different cultures have radically different moral values. In fact, often many people within the same culture have different values. Since we have no magisterium to decide for us which among the competing ethical systems we should follow, relativists argue, we should rest content with the situation as it is and allow all persons the right to determine their own ethical behavior.

The question we intend to investigate in this section does not really depend on deciding the debate between ethical absolutism and ethical relativism. We believe that a good case can be made for ethical absolutes. Not the least of the arguments in support of absolutism is that those who profess relativism in fact hide their absolutistic allegiance to certain basic values. In arguing for the right of individuals to make ethical decisions for themselves, relativists are essentially defending individual freedom and social tolerance as absolutes (that is, as binding on all persons). While I may be free to decide for or against having an abortion, for example, I am not free to be a bigot—it is absolutely wrong to be intolerant of others.

But the real point we are driving at is whether pantheism can produce a metaphysical basis for any ethical norms at all. If they are to be held reasonably, even ethical values defended by relativists (including the right to make personal choices freely and the obligation to respect the opinions of others) presumably need to be incorporated into or grow out of a total philosophy of life. An atheistic philosophy that views human life as a purposeless development within a chance universe seems to lack a ground for ethical ideals. Pantheistic philosophy suffers the same problem, though for different reasons. Can pantheism account for the experience of human beings who sense moral outrage at unfair treatment (like the Nazi extermination of Jews) or who experience a feeling of duty (like the obligation to help neighbors in a burning house)? What is the metaphysical basis for ethical concern, altruism, and conscience?

The pantheistic thrust for the perfection, infinity, and unity of the divine leads to a denial of the applicability of concepts to God. To say God is a person, for example, means that he is not impersonal. But this divides God up and subjects him to the limitations of logical opposites. The pantheist typically says, therefore, that God is above conceptual opposites. But good and evil are conceptual opposites. If the same logic follows, God (that is, reality) is beyond good and evil, and moral categories do not finally possess metaphysical grounding. In this case, our experience of moral obligation remains unexplained. To the degree that pantheism refuses to allow good and evil to have some ground in the way things are, it undercuts the rationality of ethical behavior that is fundamental to religious practice and to social and communal life. For this reason Robert Flint argues, "pantheism . . . strikes at the very roots of morality, and strives to set aside its fundamental postulates. [Every human] feels himself a free agent and responsible for his conduct. He recognizes an order or law which impresses him as sacred, and he has a conviction that he can either bring his life into harmony with it or war against it."[5]

The tendency to place the divine beyond good and evil is illustrated most graphically in Hinduism. Statues portraying the goddess Kali reflect this ambivalence toward good and evil. Kali is pictured with fangs and skulls to represent evil. The gods, therefore, are not always pictured as wholly good, but also can be described as evil. Of course, the ultimate, Nirguna Brahman, stands above good and evil in a way the personal incarnations do not.

New Agers also illustrate this principle. One of the characters in Shirley MacLaine's book, *Dancing in the Light,* explains evil this way: "It doesn't exist. That's the point. Everything in life is the result of either illumination or ignorance. These are the two polarities. Not good and evil. And when you are totally illuminated, such as Jesus Christ or Buddha or some of those people, there is no struggle any longer."[6] This is consistent with the messages typically given by New Age "channelers" who report the teachings of departed beings. Evil is not real; it cannot hurt you.

Pantheists face a dilemma. They may, on the one hand, ascribe both good and evil to the divine. Or they may, on the other hand, declare that God is beyond moral categories entirely. In the first case, the absolute perfection of God is appropriately described by concepts. But this opposes the fundamental pantheistic principle about God being beyond all categories. In the second case, our experience of moral obligation and our sense of right and wrong cannot be accounted for. No metaphysical basis for moral distinctions exists.

The best way out, it appears, is to ascribe genuine good and good only to God. This solves the problem since God's being and nature ground our valuing of 'good' and our sense of moral obligation. But we do not compromise God's perfection by calling him evil. The only difficulty with the move is that it goes against the fundamental pantheistic premise that to ascribe only one of two conceptual opposites to God somehow limits him. Theists are not afraid to take the plunge, to say that God really is good and not evil. But pantheists cannot do

    5. Robert Flint, *Anti-Theistic Theories* (London: William Blackwood and Sons, 1899), p. 396.
    6. Shirley MacLaine, *Dancing in the Light* (Toronto: Bantam, 1985), p. 247.

this without modifying their world view into something other than pantheism.

One avenue evades this dilemma. Suzuki says Zen teaches that we should just do what needs doing and move on. We need no metaphysical grounding for doing what we do; if a boy is drowning, we wade in and pull him out. We simply do the deed and move on without coveting the praise normally associated with such good deeds. The Zennist does what needs to be done without a second thought. Zen admires the "secret virtue," the "deed without merit," but it does not abandon ethics.[7]

But this answer seems to beg the question. Theists would not criticize the lifestyle of a pantheist who always helps his neighbor, protects the weak, respects property, and saves drowning children. But the issue is, Given the grounds of his world view, how does the pantheist know that helping others is good and harming them is not evil? Suzuki tells us to wade in and save the boy; theists who respect the sanctity of personal life would value that action. But why, on pantheistic grounds, would pulling the boy out be morally better than allowing him to drown? Or could walking past without regard to the boy's earthly life be an instance of "doing what needs to be done without a second thought"?

In positing this scenario, Suzuki entirely glosses over the need for a rationale behind preferring helping to hurting. If walking past without helping can be an example of a proper "deed without merit," it appears we have landed in antinomianism (a denial of law, the view that any action can be acceptable). But if walking past without helping is not an example of a proper "deed without merit," then why is helping the preferable action? This is precisely the issue. The question is not whether a pantheist would pull the boy out; presumably Suzuki thinks a Zennist would do that without thinking. The question is rather, What warrant can pantheism give for the claim that saving the boy is the morally preferable action?

Zen advocate Alan Watts takes another approach to this problem. Watts claims that Zen rejects Western-style moral laws. Rules similar to the Ten Commandments are followed by followers of Zen. But the laws are simply "voluntarily assumed rules of expediency." They function to help those who follow them achieve greater clarity of awareness. Now, breaking these rules produces bad karma not because it is ultimately wrong to break them but because any purposeful, "grasping" action leads to bad karma. Even conventionally good actions, if they grasp after the continued existence of the isolated ego, contribute to bad karma. Conventionally bad actions are

7. D. T. Suzuki, *Introduction to Zen Buddhism* (New York: Grove, 1954), pp. 130–31.

worse only because they are more grasping and build up negative karma more quickly. "The higher stages of Buddhist practice are as much concerned with disentanglement from 'good *karma*' as from 'bad.'"[8]

Watts is sharp. This answer gives morality a place in life and denies antinomianism. Yet he also denies the ultimacy of moral principles. These rules are just conventional, and we follow them voluntarily. Therefore, we need no ultimate justification for the principles. If Watts has the last word, then our criticism is blunted: presumably we need not ask about the ontological ground for preferring helping to hurting.

But this answer, too, hides some tensions. For one thing, if the "higher stages" of Buddhist moral theory emphasize "disentanglement" from all grasping, we are really saying we move through the lower stages *in order to* achieve the higher stages where grasping is overcome. Watts's phrase, "higher stages of Buddhist practice are concerned with," is a dead giveaway. What is this but a grasping for the "free, uncontrived, or spontaneous action"? Higher stages of morality "are concerned with" getting beyond being concerned with moral benefits. Of course, Watts will probably tell us that this dilemma appears only at the lower, logical level of truth. At the higher level of truth, where no logical distinctions apply, this verbal puzzle dissolves. This would be a good answer if Watts could himself consistently evade rationality. As we shall see, however, he cannot.

But even if Watts deflects this question, his basic answer may still fail to solve our problem. He says that all conventional rules are simply followed as an expedience in order to help Zennists achieve the totally spontaneous life Zen admires most. But this fails to detect that Watts is working with two levels of norms. While the lower-order ethical norms may be purely conventional, the higher-order norms are not. At the higher level, the Zennist is supposing that certain principles have a validity that is more than conventional. How are these principles justified?

For example, Watts assumes that rules against taking life, lying, or intoxication are lower-level, conventional rules. But as a higher-order principle, he also presupposes the correctness of prohibiting grasping. I can "break" the higher-order law of grasping even if I follow all the conventional norms. Obeying the law against lying might not be required, but obeying the "law" against grasping surely is. Watts believes all grasping is wrong. The principle extolling "free, uncontrived, or spontaneous" action and the norm admonishing the "deed without merit" and the "action without thought" are different from

8. Alan Watts, *The Way of Zen* (New York: Random House, Vintage Books, 1957), p. 52.

the conventional rules and operate at a higher level. We still want to ask why it is or how we know that grasping is wrong and spontaneous action is right.

The dilemma faced by a pantheist at this point is created once again by the hesitancy to allow that conceptual categories apply to the divine. If God is all, and God's unity demands that no rational distinctions can be ultimately true of God, then the good/evil distinction is groundless. In this case, it is hard to see how ethical behavior could have a basis and how one action could be morally preferable to another. To evade antinomianism, Suzuki and Watts are forced to advocate moral principles they cannot defend.

Christmas Humphreys, another Buddhist advocate, spells out a more consistent ethical implication of this philosophy. He writes that ethics has "no intrinsic validity." If there is "a washing-up to be finished, or a war to be won; let them be done." We should not repress emotions, he says; if our emotions run high, then "use them, develop them, express the highest in you by their means." (He does not say how we know what is "highest.") We should take our emotions out "for a run" and not be afraid to "sing, shout, get excited, whether with great beauty, a local football match or, best of all, great fun." We can compete in "sport, trade or politics, so long as [we] do not imagine that it matters in the least who wins." The important thing is "the excitement itself, the letting off of steam. . . . The game, whether of football, national politics, or international war, has no intrinsic validity."[9] Humphreys, it appears, is more consistent with pantheistic premises.

If, however, good really is good and therefore preferable to evil, we are justified in asking why this is so. If it is suggested that God is good and not evil, then the fundamental pantheistic principle about ascribing concepts to God is abandoned. If this seems like a small matter, recall that the effect of it is to modify pantheism significantly in a theistic direction. To admit that conceptual opposites apply adequately (if not exhaustively or univocally) to ultimate reality suggests that reality is not really one in the way pantheists want to maintain that it is. To whatever degree the pantheists are willing to admit that conceptual categories of good and evil are in God, they erode the unity of God that is the central tenet of their world view.

Concepts and Reality Revisited

Despite these problems, pantheists almost universally find that ethics is useful to achieve salvation. In Plotinus and the Oriental pan-

9. Christmas Humphreys, *Zen Buddhism* (London: William Heinemann, 1949; reprint ed., London: Allen and Unwin, 1961, 1988), p. 158.

theists, ethical discipline becomes the avenue through which a person prepares herself for enlightenment. In the first stage of mystical ascent toward the divine, ethical discipline helps one shut out the world. In one sense, this emphasizes that this world is not the sum total of reality; a spiritual realm exists. Those who possess religious convictions, regardless of their tradition, share a belief that this world is not all there is to life. We do not question this basic conviction.

The issue we are raising here is different: Why is ethical behavior generally recognized as good (instead of evil or at least neutral) chosen to emphasize the transitory nature of this life? Why not some other nonmoral practice? Zen does use art and sport to accomplish its goals. Poetry, calligraphy, and archery are among the disciplines Zen has molded for its own purposes. But could a person develop discipline necessary for the mystical ascent through some grotesque activity, say, becoming the world's top contract killer? If no ethical, moral qualities constitute the nature of the ultimate reality, there appears to be no reason why the discipline, self-denial, and other qualities allegedly necessary for enlightenment could not be achieved through demanding but immoral acts. But this conclusion is counterintuitive. And we observe that pantheists almost universally advocate morally good activities as the prelude to enlightenment. This is curious if indeed no moral qualities obtain in the highest levels of reality.

Additionally, the one who accomplishes enlightenment often works to help others achieve it as well. In Hinduism, the last of the four stages of life does involve exclusive attention to personal salvation as a man leaves society to become a hermit. But even here the earlier stages include service to others. Mahayana or Larger Vehicle Buddhism, of which Zen is a part, especially emphasizes the moral responsibility of the enlightened person for helping others. This ideal is expressed in the *bodhisattva* concept.

The Western pantheists taught their disciples and wrote their books presumably intending to help others achieve enlightenment. But if no moral qualities obtain in the highest reality, what motivates the pantheist to help others achieve salvation? How do we explain all the pantheists' arguments, teachings, and writings? Do not pantheists feel the moral obligation to serve others? If God is a personal God of love who himself possesses moral qualities, our ethical responsibilities to others have a ground. But in a God beyond all conceptual distinctions, where do we locate the foundation of the moral obligation to help others achieve salvation?

As in the chapter on metaphysics, so in this chapter we find that the issue of applying concepts to God becomes the focal point of discussion. It is not surprising to find the pantheist facing a dilemma, for the same problem we encountered in our discussion of metaphysics is repeated here. Just as difficulties arise in the attempt to rise above the personal/impersonal distinction, for example, so they surface in the attempt to move beyond the good/evil contrast. Pantheists cannot have it both ways; they cannot have their philosophical cake and eat it too. If concepts do not apply to God and God alone exists, then they can incorporate concepts like good and evil only through some interpretive sleight of hand.

We have consistently resisted the attempt to rise above all concepts into the realms of reality that allegedly lie beyond rationality. We cannot avoid the fundamental conviction that what is conceptually contradictory is not only rationally impossible but metaphysically impossible as well. At this point our critics may feel compelled to conclude that the basic disagreement we have with pantheism is grounded simply in an arbitrary decision about how we relate rationality and logic to what we believe is ultimately real. Some may feel a temptation to assume that there are simply two points of view: one posits, without defense, the rationality of all existing things, while the other assumes, as an unsupported first principle, the necessity of leaving rationality behind to move to the highest reality. This issue is critically important. Its centrality in evaluating pantheism in general and New Age thinking in particular cannot be overestimated.

The pluralistic or relative point of view is common today. In selecting this understanding, a person chooses to believe that different world perspectives simply begin with different basic interpretive principles. World View A makes up its rules, on the basis of which it turns out to be the "true" world view. But World View B makes up its rules, on the basis of which B turns out to be "true." No decision can be made about A and B or their fundamentally different principles except from within the systems of thought. Therefore, we reach an impasse: each world view tries to criticize the other, but both miss the target because they have no common standards for making world view decisions.

This interpretation attracts many in our shrinking, modern global village of instant communication. But we still believe that one undeniable factor forces us to reject it. Suppose that, in the course of explaining their view, pantheists did in fact utter statements that appeal to rational principles or took actions we would expect based on the dictates of rationality. In these cases, we believe they reveal that their verbal denials of rationality cannot be sustained.

Even at the highest levels of their thought, pantheists do in fact sense conceptual problems that are forced on them by rationality. Further, they respond to these problems by giving answers or performing behaviors we would expect to find a rational person giving or performing. These responses, whether verbal or behavioral, indicate an acknowledgment of rational principles. Pantheists wish to deflect conceptual criticisms by questioning the validity of rationality. But their words and actions reveal that this rejection of rationality is not and cannot be sustained consistently. The denigration of logical principles is an ad hoc procedure used to ease conceptual pressure; it cannot be a consistent principle in any world view.

Consider several examples. Plotinus says that the One is beyond being. An important reason for this approach is the Greek idea that *being* refers to something that has form and therefore is limited. Given this definition, the One could not have being. Why could Plotinus not just say, "Having being entails form and limitation. The One is being, but the One has no form or limitation. This is irrational, but it does not matter for rationality does not obtain"? As we would expect, Plotinus solves this interpretive dilemma by placing the One entirely beyond being.[10] This solution is exactly what we would expect from someone interested in coherence. In the last analysis, Plotinus reveals his unwillingness to reject rationality.

The classic Hindu solution to the problem of ascribing concepts to God suggests a dependence on the principle of consistency. Some recognize that Brahman has no attributes, but others wish to describe Brahman by using concepts. If consistency and coherence did not matter, then Shankara could have said both groups are right: "Saguna Brahman is describable and Nirguna Brahman is not. But Saguna and Nirguna Brahman are the same. Now, this is inconsistent, but it does not matter, for consistency is irrelevant to truth." But this solution is rationally repugnant. Ultimately, Shankara tells us, those who accept Saguna Brahman view Brahman as an object of ignorance. In this way, Hinduism in general and Shankara in particular avoid incoherence.[11]

The Zen masters wish to avoid serious answers to questions about the nature of reality. They recognize that if they claim they cannot use logic to describe reality and then give logical answers, they will contradict themselves. But they resist contradiction. They do not say, "I cannot tell you anything rationally about reality, for conceptual opposites distort reality. Reality is everywhere one, and the divisions we see are illusions created by the conceptual mind. This answer is contradictory, but it does not matter, since rationality does not apply to reality." Instead, as everyone knows, the Zennists deliver nonsensical answers, puzzle their students with *koan*, and opt for mutism on questions about ultimate reality. These evasive answers are logically

---

10. Plotinus, *The Six Enneads*, trans. Stephen MacKenna and B. S. Page, 6 vols. (Chicago and London: Encyclopaedia Britannica, 1952), 5.2 [1].

11. Shankara, *The Vedānta Sūtras of Bādarāyaṇa with the Commentary by Śaṅkara*, trans. George Thibaut, 2 parts (New York: Dover, 1962), 2.1.14.

necessary; they help the Zen masters to avoid self-contradiction and self-destruction.

Watts provides a graphic example of this phenomenon. He had written a number of books explaining with care and wit that words distort and rationality confuses. But these claims naturally provoked the objection: If words distort, why are you writing books? If rationality confuses, what sense are we to make of your rational statements? If Watts truly thought rationality to be irrelevant to truth, he should have said, "All words do distort, but my words telling you that words distort do not distort. This is self-referentially inconsistent, but since rational principles like consistency are irrelevant and meaningless, my words are true." But Watts does not say this. Instead he wrote,

> If, then, I am not saying that you *ought* to awaken from the ego-illusion and help save the world from disaster, why *The Book*? Why not sit back and let things take their course? Simply that it is part of things "taking their course" that I write. As a human being it is just my nature to enjoy and share philosophy. I do this in the same way that some birds are eagles and some doves, some flowers lilies and some roses. I realize, too, that the less I preach, the more likely I am to be heard.[12]

This is a surprisingly consistent response, given Watts' sustained campaign against rationality. It seems that Watts is in essence admitting that his books tell us nothing about reality. Suppose he had said, "Words do not tell us anything meaningful about reality, but the words I just used to tell you this are meaningful." This obviously self-defeats and so breaks rational principles. If Watts really rejected rational consistency, he should have been willing to claim he was meaningfully telling us that it is impossible to tell us anything meaningfully. But he cannot bring himself to claim consistently and meaningfully that no words can speak about reality. He cannot summon the courage to be truly irrational. In short, Watts would rather acknowledge the meaninglessness of all he wrote than to deny the basic rational principle of consistency. Thus, in the very process of overtly discussing the irrelevance of rationality, his maneuver implicitly affirms it.

This move is particularly interesting because rational consistency is not one of the basic principles of Zen. In fact, it is a principle that Zen life and practice are explicitly calculated to destroy. Why, then, should Watts be concerned about having a rationally consistent version of Zen? Is it not inconsistent for him to insist on a rationally consistent form of a philosophy that denies the need for rational con-

---

12. Alan Watts, *The Book: On the Taboo against Knowing Who You Are* (New York: Random House, Pantheon Books, 1966; reprint ed., P. F. Collier and Son, 1970), p. 20.

sistency? Perhaps this is a tacit admission that rationality is unavoidable, even in a system that eschews it.

We believe these illustrations show that the choice between the rational perspective and the alleged suprarational way is not entirely arbitrary. The basic principles by which we elaborate and defend world views are not chosen at random. Even though pantheists overtly deny the fundamental principles of rationality, they establish these principles implicitly in the very process of spelling out their views—even when they are defending an extreme form of antirationalism. The Zennists, for example, are to be commended for the rigor with which they seek to carry out their program of finding reality without recourse to rationality. But even they reveal their dependence on the very principles they so profoundly dislike. The price one pays for denying basic principles like consistency and coherence in the hope of achieving contact with reality in some suprarational way is very high indeed.

Conclusion

We conclude again, therefore, that the pantheistic tendency to resist the use of rational categories creates far more difficulty than it is worth. There is something right about resisting human, abstract categories, for not even finite reality is ever fully captured in abstract concepts. And if God is infinite, how much more can it be said that God is never fully described conceptually? But by no means does this require the complete abandonment of conceptual patterns of thought. In his response to Buddhism, Hackett writes these incisive words to defend the significance of conceptual thinking:

> Of course substance and attribute, cause and effect, and indeed all concepts without exception can only be understood reciprocally: but that is no basis for rejecting either the ultimacy of conceptual reason or the complex of reality to which it applies; it is rather an attempt at clarifying the very nature of rational intelligibility. To identify something and explain it for what it is is unquestionably important; but it is no reason at all for casting it aside on the supposition that it is not some other thing, especially when it never really claimed to be anything but itself.[13]

The last-ditch move of a mystical pantheist in response to our critical probings could be something like this: "All your criticisms make good sense from a rational point of view. But we just don't see the necessity of this highly abstract, overly rationalistic method. We would rather base our decision on our own firsthand experience." We

13. Hackett, *Oriental Philosophy*, p. 120.

believe, however, that this maneuver does not squarely face the evaluative comments we have made. If someone refuses to acknowledge that even the pantheists answer questions and choose positions on the basis of rational criteria, then he reveals his determination to believe what he has always believed no matter what. If truth is an important matter, this attitude is rationally inconsistent and potentially dangerous. Far better, we believe, to begin walking the path toward a world view that is both rationally defensible and personally fulfilling. Pantheism in general and New Age philosophy in particular are neither.

Conclusion
Apologetics in the New Age

Of all the horrible religions the most horrible is the worship of the god within.—G. K. Chesterton

We began by considering three basic world views: Epicurean humanism, Christian theism, and Stoic pantheism. Pantheism, which now presents itself most prominently as New Age thinking, is not just an Oriental philosophy. And it is not new. It has attracted followers for millennia because it proffers an appealing message: you are valuable; you are worth something; you are divine.

Pantheism finds fertile soil in egocentric Western culture. Its message declares what a self-centered society wants to hear. This makes pantheism particularly dangerous, for it caters to our narcissism. Should we worship ourselves? G. K. Chesterton has warned, "That Jones shall worship the god within him turns out ultimately to mean that Jones shall worship Jones. Let Jones worship the sun or moon, anything rather than the Inner Light; let Jones worship cats or crocodiles, if he can find any in his street, but not the god within."[1] Recognizing the attractions the New Age has to offer spiritually thirsty people today, how shall we approach the New Age?

Developing an Apologetic Stance

The critical issue in dealing with New Age thinking is its strong aversion to rationality. New Age pantheistic thinking follows long-standing tradition in its distaste for rationality. New Agers resist the conceptual, evidential, and analytic approach to religion and faith. But those who speak with New Agers recognize that every meaning-

1. G. K. Chesterton, *Orthodoxy* (Garden City: Doubleday, Image Books, 1959), p. 76.

223

ful interaction between two thinking persons requires a common playing field on which the discussion can take place. This court needs to be defined in part by the rules of rationality. If the field is defined so that a New Ager can evade rational criticism by an appeal to subjective, intuitive knowledge or insight, any apologist will be frustrated. The ground rules of the game must include rational principles that delimit what both participants will accept as truth and whose ideas have evidence and are "reasonable." If total agreement is not possible, at least some common principles are needed.

The rational ground rules should include several things. First, commitment to *consistency* and *coherence* is important. It is not acceptable to hold contradictory ideas. We must discipline ourselves to weed out ideas that entangle us in inconsistencies. And we must be committed to consistency all the time—not just when it appears to be in our favor. Second, emphasis on *proper evidence* is significant. New Agers (like many cultists) will want to appeal to personal experience. But while personal experience is helpful, it is never sufficient. Many factors distort individual interpretations of experience. We must be committed to confirmation of personal feelings by reliable, external principles. Third, achieving *clarity in concepts* is critical. We only communicate in dialog when both participants use words in the same way. This is a special problem because New Agers often use Christian terms in decidedly non-Christian ways.

This raises the question of reason's relation to our faith. This ancient problem is at the heart of apologetics. 'Faith' (or what the Bible calls 'belief in') is a personal trust in and commitment to another person. Faith involves knowing someone in contrast to knowing about that person. As such, faith is primarily an act of our wills, although it includes our whole personalities. The best illustration of faith is the marriage vow. When the groom says, "I do," he is performing, first and foremost, not an act of the mind (although thought is included), but an act of the will. "I do" means a promise to trust, to be true. And it includes the promise to forsake all others and cleave only unto her. So faith in Christ means turning from other gods, including self, and exercising a whole-soul trust in the person of Christ.

'Reason' (or what the Bible calls 'belief that') is a cognitive understanding of something. Reason is knowing about something as distinct from knowing a person. As such, reason is primarily an act of the mind (although the other dimensions of personality are included). Rationality simply means the rules by which human thinking ought to work. When we think properly, we are rational; if not, we are irrational.

Reason and faith cannot be separated. At the same time, reason and faith cannot be identified. They are different, but never divided. They are related in this way: it is *possible* to believe that Christ is the Savior (reason) without believing in Christ (faith); it is *impossible* to believe in Christ (faith) without believing that Christ is the Savior (reason). So reason and faith are asymmetrically related. Logically, understanding the gospel comes before personally accepting it; personally appropriating the gospel carries one beyond merely grasping it intellectually. "Faith comes by hearing, and hearing by the Word of God," says Paul.

Given these comments, we can see the relevance of rationality to apologetics. Rationality helps one move to the place of comprehension. In that role it is *critical,* but not *sufficient.* Rationality is important to faith, but it does not replace faith. Tires are important to your car, but they do not replace the spark plugs. While we acknowledge rationality, we reject rationalism. Rationalism says that certain knowledge is possible through purely human reasoning and implies that knowledge is an end in itself. In the Christian faith, knowledge is a means to an end, namely, love. Though philosophers have defined humans primarily as knowers, Christian faith defines persons primarily as lovers: we were built to be in love with God. Thus, rational knowledge is important, but it is not the goal of life. We recognize as apologists that the Christian faith is a spiritual affair and demands spiritual tools as well as rational ones.

Recognizing both the importance and the insufficiency of rationality, we should seek to define the parameters of discussion by illustrating and defending the claim that we are interested in finding truth. We want the world view that is true. We are not interested primarily in exciting experiences, heart-warming feelings, practical tips, or leaps of faith. We want truth, and we believe the Christian gospel because, first and foremost, it is true.

We believe it is helpful in apologetic conversations to seek to join forces with the dialog partner in a cooperative journey toward truth. If possible, it is helpful to set the stage in such a way that the battle is not between you and me, but between us and falsehood. You and I together are doing our best to root out what is false and find what is true. So we cooperate, helping each other to achieve this goal. If both dialog partners make a commitment to truth early on, it becomes more difficult later to say, "Well, what you say is logical, but I still believe. ... ."

This attitude, whether expressed or not, will go a long way toward relieving some anxieties about apologetics. Many express these fears by saying, "You can't argue people into God's kingdom," to which we say, "Exactly right! And you can't preach them in or witness them in either." Apologetics, with its commitment to finding truth through clear thinking, does not mean browbeating people into accepting the gospel—a sort of cognitive crusade or intellectual inquisition. Apologetics is a rational defense of the faith offered in the spirit of concern and genuine care for the other. It is "speaking the truth in love"; and both *truth* and *love* are important.

Truth is important because depending on intuition, hunches, experiences, and hearsay often can be wrong. While intuition may give us brilliant insights, it also can mislead. We believe it is acceptable to use intuition as a source of potentially great ideas. But intuition also needs the checking procedures of rationality. With New Agers, cultists, and even many Christians, the unreliable nature of subjectivism must be illustrated and the authority of the intuitive made subject to the guidance of rationality.

Love is important because, in the final analysis, we are more interested in persuading the heart than in merely convincing the mind. If a person's mind is changed but her heart remains unchanged, apologetics has not done what we hope it will do. We can argue helpfully by presenting evidence for a position in a manner that is warm, enlightening, even stimulating and enjoyable. We can argue harmfully by debating and attacking in a manner that does more damage than good. Psychological studies have shown that how well the audience likes the messenger profoundly affects the level of persuasion. Here as much as anywhere, the medium is the message.

The requisite attitude for speaking with those who think with their feelings is patience and confidence. Patience may mean going back through arguments many times until they sink in. This is especially true with respect to the problem of intuitive insight and rational truth. New Agers, like cultists, will be rational as long as the results seem to go their way. But when it appears that clear thinking will yield an unacceptable conclusion, they suddenly question its validity. This is why a mutual commitment to truth early in the conversation is important. It gives a benchmark from which to work when the New Ager or cultist takes a subjectivistic dodge. It takes great patience and strong confidence in the truth to continue to draw the conversation back to the questions of consistency, evidence, and clarity.

Naturally, the degree to which these admonitions are relevant is person-relative. But this suggests an important proviso for any apologist: no two people are exactly alike. No two New Agers will say the same thing. In many cases, people (including Christians) are minimally committed to some New Age ideas without being totally committed to the system. Apologetics is a concrete business. It means talking to people, individuals, not answering generic arguments that all persons in a class have in common. In our discussion, we have tried to emphasize the kinds of arguments New Agers and other mystical pantheists use. You are responsible to work with this raw material and present it in the appropriate way to the right person.

This implies that we must respond to a person at his or her level. Is this person a committed New Ager or a dabbler? Is she emotionally secure or in the midst of a crisis? Is he highly educated or fairly simple in thinking? Is he a professing Christian or not? Apologetics is not a discipline geared to teaching you, "If he says such-and-such, then you say so-and-so." It provides tools, raw materials, from which individual answers are shaped to meet particular needs of particular persons at their particular level. This means hearing whether the question is primarily emotional or cognitive. It means neither oversimplifying nor overcomplicating the issue—both have disastrous effects. This is a tall order. None of us does it perfectly. But the one who has thought through the issues clearly for herself and listens carefully to her dialog partner is in a good position to be led by the Holy Spirit to say just the right word at just the right time. We only prepare ourselves to be the best vessels we can be. Only the Spirit fills and uses those vessels.

Reviewing the Arguments

1. Metaphysics. The arguments we have spelled out involve the New Age pantheistic world view in difficult conceptual tangles. In discussing the world view itself, the main issue involves the unwillingness to ascribe concepts to God. Pantheists want to affirm God as unconditioned and infinite. If concepts are used to describe God, they believe, this absoluteness is compromised. Then God is not everything there is; he becomes one thing and not another. For example, he becomes good, but not evil. Applying concepts to God makes him subject to concepts that divide up his unity and restrict his being. Pantheists claim these descriptions confine God so he is no longer completely unlimited and unconditioned.

While we observed the noble motive behind this move, we believe this way of defending God's absoluteness is too costly. For if *God* is a word of which no concepts can be predicated, then *God* has no meaning. We say nothing about God. Our idea of God becomes shapeless and formless. In their quest to make God absolute, New Agers, like other pantheists, sometimes affirm that we cannot describe God cognitively.

But some New Agers are not willing to live with the consequences of this move. If *God* is without any cognitive shape at all, it is not meaningful to call God good or personal or anything else. Yet some pantheists will in the next breath talk about God in various ways. It is inconsistent to deny concepts of God at one time and at another time to talk about God as if we had some meaningful idea of what *God* means. If we say that no concepts apply to God, then we should not even use the word *God*. It is unfair for pantheists to deny any meaningful concept of *God* and then to use the word by plundering meaning from the theist's idea of God. If *God* has no cognitive meaning, then *God* has no cognitive meaning, and we should not try to sneak meaning in under cover.

On the other hand, if, to restore God as a topic of discussion, pantheists admit that *God* has meaning, two consequences follow. First, they compromise a fundamental premise of pantheistic thinking that says that God cannot be limited by concepts. Second, they open the door for a discussion of views of God in the conceptual arena. They enter the realm of rational discussion and no longer can retreat into the impregnable castle of subjectivism and nonrationality when it suits them.

2. Epistemology. In the context of knowledge, the mystical consciousness of New Age pantheists entangles them in difficulties. Pantheists who use a mystical way of knowing must try somehow to distinguish two modes of knowing, the mystical mode and the empirical mode. The first of these is unitive, unmediated, nonconceptual, nonlogical, and noninferential. By contrast, the second is divided, conceptual, logical, and inferential. Mystics claim that the mediated nature of empirical knowledge makes it subject to error. Because it involves sensory apparatus as well as logical deductions, empirical knowledge systematically misleads us. Thus, noninferential, unmediated mystical knowing is the solution. It promises knowledge unsullied by the flaws inherent in ordinary knowing.

While this approach is attractive at first, we wonder whether it really succeeds. For one thing, mystics (or at least philosophers of pantheism) present several reasons to think that mystical knowing is entirely different from ordinary modes of knowing. These reasons include mysticism's allegedly self-authenticating, immediate, and ineffable nature.

But after examining these characteristics of mystical knowing, we found that the two modes of knowing are not radically different. Mystical knowing is not absolutely self-authenticating, for testing procedures are relevant to mystical knowing, as they are to other modes of knowing. And mystical knowing is not strictly ineffable or indescribable, for mystics do describe their experiences and others (including nonmystics) do understand their descriptions. In fact, philosophers develop arguments like the Argument from Unanimity because they meaningfully apprehend those descriptions.

To solve these dilemmas, some mystical pantheists revert to

mutism. They refuse to discuss their experiences and simply indicate that we, too, must have such experiences to be "in the know." But this move presupposes the very logical principles it seeks to by-pass. Zennists provide the most graphic example. Their mutism is itself a result of logical inference. They know that if they speak, they will self-defeat. They do not want to self-defeat. So they do not speak. This mutism is a very logical option. If logical principles really do not apply, they should say, "It is irrational for me to say this, but because ordinary knowing and speaking assume logic, they are systemically misleading. You may think I should not make this statement, but since logical principles are irrelevant, I can say it anyway." No one is really willing to live consistently with the implications of an utter denial of logical principles.

Additionally, to speak or act as though there were two different modes of knowing posits a conceptual distinction. The move to discredit ordinary modes of knowing in favor of the higher mystical mode of knowing depends on the logical distinction between the two modes of knowing. Far from overcoming rational principles, this move affirms them. New Agers who appeal to the right-/left-brain distinction commit this oversight. Though they hope to abandon logical, analytical, left-brain thinking in favor of unitive, mystical, right-brain thinking, they are in that very move affirming the logical distinction between left-brain thinking and right-brain thinking. This is a very left-brained thing to do. It reveals the necessity, if not the sufficiency, of rational ways of thinking.

To recognize the necessity of logical modes of thinking in the human knowing process has a very important implication. A mystical pantheist who recognizes the force of what we have said must come out of the castle and onto the jousting field. His ideas cannot be defended as beyond question simply because they are mystically generated. These ideas must join the rough-and-tumble of the playing field and defend themselves as every other idea does. Those who are interested in what is really true (as opposed to finding reasons to support their previous inclinations) will have to take this point seriously. We have found no way to avoid the necessity of left-brain thinking.

3. Religious experience. When discussing the concept of salvation, mystical pantheists speak about their epistemology. Since the usual pantheistic analysis of evil locates the cause of all human problems in ignorance, the remedy must include the elimination of ignorance. For the mystic, of course, the mystical consciousness eliminates ignorance.

But an important aspect of New Age and pantheistic thinking on religious experience is the claim that those in every religion are in contact with God. This pluralistic belief fits nicely with the pantheists' resistance to conceptual modes of thought. Those who think experience is more critical than doctrine will find it much easier to overlook doctrinal contradictions than those who take rationality seriously. And an enticing corollary of this approach is the claim that tolerance and mutual understanding between people of all religious perspectives is possible.

As attractive as pluralism seems at first, it is not without difficulties. Pluralism is parasitic on exclusivism; it is exclusive at heart, although its commitment to exclusivism becomes evident at a different, more general level. At some point, pluralists must stop being tolerant of any and all positions. If they do not, then they slide all the way to complete relativism. When they draw the line, when they say that no more pluralism can be permitted, then they become exclusivists. Pluralists believe exclusively that pluralism is true.

Consider this simple example. We can identify several levels at which debates on religious truth can take place: (a) the debate between the religious perspective and the irreligious viewpoint; (b) the debate between religions (say, between Christianity and Islam); (c) the debate between particular expressions of a religion (say, between Presbyterianism and Methodism). Hick believes it is critical to be exclusive at level a, but not at b or c. Many Christians believe it is crucial to be exclusive at levels a and b, but not at c.

This set of examples is simplistic because there are many factors that cut across these illustrations. For example, the commitment to a supernatural religion in contrast to a purely natural religion may be more important than level c debates. Yet this issue could arise between two Presbyterians. But recognizing these limitations, the example suggests that the difference between pluralists and exclusivists is not absolute. The difference lies in the choice of where to draw the line at which the slide to complete relativism is halted. Sooner or later, pluralists become exclusivists.

Further, pluralists are wrong when they claim that tolerance depends on pluralism. Exclusivists can be tolerant in accepting the right of others to have different beliefs. Pluralists can be intolerant in telling adherents of all religions that they are wrong when they hold exclusive beliefs. Indeed the whole notion that one needs to accept as true the other person's belief in order to tolerate that person is a misuse of language. It makes no sense to speak of tolerating ideas with which we agree—we tolerate those beliefs with which we disagree. In a sense, tolerance demands a compassionate exclusivism, not an amorphous pluralism.

4. Good and evil. Every world view must deal with the omnipresent human experience we call evil. Evil is a theoretical problem for world views: How can we explain its origin and its existence? But

evil is also an existential problem: How can we deal with evil in our lives?

Pantheism feels a constant rational pressure to take an extreme view: evil is not real. Of the various views of evil's origin, most place evil outside God's own being. But if we place evil outside God, the unity of all reality as God is compromised, for something which is not God must exist as such. A pantheist cannot push this move too far without eroding the central tenet of his philosophy. But if he emphasizes the unity of all reality in God, then whatever appears to exist outside God must be thought to exist within the divine being or as an extension of God. In this case, either evil is real (and in God) or evil is not real. The first option is unpleasant. Who wants to say God is or contains evil? The second option is left. Though pantheists resist this conclusion, the inner logic of pantheism inexorably presses them toward the illusionist view of evil.

A solution to the practical problem of evil must find its roots in the theoretical answer. Telling a person his cancer is an illusion is cruel and inhumane unless it really is an illusion. If we had good reason to believe that evil is simply a nightmare, then helping people to see this would be a good thing to do. But we do not have such good reasons. Since calling evil unreal seems implausible as an explanation, counseling people to act as though evil were unreal in their everyday struggles does seem cruel. To suggest the unreality of evil to a suffering person is seriously out of touch, both theoretically and practically, with the vast and pressing human experience with evil.

The other aspect of good and evil is moral obligation. How do we ground the ought we feel to follow certain moral guidelines? How do we explain the guilt we feel when we fail to follow these guidelines? The pantheists' propensity to deny that conceptual opposites are real in God means undercutting the ontological basis for concepts like 'right' and 'wrong.' To the degree our experience of right and wrong motives and actions is real, we must find a metaphysical basis for these values.

Zennists try to evade this problem by saying simply, "Do what needs to be done. Don't give it a second thought. If it needs to be done, do it, and be on your way!" But this answer is circular for it assumes we know what *needs to be done* means. Suzuki says we should pull the drowning child out of the water and be gone. Could we push the drowning child further from the shore and be gone? If we have no standards of moral behavior, we are hard pressed to say that harming instead of helping would be wrong.

The numerous difficulties we have reviewed briefly here are caused by the pantheists' unwillingness to limit God with human concepts. This seems like a noble idea. On the other hand, Christian theists do "limit" God by ascribing concepts to the divine. Is this position flawed?

Orthodox Christians have taught that God uses concepts for himself in the Bible. They have admitted that this truth, which comes in conceptual form, is a condescension on God's part: the Holy Spirit comes down to speak in terms that finite humans can understand, much as a parent would in explaining something to a small child. Thus no one claims that what we say about God exhausts the divine reality. In fact, human conceptual knowing scratches the surface of God's reality. But the inadequacy of our understanding of God does not entail its falsity. Christians believe that humans can think God's thoughts after him in a limited, inadequate, yet true manner. If this is so, many of the difficulties caused by the unwillingness to ascribe concepts to the divine being evaporate.

The Strength of Christian Theism

Despite the arguments we have detailed in the book, many people are still attracted to New Age pantheism. It must be offering something people want. We believe that the New Age message does have some positive aspects. But what is good in the New Age is counterfeit of the Christian gospel. The aspects of the message that are half right, that have some validity, can be found in the gospel as well, but there they are completely right. The gospel not only is more adequate rationally and philosophically than New Age teaching, but also is more satisfying and richer emotionally and spiritually. Consider as examples these areas:

1. A sense of divine mystery. Many people want mystery, awe, inspiration, and wonder in their lives. Humans are not laboratory rats. They are not satisfied to live sterile, technological, mechanical lives. They are persons and crave the personal dimensions of existence. They are bored with the mundane, the everyday. They want a little excitement and romance. This need for wonder and the magical in life leads some to deny the cold, barren, antiseptic, analytical aspects of the human brain and its technological and scientific creations. To those who sympathize with this point of view, the New Age, with its mystical and magical claims, can be irresistible.

The Christian faith also provides this sense of mystery and awe. We are invited to worship the God of creation, whose majesty and sovereignty boggle our minds and lift our hearts. Anyone who reads the Psalms, for example, recognizes this depth in human experience with the biblical God. Sometimes the practice of Christian faith has been reduced to dry rituals, dead rules, and dusty rigamarole. When this happens, the defection to the New Age is understandable. People are looking for something and believe that the New Age will provide it. But at its best, the Christian gospel offers a loving relationship with the majestic God that far exceeds what New Agers hope to find in the Age of Aquarius.

In order to heighten its sense of wonder and worship, the New Age movement denigrates rationality. New Agers use the left-/right-brain distinction to abandon the analytical left brain and highlight the intuitive right brain. The mystery in the New Age is gained at the expense of a very important dimension of human existence—conceptual thought. From a human point of view, the human progress we have made in building civilization, creating art, conquering disease, and developing science has been made possible by humans who have thought clearly about the problems they faced and set out to solve them. New Agers barter away rationality in order to gain the renewed sense of spirituality. The New Age benefits come with heavy negative baggage.

The biblical faith of Christians preserves both the mystery of an awe-inspiring God and the rationality upon which we so obviously depend. In its full-blown form, the Christian gospel provides what the New Age claims to give but without the excess baggage and the negative side effects. The gospel of Christ (I Cor. 15:1–4) provides both the mystery and awe of a majestic and sovereign God who condescends to love us where we are and the positive sense of human rationality as a gift of that majestic God to his creatures. Those who think the New Age offers something that a relationship with Christ does not need to rethink their conclusion. In Christ, we have the resources both for deep spirituality and for deep understanding.

2. A sense of human worth. Many feel that life tramples them down. They feel that the rat race is over and the rats have won. They feel like insignificant, unimportant nobodies. Many suffer from a debilitating self-concept; others feel the pain of nagging self-doubts. The New Age offers a solution to these negative feelings. What could be more uplifting than to realize that we are God? We are not just insignificant specks of dust on an unimportant little planet in an out-of-the-way solar system. We are part of the divine being. This is an intoxicating message, and its widespread appeal comes as no surprise.

The Christian gospel emphasizes the tremendous worth of each person. Because God created each person in his own image, each one is valuable. Jesus tells us explicitly that animals are valuable, for God takes care of them. Yet humans are worth much more than animals. The Christian truth of human worth is lost sometimes in Christian teaching because of the emphasis on human sinfulness. But the two ideas are both true. And the gospel, when it is understood in its fullest sense, maintains both worth and sinfulness in proper balance.

In the Age of Aquarius, the truth of human worth is exalted without the balancing idea of human sinfulness. The New Age teaches the basic divinity of each human person. If we are all God, we are obviously of great value. And this inference is clear to New Agers. This distinctive, however, is purchased at a high cost, for the New Age is not realistic in its understanding of human evil. It fails to account fully for the basic, self-centered twist of human nature that inflicts us all. This ego-centrism, the sinful nature, is the source and root of specific sinful acts. Indeed, the New Age caters specifically to this self-centeredness with its message of God within instead of challenging that most basic root of evil within us. The New Age, in its obsession with divinity, cannot include this dimension of human existence and so purchases its emphasis on human worth at the cost of presenting an unrealistically optimistic view of human nature.

The Bible preserves both the worth and the sinfulness of the human person in magnificent balance. Humans are of great worth to God. But humans are sinful and unworthy of God's favor. Thus God chooses to give us his spiritual resources to turn from our basic selfishness and cast our destinies into his hands. The central Christian symbol, the cross, pictures both our worth and our sinfulness. It demonstrates that we are of great worth to God because God willingly gave the life of his Son to save us from sin and self. It proves that we are unworthy of God's favor and in need of his work on our behalf because God had to give the life of his Son to save us. Thus, in the cross we have a message that emphasizes human value in a way far richer than the New Age ever could, yet without the negative baggage of an unrealistically optimistic view of humanness that New Age thinking carries along.

These examples illustrate our claim that the New Age message offers something modern humans yearn for. But what the New Age gives us can be found more fully in the gospel of Jesus Christ. The message of the Bible meets human needs in every way New Age teaching does and more. The New Age gives a sense of awe and mystery, but no rational ground for its teachings. The New Age tells us we have great worth and potential, but does not recognize our entanglement in sin. In Christ the plusses of New Age thinking are found without the minuses. If the gospel is presented properly, the strongest response to the New Age is contrasting it with the riches of the gospel. The best way to spot a counterfeit is to know the original exhaustively.

In both of these areas, the concept of God and the idea of humanness, the Christian faith offers reality that the New Age can only counterfeit. The cross of Jesus Christ offers genuine hope for the suffering and pain, the selfishness and rebellion, the sin and self-condemnation we all experience as fallen human beings. The New Age thrives on hope. That is the point of the New Age—a Utopia, a perfect earth, a new era of peace, prosperity, and unity. That many flock to the New Age suggests that people today crave this hope. Yet it is a false hope, a pipe dream. It lacks substance. The evidence that such a transformation will take place is sadly lacking. Hope without realism is cruel.

The Christian message of the cross is this: the hope for genuine personal transformation, social revolution, and cosmic reconciliation comes not from us but from God. Through the cross of Christ, the evil we all experience and long to overcome has already been defeated. Through the cross, human values can be enhanced and human redemption achieved. In Jesus Christ, the living Water, the thirst for peace and hope that drives the New Age will be quenched.

Glossary

Absolute, the: a pantheistic term for God.

Absolute pantheism: the religious world view of one branch of Hinduism, in which God alone is real and all else is unreal.

Absolute Self: in Eastern thought, God or the All *(see* Cosmic Ego).

Absolutism: in ethics, the view that the same moral obligations apply to all people; opposed to moral *relativism* (which see).

Advaita: the principle of nonduality, that all Reality is a single, inclusive whole not subject to any distinctions.

Analogous: having similar meaning in different applications; distinguished from *univocal,* having the same meaning in different applications.

Anatman: individual self, part of, or an expression of, the Cosmic Self, Atman (or Brahman).

Atman: the Cosmic Self, Brahman, the All, God, in Hindu philosophy.

Atheism: belief that there is no God.

Bhagavad Gita: a lyrical commentary on the *Veda* (which see), informally accorded the authority theoretically reserved for the Hindu scripture.

Bhakti: in Hindu thought, the path to salvation through devotion to a personal god.

Bodhisattva: in Mahayana and Zen Buddhism, one who has attained enlightenment but postpones entrance into the state to keep a vow to assist all life to achieve salvation.

Brahman: in Hindu philosophy, originally, the power inherent in sacrificial ritual, later and more importantly, the mysterious One out of which all action proceeds; God, the All, World Soul.

Channeling: a New Age term for divination, consulting mediums, or

237

receiving and transmitting information from supposed disembodied spirits or higher beings.

Coherence: the presence of genuine unity and relatedness among claims in a world view; as an epistemological test, it eliminates perspectives that fail to relate their various elements.

Comprehensiveness: inclusiveness, completeness; as an epistemological test, it asks how well a world view can accommodate large ranges of experience.

Congruity: the fit of the theory to the facts; as an epistemological test, it asks whether facts fit a world view neatly and comfortably or whether the world view must be modified significantly to account for facts.

Consistency: lack of logical contradiction; as an epistemological test, it operates negatively, eliminating perspectives that are self-contradictory.

Cosmic Ego: in Eastern thought, the All, or God, of which all apparently individual selves are mere manifestations (*see* no-self).

Creation: in theistic thought, refers to things distinct from God brought into being by a free act of God; in pantheistic thought, refers to things ultimately indistinct from God and given expression necessarily because of God's nature.

Deism: belief that God, though he created the world, takes no active part in its ongoing affairs.

Determinism: the philosophy that every event is determined by a sequence of cause and effect, hence that there is no personal freedom of will.

Dharma: the Hindu principle of right action, of living according to the truth of things.

Emanational pantheism: the world view of Plotinus, in which God's being overflows into the world as a flower grows from the bud.

Enlightenment: in pantheistic philosophy, the mystic state of realizing one's identity with the divine.

Epistemology: the study of knowledge and how it is attained.

Exclusivism: the view that only one religion is correct in its apprehension of God, salvation, or morality; opposed to philosophical/normative *pluralism* and *inclusivism* (which see). One who embraces exclusivism is an *exclusivist*, and his view of the relations of religions is *exclusive*.

Fideism: the view that one should believe without reason or even contrary to reason; a *fideist* is an adherent of fideism.

Gnosticism: a heretical mixture of early Christian thought with the doctrines of mystical Greek religious and philosophical sects emphasizing privileged access to special knowledge; Gnosticism tended to see mystic or occult knowledge, not faith, as the path to salvation.

Imagination: in the epistemology of Spinoza, the lowest level of knowledge (*see* opinion).

Inclusivism: the view that one particular religion is true but that adherents of other religions are covert followers of the one true faith; opposed to *exclusivism* and to philosophical/normative *pluralism* (which see).

Ineffability: the quality of being indescribable, of being beyond the capacity of language to communicate. Most forms of pantheism affirm that God is ineffable, not subject to linguistic description.

Intuition: knowing something immediately (without mediation) apart from the use of reason (inference) or observation. Pantheism normally views intuition as a higher form of knowledge than knowledge gained by logic or empirical experience. Analysis indicates that even knowledge claimed to be intuitive depends on inference (mediation) from the elements of a world view. In the epistemology of Spinoza, *intuition*, the highest level of knowledge, differs from reason not by being unmediated but by being "more potent," grasping the whole of reality as a total system.

Karma: the law of merit and demerit, which teaches that every person receives in this life the rewards or punishments for previous lives; the law of moral cause and effect.

Koan: in Zen, an absurd dialogue, question and answer, or anecdote that opens a novice's experience to *satori* (which see) without using direct teaching.

Liberation: in pantheistic thought, release from the illusion of individuality or of distinction from the All (*see* enlightenment, self-realization, satori).

Maya: in Vedantic Hinduism, an illusory appearance of Brahman, what we see as the world around us. *Maya* does not imply solipsism or non-existence. Rather, *maya* acknowledges that the world is something, but it is not what it appears; it really is Brahman.

Mechanism: the view that all reality is so interconnected that whatever happens in nature happens by necessity and hence there is no freedom in nature; a form of *determinism*.

Metaphysics: the philosophical study of being (*see* ontology) or reality; the origin, nature, and structure of all that is.

Metempsychosis: *see* reincarnation.

Modal pantheism: the world view of Benedict de Spinoza, in which the finite world and all things in it are modes, or modifications, of God's infinite being.

Moksa: Sanskrit for "release" or "freedom," gained in enlightenment from ignorance (the illusion that one is an individual self distinct from Brahman) and reincarnation; in Vedantic pantheism, the experience of realizing one's identity with Brahman, the Cosmic Self. Shankara taught that *moksa* is Brahman.

Mondo: in Zen Buddhism, a paradoxical question-and-answer dialogue designed to overcome attachment to logic and reason.

Monism: the idea that all of reality is one.

Mother Earth: in New Age pantheism and various pagan religions, earth viewed as divine; also referred to as *Gaea, Gaia,* and *Ge* (all forms of the Greek name for the earth goddess).

Multilevel pantheism: the religious world view in which God is the ultimate reality and other things exist only at lower levels of reality; also called manifestational pantheism.

Mysticism: belief that it is possible or necessary to achieve communion with, knowledge of, or identity with God through direct contemplation unmediated by human reason, logic, or observation.

Neti, neti: Sanskrit for "not this, not that," the doctrine that *Nirguna (Unqualified) Brahman* has no attributes either positive or negative and so can be described as neither A nor non-A.

Nirguna (Unqualified) Brahman: the Ultimate (God, the All) perceived without qualities; opposite of *Saguna (Qualified) Brahman.* Viewed from the perspective of ignorance, the Ultimate is *Saguna Brahman;* from the perspective of knowledge, it is *Nirguna Brahman.*

Nonduality: the principle in Vedantic Hinduism that all reality is a single, inclusive whole not subject to any distinctions (also called *Advaita*).

No-self: Buddhist doctrine that denies any substantial existence to individual egos but sees all selves as manifestations of the All (also called *non-ego*).

Nous: Latin for "mind," "intelligence," or "spirit," the second level of reality in the emanational pantheism of Plotinus.

Occult: secret, esoteric, beyond human understanding; having to do with mysticism, magic, alchemy, astrology, and forms of divination.

One, the: the ultimate level of reality in the philosophy of Plotinus, the level beyond being and absolutely without distinction and multiplicity; the Absolute; (impersonal) God (without attributes); the Source of all reality.

Ontological argument (for the existence of God): the argument that since God is defined as the absolutely perfect Being, and since to lack existence would entail imperfection, God must exist.

Ontology: the study or philosophy of being or existence.

Opinion: in the epistemology of Spinoza, the lowest level of knowledge, including ideas derived from the senses; also called *imagination*.

Pantheism: generally defined, the theory that God is the world and the world is God. Five varieties of pantheism are examined in this book: permeational pantheism (chapter 1), absolute pantheism (chapter 2), multilevel pantheism (chapter 3), emanational pantheism (chapter 4), and modal pantheism (chapter 5). For definitions of the varieties, see the separate entry for each.

Permeational pantheism: the religious world view of Zen Buddhism, in which a oneness like a Life Force underlies and permeates all reality.

Pluralism: in this book, two kinds of pluralism concern us: (1) phenomenological/factual pluralism, which refers to the sociological fact that different people have different religious perspectives, and (2) philosophical/normative pluralism, the theory that many religions, with their different and even inter-religiously contradictory concepts and practices, can be appropriate or even equally true or adequate modes of expressing our experience of God, that is, the notion that there is no single true religion or no religion that is truer than or morally preferable to any other religion. The second kind of pluralism is opposed to *exclusivism* (which see).

Polytheism: belief in the existence of many gods; some forms of polytheism view the many gods as lower-level manifestations of the All (Brahman, God, the One, etc.).

Prajna: in the epistemology of Zen Buddhism, intuition, the basic knowing principle that makes possible a synthetic realization of something in its wholeness; opposite of *vijnana* (which see). See also *two-truth* theory of knowledge.

Reason: (1) in general, the faculty of rational beings by which they, using evidence, can arrive at sound conclusions; (2) in the epistemology of Spinoza, the second level of knowledge, necessarily true because adequate, going beyond concrete objects to a system of abstract statements revealing the essential properties that all objects in a class share.

Reincarnation: the return of the soul into another body after death; also called *transmigration* and *metempsychosis*.

Relativism: the doctrine that there is no truth, that any view is acceptable, that truth depends on (is relative to) perspective; the view that there are no absolutes in either truth or morality; opposed to ethical *absolutism* (which see).

Saguna (Qualified) Brahman: the Ultimate conceived to possess attributes or qualities; the personal god, Īśvara, lord of this world; opposite of *Nirguna (Unqualified) Brahman*. Viewed from the perspective of ignorance, the Ultimate is *Saguna Brahman;* from the perspective of knowledge, it is *Nirguna Brahman.*

Satori: in Hinduism and Buddhism, the experience of *enlightenment* (which see); perception of Reality itself in its wholeness without specific content.

Self-realization: in pantheistic philosophy, the realization that the individual self is an illusion and that the true self is identical to (or a manifestation of) the All (God).

Soul, or **World Soul:** the third level of reality in the philosophy of Plotinus, including the universal Soul and individual souls.

Sunyata: 'emptiness' or 'void', a central concept of Mahayana and Zen Buddhism, not an absence of reality but an absolute emptiness that transcends all dualities (e.g., God versus the world or subject versus object); a negative expression of *tathata* (which see).

Sutra: Sanskrit word for thread or string; in Hinduism, a precept or maxim; in Buddhism, scriptural narratives or the dialogues of the Buddha (*see* Vedanta-sutras).

Tat tvam asi: Sanskrit for "that art thou," a central doctrine of Shankara's *Advaita Vedanta* Hinduism, identifies the individual self *(anatman)* with the Cosmic Self *(Atman).*

Tathata: 'suchness' or 'thusness', a basic concept of Mahayana and Zen Buddhist metaphysics, that things have no underlying substance or nature but simply are what they appear to be; opposite of *sunyata* (which see).

Theism: belief in one infinite, eternal, and personal God who as Creator is distinct from but rules over creation; distinct from *atheism, deism, pantheism,* and *polytheism.*

Tolerance: recognizing other people's views, respecting other people, and permitting them to hold their views, despite disagreement with those views. Tolerance does not require philosophical/normative *pluralism* (which see), but makes sense only from the perspective of *exclusivism* (which see).

Transmigration: *see* reincarnation.

Two-truth theory of knowledge: the view that there are two distinct kinds or levels of truth or knowledge, the one mystical and unmediated, not tied to observation or logic, and the other rational, logical, mediated, often tied to observation. Pantheism generally emphasizes mystical knowledge, though it also sometimes claims that each level, despite its contradictions with the other level, is valid in its own sphere. *See* prajna and vijnana.

Unaffirmability principle: the principle that statements that self-destruct must be false (e.g., the statement "I cannot speak one word of English" when uttered in English).

Undeniability principle: the principle that some truths are undeniable because their denial depends on their truth; for example, the statement "Logic is always misleading" assumes logic as a condition of its meaningfulness and therefore self-destructs, leading to the conclusion that logic is undeniable.

Univocal: having a single meaning in all applications; opposed to *equivocal*, having different meanings in different applications, and to *analogous*, having similar meanings in different applications.

Upanishads: additions to the *Vedas* (which see) written after 1000 B.C.; part of the Hindu scriptures.

Utopia: a hypothetical place or time of perfection (from Greek *ou*, "not," and *topos*, "place").

Veda, Vedas: the Hindu scriptures, composed 1500 to 1000 B.C.; *Veda* sometimes refers to the *Vedas* plus the *Upanishads* (which see).

Vedanta: literally, "end of the Veda," expresses certain philosophical and religious speculations on the Upanishads.

Vedanta-sutras: two- or three-word statements that systematize the teachings of the Upanishads.

Verification Principle: an axiom of logical positivism that only two kinds of statements count as meaningful: definitions and facts (with facts defined as statements that are empirically verifiable). The Verification Principle is self-defeating and therefore false because it is itself neither a definition nor empirically verifiable.

Vijnana: in the epistemology of Zen Buddhism, rational or conceptual knowledge based on analysis and differentiation; opposite of *prajna* (which see). *See also* two-truth theory of knowledge.

World Soul: in Eastern and related forms of pantheism, the All, the Absolute, God; in the emanational pantheism of Plotinus, the third level of reality. *See* Soul and Emanational Pantheism.

Yoga: the Sanskrit word for "union;" *yoga* is a mystical form of meditation whose goal is realization of the soul's identity with the All (Brahman, the Absolute, God, etc.), often employing strict disciplines of posture, breathing, and concentration.

Zen: a Japanese word corrupted from the Chinese *Ch'an*, which is corrupted from the Sanskrit *dhyana*, "meditation"; the Buddhist school represented by D. T. Suzuki.

Suggested Readings

Chandler, Russell. *Understanding the New Age.* Waco: Word, 1988.

Clark, David K. *The Pantheism of Alan Watts.* Downers Grove: InterVarsity, 1978.

Geisler, Norman L. *Christian Apologetics.* Grand Rapids: Baker, 1976.

Geisler, Norman L., and J. Yutaka Amano. *The Reincarnation Sensation.* Wheaton: Tyndale House, 1986.

Groothuis, Douglas. *Unmasking the New Age.* Downers Grove: InterVarsity, 1986.

Hackett, Stuart C. *Oriental Philosophy: A Westerner's Guide to Eastern Thought.* Madison: University of Wisconsin Press, 1979.

Johnson, Arthur L. *Faith Misguided: Exposing the Dangers of Mysticism.* Chicago: Moody, 1988.

Johnson, David L. *A Reasoned Look at Asian Religions.* Minneapolis: Bethany, 1985.

Miller, Elliot. *A Crash Course on the New Age.* Grand Rapids: Baker, 1989.

Owen, H. P. *Concepts of Deity.* New York: Herder and Herder, 1971.

Plumptre, Constance E. *A General Sketch of the History of Pantheism.* 2 vols. London: W. W. Gibbings, 1878.

Sire, James W. *The Universe Next Door.* Updated ed. Downers Grove: InterVarsity, 1988.

Watkins, William D., and Norman L. Geisler. *Worlds Apart: A Handbook on World Views.* 2d ed. Grand Rapids: Baker, 1989.

Yamamoto, J. Isamu. *Beyond Buddhism.* Downers Grove: InterVarsity, 1982.

Index

The authors wish to acknowledge Sharon Coomer, Mark Foreman, Lisa Johnson, and Renée Willard, who assisted in preparing the index.

Abandonment of senses, 122
Absolute: ego, 23, 41; emptiness, 21, 26; oneness, 43, 126; pantheism, 13, 37,53, 237, 241; reality, 40–44, 57–74, 142; unity, 40–44, 49, 78, 133
Absolute, the, 237, 240, 243; Brahman and, 68–70; Hinduism and, 37–56, 57, 59–64, 73; as infinite being, 93–114, 142; as intuitive knowledge, 64–68 *See also* All; Cosmic Self; Ego; God; One; Ultimate
Absolute Knower. *See* Knowledge
Absolute Self. *See* Cosmic Self, Ego; Self
Absolutism, 21, 210–11, 237, 241
Absorption into Ultimate, 22, 53. *See* Ultimate
Adviata: concept, 40–44, 60; *Adviata Vedanta*, 40, 58, 60–61, 74; in Hinduism, 242
Agni, fire god, 38
Akbar, Emperor, 61
All, the, 53, 118, 147–149, 157, 237 *See also* Absolute; Cosmic Self; Ego; God; One; Ultimate
Allah, 188, 194
Analogy, 177–78, 180, 237, 243
Anatman, individual self, 43, 63, 237, 242
Anselm of Canterbury, 104
Antinomianism: moral law and, 33–34; in pantheism, 128–29, 213–14

Apologetics, 12, 223–35
Aquarian Conspiracy, The (Ferguson), 9, 124
Aristotle, 96, 106
Aryans, 37
Asceticism, 20
Atheism, 7, 12, 237, 242; philosophy of, 211; psychology of, 170
Atman, Cosmic Self, 43, 51, 68, 237, 242; and individual, 48
Atonement, 200
Augustine, 78, 91, 144
Avidya, ignorance, 53
Axiom, 100

Bacon, Francis, 102
Barth, Karl, 125
Being: God's, 205, 212, 218, 240; metaphysical nature of, 117–31, 144–47, 218; ontology, 241
Bhagavad Gita, 11, 39, 51, 237
Bhakti, 39, 58–59, 237
Bible, 187, 224, 232, 234
Blavatsky, Helena Petrovna, 11
Blyth, R. H., 32
Bodhidharma, Zen Buddhism, 18–19, 22, 29
Bodhisattva, 33–34, 129–30, 216, 237
Brahman, 39, 237; absolute theory of, 49; Adviata and, 42; being of, 41, 43, 45, 47, 49, 50, 59, 68, 129, 150, 155, 164–65, 218; causality, 45; coherence in scriptures, 45; desires and, 54; godhood of, 194; immutability and, 46; karma and,